CiviCRM Cookbook

Master this web-based constituent relationship
management software for nonprofit and civic
sector organizations

Tony Horrocks

[PACKT] open source ✽
PUBLISHING   community experience distilled

BIRMINGHAM - MUMBAI

CiviCRM Cookbook

First published: June 2013

Production Reference: 1310513

Published by Packt Publishing Ltd.
Livery Place
35 Livery Street
Birmingham B3 2PB, UK.

ISBN 978-1-78216-044-1

www.packtpub.com

Cover Image by Abhishek Pandey (abhishek.pandey1210@gmail.com)

Credits

Author

Tony Horrocks

Reviewers

Erik Hommel

Kurund Jalmi

Andrew Wasson

Acquisition Editor

Usha Iyer

Lead Technical Editor

Dayan Hyames

Technical Editors

Jalasha D'costa

Pushpak Poddar

Varun Pius Rodrigues

Lubna Shaikh

Project Coordinator

Anugya Khurana

Proofreaders

Maria Gould

Paul Hindle

Indexer

Tejal Soni

Production Coordinator

Nitesh Thakur

Cover Work

Nitesh Thakur

Foreword

This year CiviCRM celebrated its eight birthday. Leveraging the open source model of collaboration and transparency, a global network of passionate people have built an enterprise quality CRM solution, which provides a compelling alternative to closed source proprietary products, and supports the mission critical activities of thousands of nonprofit and civic-minded organizations in more than 25 countries and five continents. Nonprofits of all sizes are adopting CiviCRM, from local arts groups (such as San Francisco Center for the Book), to multinational membership associations (International Mountain Biking Association), political parties (British Columbia NDP), advocacy organizations (Electronic Frontier Foundation), national charities (Leukemia & Lymphoma Research), and government entities (New York State Senate).

This "Cookbook" represents another exciting milestone in the evolution of the project. As an enthusiastic chef, I learned long ago that cookbook recipes provide a launching point for creativity. Good cooks take a recipe, test it out, and then modify and improve it based on their personal taste *and* knowing their "audience" (family, friends, and guests). Cookbook recipes are a perfect analog for sharing, leading to innovation.

CiviCRM's strength is based on shared innovation. In the two years since Packt's *Using CiviCRM* was published, we've seen an explosion of invention as users and implementers shape CiviCRM-based solutions to increasingly complex problems. Some of these are one-off customizations, but many have developed into full-fledged projects such as the CiviCRM-Webform integration module highlighted in this book. The power of these tools was brought home to me at a recent CiviCRM meetup, where Lisa Hubbert demonstrated the complex summer camp management interface she had built as a volunteer for San Francisco Arts Ed – a wonderful nonprofit that runs arts programs for inner-city kids. Lisa is not a software engineer, but a curious and passionate "cook". She developed an effective solution for her organization, *and* she taught and inspired others by sharing her work at a meetup and on the `CiviCRM.org` blog.

The introduction this year of "native" CiviCRM extensions, a built-in extension browser for site administrators, and a searchable Extensions Directory (`http://civicrm.org/extensions`) on `CiviCRM.org`, will facilitate even more shared innovation—including sharing major new extension-based functionality such as the forthcoming CiviVolunteer module across all three CMS platforms.

For those of you working with CiviCRM in a Drupal environment, this book includes a wide array of techniques. Take advantage of the integration capabilities and openness of both platforms. For those of you working with CiviCRM in WordPress or Joomla!, my hope is that these recipes will stimulate you to explore, build, and share analogous integrations with those CMSs.

This Cookbook is well-suited to bridge the gap between nontechnical end users and software engineers. Whether you are a volunteer, in-house staff person, or a consultant—I'm confident it will provide you with ideas for using CiviCRM more effectively.

Ultimately, the strength of any open source project is the strength of the community behind it. If CiviCRM helps your organization (or your clients' organizations) with mission critical tasks, I urge you to participate actively in the community. Sponsor new features and improvements via the "make it happen" campaigns (`http://civicrm.org/mih`), post new recipes and modules on the Extensions Directory (`http://civicrm.org/extensions`), use social media to share success stories, introduce your peers at other nonprofits to CiviCRM, join a local meetup (or start one), help others who are getting started, and ensure the long-term sustainability of the project with a recurring contribution at `http://civicrm.org/contribute`!

David Greenberg,
Co-founder of CiviCRM

Looking for more learning resources? Check out:

- *Using CiviCRM* by *Packt Publishing*
- CiviCRM User guild and Developer guide (`http://book.civicrm.org`)
- Extension Developer guide and reference (`http://documentation.civicrm.org`)

And remember, CiviCRM is continually evolving and growing, so make sure you're on top of the latest news, by subscribing to the community newsletter at `http://civicrm.org`.

About the Author

Tony Horrocks is the owner of Fabriko Limited (`http://fabriko.co.uk`), a web development company that specializes in CiviCRM and Drupal. Tony has worked for membership organizations for over 25 years and has been developing websites since 1994.

He now works primarily as a Development Consultant for the nonprofit sector.

Thanks, of course, to the superstars of Packt Publishing for their assistance and encouragement, and the reviewers far and wide who I have never met.

Also, thanks to the CiviCRM core development team and the wider CiviCRM community for their dedication.

Thank you to all those people and organizations who donate to the CiviCRM project (`http://civicrm.org/content/make-it-happen`).

Lastly, thanks to Jackie, without whom none of this would have been possible, and also thanks to Rosie, who now has a book dedicated to her.

About the Reviewers

Erik Hommel has been an active member of the CiviCRM community since 2009. As project manager and developer with EE-atWork (`http://www.ee-atwork.nl`), he has worked on several projects implementing CiviCRM and developing customizations to CiviCRM. You can spot Erik regularly in the CiviCRM community on IRC or on the forum.

Kurund Jalmi is one of the core developers of CiviCRM, and he has been associated with the project since its inception. He has also worked on a CiviCRM book at `flossmanuals.net`. When not coding, he likes to spend his time outdoors exploring nature. He loves traveling and is very passionate about photography. For more information, check out `kurund.com`.

Andrew Wasson is partner and lead developer at Luna Design, a graphic design and web development studio in North Vancouver, British Columbia, Canada.

Keenly interested in electronics and technology from an early age, Andrew built his first computer from scratch while in high school in the early 80s. His journey in computer programming began with machine language assemblers, graduating to variations of Basic, C, and he eventually made the leap to web technologies in the mid-1990s when the Internet burst on to the scene.

Andrew has been developing and producing websites since 1998, and today he specializes in developing online membership management systems using Drupal and CiviCRM. Andrew was the technical reviewer for *Designing Next Generation Web Projects with CSS3* (2013), Packt Publishing.

When he is not sharing the responsibilities of running their business with his wife Fiona, Andrew can be found riding or restoring his vintage ex-racing motorcycles.

www.PacktPub.com

Support files, eBooks, discount offers and more

You might want to visit www.PacktPub.com for support files and downloads related to your book.

Did you know that Packt offers eBook versions of every book published, with PDF and ePub files available? You can upgrade to the eBook version at www.PacktPub.com and as a print book customer, you are entitled to a discount on the eBook copy. Get in touch with us at service@packtpub.com for more details.

At www.PacktPub.com, you can also read a collection of free technical articles, sign up for a range of free newsletters and receive exclusive discounts and offers on Packt books and eBooks.

http://PacktLib.PacktPub.com

Do you need instant solutions to your IT questions? PacktLib is Packt's online digital book library. Here, you can access, read and search across Packt's entire library of books.

Why Subscribe?

- Fully searchable across every book published by Packt
- Copy and paste, print and bookmark content
- On demand and accessible via web browser

Free Access for Packt account holders

If you have an account with Packt at www.PacktPub.com, you can use this to access PacktLib today and view nine entirely free books. Simply use your login credentials for immediate access.

Table of Contents

Preface

A good implementation of CiviCRM can transform your organization. Online management of contacts, members, communications, campaigns, funding, and casework used to be beyond the means of small non-governmental organizations (NGOs). But not anymore.

CiviCRM is loaded with features designed and developed by NGOs that make it a second-to-none management tool.

This book takes you from a CiviCRM installation and guides you through, by example, how to exploit the features that make it so popular.

We cover the post-installation setup and all the core and component parts of CiviCRM. In some cases, the recipes focus on CiviCRM, while in others, we cover using CiviCRM with Drupal.

The recipes in this book are not just meant to provide solutions to specific problems. They are there for you to explore and adapt to your own situation.

You don't need to be—and are not expected to be—a CiviCRM expert or a coding ninja. Far from it. What you do need, however, is the will and enthusiasm to use CiviCRM to take your organization from where it is now to where you want it to be.

What this book covers

Chapter 1, Setting Up CiviCRM, covers the important post-installation tasks that will get you going quickly. We look at some of the hard-to-do and hard-to-find settings and explore some of the ways of implementing workflows using Scheduled Reminders and CiviCase.

Chapter 2, Organizing Data Efficiently, covers the role of tags and groups. We also explore importing and exporting data, and some techniques to make these processes trouble-free.

Chapter 3, Using the Power of Profiles, covers how you can exploit the power of CiviCRM profiles to improve usability, speed up data entry, and control listings and directories.

Chapter 4, Controlling Permissions, demystifies permissions and shows you how you can use them in a variety of contexts to control access to viewing and editing data.

Chapter 5, Managing Communications, covers how to get the best out of CiviMail. We explore the mail templating system and a Drupal-based alternative to authoring your mailings. We also cover techniques for managing mailing subscriptions and allowing users to update information easily.

Chapter 6, Searching and Reporting, focuses on the search capabilities of CiviCRM. We look at how you can use searching to find and group data easily. We also explore how you can customize the search result display, and finally we will look at a search technique in Drupal that is not possible within CiviCRM itself.

Chapter 7, Integrating CiviCRM with Drupal, covers integrating CiviCRM with Drupal Views and using the power of the Drupal Webform CiviCRM module to do things CiviCRM can't. Finally, we explore some experimental modules that enable you to create user accounts on the fly and to organize contacts using Drupal taxonomy terms.

Chapter 8, Managing Events Effectively, uses CiviEvents to explore how you can use jQuery to alter the display and behavior of CiviCRM forms. We also look at how you can use Webform CiviCRM to control registration workflow for paid-for events.

Chapter 9, Using Campaigns, Surveys, and Petitions Effectively, covers in detail how to set up campaigns, surveys, and petitions. We also look at how you can use Drupal Views to create a Campaign Dashboard so you can get at-a-glance information about the progress of your campaigns.

Chapter 10, Working with CiviMember, explores **CiviMember**, a CiviCRM component used for membership management. We look at a popular requirement—displaying a membership directory—and then explore how to link common membership tasks with other CiviCRM components.

Chapter 11, Developing with CiviCRM, looks at the software, skills, and resources you need to start developing CiviCRM in earnest. We also cover developing a simple Drupal module and exploring the CiviCRM API.

What you need for this book

You will need an installed version of CiviCRM. For several recipes, the CMS of choice should be Drupal. There are no specific recipes for Joomla! or WordPress.

For some of the recipes you should have a good text editor.

Who this book is for

This book is for the nontechnical CiviCRM user. You will know how to get CiviCRM installed, but will now want to find out the tips, tricks, and techniques to get the best out of CiviCRM for your particular situation. You should understand the basic operation of CiviCRM and Drupal. For some recipes, it helps if you are familiar with a coding environment as we will be doing some PHP scripting, but you do not need any programming or technical skills as you will learn everything you need in this book.

Conventions

In this book, you will find a number of styles of text that distinguish between different kinds of information. Here are some examples of these styles, and an explanation of their meaning.

Code words in text are shown as follows: "In the previous recipe, we used a URL to access the profile we created, that is, `civicrm/profile/create?gid=N&reset=1`, where N was the ID of our profile."

New terms and **important words** are shown in bold. Words that you see on the screen, in menus or dialog boxes for example, appear in the text like this: "Navigate to **Administer | Customize Data and Screens | Profiles** and add a new profile that will contain the fields you wish to display on your directory."

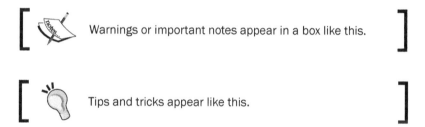

Warnings or important notes appear in a box like this.

Tips and tricks appear like this.

Reader feedback

Feedback from our readers is always welcome. Let us know what you think about this book—what you liked or may have disliked. Reader feedback is important for us to develop titles that you really get the most out of.

To send us general feedback, simply send an e-mail to `feedback@packtpub.com`, and mention the book title via the subject of your message.

If there is a topic that you have expertise in and you are interested in either writing or contributing to a book, see our author guide on `www.packtpub.com/authors`.

Customer support

Now that you are the proud owner of a Packt book, we have a number of things to help you to get the most from your purchase.

Errata

Although we have taken every care to ensure the accuracy of our content, mistakes do happen. If you find a mistake in one of our books—maybe a mistake in the text or the code—we would be grateful if you would report this to us. By doing so, you can save other readers from frustration and help us improve subsequent versions of this book. If you find any errata, please report them by visiting `http://www.packtpub.com/submit-errata`, selecting your book, clicking on the **errata submission form** link, and entering the details of your errata. Once your errata are verified, your submission will be accepted and the errata will be uploaded on our website, or added to any list of existing errata, under the Errata section of that title. Any existing errata can be viewed by selecting your title from `http://www.packtpub.com/support`.

Piracy

Piracy of copyright material on the Internet is an ongoing problem across all media. At Packt, we take the protection of our copyright and licenses very seriously. If you come across any illegal copies of our works, in any form, on the Internet, please provide us with the location address or website name immediately so that we can pursue a remedy.

Please contact us at `copyright@packtpub.com` with a link to the suspected pirated material.

We appreciate your help in protecting our authors, and our ability to bring you valuable content.

Questions

You can contact us at `questions@packtpub.com` if you are having a problem with any aspect of the book, and we will do our best to address it.

1

Setting Up CiviCRM

In this chapter we will cover:

- ► Setting up a CiviCRM theme in Drupal
- ► Setting up cron using cPanel
- ► Adding items to the CiviCRM navigation menu
- ► Refreshing the dashboard
- ► Changing display preferences
- ► Replacing words
- ► Setting up geocoding
- ► Autofiling e-mails
- ► Creating new activities
- ► Adding custom fields
- ► Using Scheduled Reminders for activities
- ► Using CiviCase to create an HR system
- ► Installing languages and localizing CiviCRM

Introduction

This chapter provides recipes to help you set up your CiviCRM installation. You will find that most of them work in Drupal, Joomla!, and WordPress. Some recipes are **Content Management System** (**CMS**) specific and we have chosen Drupal to illustrate these.

Setting up a CiviCRM theme in Drupal

CiviCRM administration screens take up a lot of browser real estate. How CiviCRM looks is determined by what themes you are using in your CMS. Problems arise when you use your main website theme to display CiviCRM pages. All the customizations, blocks of information, and layouts suddenly get in the way when you want to administer CiviCRM. The trick is to use a different theme for CiviCRM.

How to do it...

This is very easy to accomplish, and just uses a configuration screen in Drupal.

1. Make sure you have the CiviCRM theme module enabled.

2. Navigate to `admin/appearance` in Drupal by clicking on the **Appearance** button. This page shows the themes that are currently installed within our CMS—in this case, Drupal.

3. Make sure that any themes you wish to use are enabled.

4. At the foot of the screen, configure **CiviCRM Administration theme**.

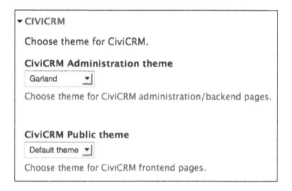

How it works...

Drupal uses the page URL to check if you are administering CiviCRM. If you are, the pages are displayed using the CiviCRM administration theme.

It's a good idea to select a flexible-width theme with sidebars. Garland is a good example. The flexible width accommodates CiviCRM displays nicely.

Once the administration theme is selected, navigate to `admin/structure/blocks`. Here you will see various blocks provided by the CiviCRM module. You can now place these blocks within your administrative theme.

Pay special attention to the visibility settings for these blocks, so that they only appear when using CiviCRM.

There's more...

In Drupal, there is an additional setting that controls which theme is used to display public CiviCRM pages, for example, event sign-up pages.

See also

▶   You can explore hundreds of contributed Drupal themes at `http://drupal.org/project/themes`

Setting up cron using cPanel

Cron is a time-based scheduler that is used extensively throughout CiviCRM. For example, you might want to use CiviCRM to send out an e-mail newsletter at a particular time, or you might want to send out a reminder to participants to attend an event. CiviCRM has settings to accomplish all these tasks, but these, in turn, rely on having "master" cron set up. Cron is set up on your web server, not within CiviCRM.

How to do it...

There are many different ways of setting up cron, depending on your site-hosting setup. In this example, we are using cPanel, a popular control panel that simplifies website administration.

1.   Make a note of your CMS site administrator username and password.

2.   Make a note of your CiviCRM site key, which is a long string of characters used to uniquely identify your CiviCRM installation. It is automatically generated when CiviCRM is installed, and is stored in the `civicrm_settings.php` file. Using a text editor, open up the CiviCRM settings file located at `/sites/default/civicrm_settings.php`. Around line 170, you will see the following entry:

```
define( 'CIVICRM_SITE_KEY',
    '7409e83819379dc5646783f34f9753d9' );
```

Make a note of this key.

3.   Log in to cPanel and use the cPanel File Manager to explore the folders and files that are stored there. You are going to create a file that contains all the necessary information for cron to work. You can choose to create the cron file anywhere you like. It makes sense to keep it in the home directory of your webserver—that is, the first directory you get to once you start exploring.

4. Create a file called `CiviCron.php`. The naming does not particularly matter, but it must be a PHP file.

5. Insert the following code:

```php
<?php
// create a new cURL resource
$ch = curl_init();
// set URL and other appropriate options
curl_setopt($ch, CURLOPT_URL,
    "http://myDrupalsite.com/sites/all/modules/civicrm/bin/
    cron.php?name=admin&pass=adminpassword&key
    =01504c43af550a317f3c6495c2442ab7");
curl_setopt($ch, CURLOPT_HEADER, 0);
// grab URL and pass it to the browser
curl_exec($ch);
curl_close($ch);
?>
```

- Substitute `http://myDrupalsite.com` with your own domain
- Substitute `admin` with your own CMS admin username
- Substitute `adminpassword` with your own CMS admin password
- Substitute the key value with the site key from `civicrm_settings.php`

6. Save this file and then navigate to `cron` in cPanel.

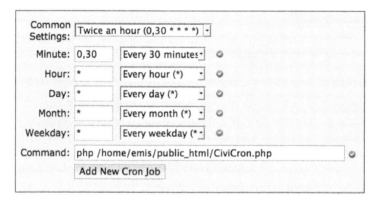

7. Select an appropriate cron interval from the **Common Settings** list. Choosing an appropriate cron interval may take some experimentation, depending on how your site is set up. In the **Command** field, enter the following address:

php /home/site_account_name/public_html/CiviCron.php

The portion after `php` is the absolute path to the `CiviCron.php` file you created in step 4.

8. Click on **Add New Cron Job**.

How it works...

All cron does is execute the URL that is constructed in the cron file.

The following piece of code does the work:

```
curl_setopt($ch, CURLOPT_URL,
  "http://myDrupalsite.com/sites/all/modules/civicrm/bin/
  cron.php?name=admin&pass=adminpassword&key=
  01504c43af550a317f3c6495c2442ab7");
```

The URL contains the information on permissions (the username, the password, and the site key) to execute the `cron.php` file provided by the CiviCRM module.

Getting cron to work is critical to getting CiviCRM working properly. If you get into difficulties with it, the best solution is to contact your hosting company and seek guidance.

> To test that your cron job is actually working, carry out the following instructions. In the cPanel cron screen, set it to send you an e-mail each time the cron command is run. The e-mail will contain an error message if the cron fails. Failures are generally due to an incorrect setting of the path, or a permissions problem with the username, password, or site key.

Adding items to the CiviCRM navigation menu

As you begin to use CiviCRM, you will want to provide administrative shortcuts. You can do this by adding custom menu blocks within your CMS or editing the navigation menu in CiviCRM.

How to do it...

CiviCRM has a fully customizable navigation menu. You can edit this menu to get one-click access to the features you use most.

1. Navigate to a page that you want to use as the link destination for a menu item. For example, you could navigate to **Contacts | Manage Groups**, and then select a suitable group.

2. Copy the page URL in the browser location. In this example, it would be as follows:

   ```
   civicrm/group/search?reset=1&force=1&context=smog&gid=2
   ```

3. Navigate to **Administer | Customize Data and Screens | Navigation Menu**. This displays the CiviCRM navigation menu in tree form.

4. Click on the left arrow on each **Parent** menu item to expand it. You can now explore all the child menu items.

5. Click on the **Add Menu item** button at the top of this screen. This brings up the **Add Menu Item** edit screen.

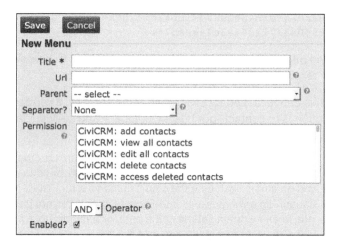

6. Enter the name of the menu item in the **Title** field.

7. Enter the URL (that you copied) into the **URL** field.

8. Select a parent to make the menu item appear as the child of another menu item. If you don't select a parent, the item will appear on the main CiviCRM menu bar.

9. Select one or more permissions in the **Permission** field to control who can use the menu item. These are CMS permissions, so we must ensure that these are set correctly in our CMS for the menu item to behave properly.

How it works...

CiviCRM stores new menu items, and displays them according to where they are placed in the menu tree and what permissions a user may have to use them.

See also

▶ You can fully explore CiviCRM customization at http://book.civicrm.org/ user/current/initial-set-up/customizing-the-user-interface/

Refreshing the dashboard

By default, CiviCRM sets the auto-refresh period for the home page dashboard to 1 hour. In a busy setting, this is too long, and you constantly have to click on the **Refresh Dashboard data** button to get the information on the dashboard up to date.

How to do it...

Changing the setting is simply a matter of visiting the CiviCRM administration pages:

1. Navigate to **Administer | System Settings | Undelete, Logging and ReCAPTCHA**.
2. Change the **Dashboard cache timeout** value from **1440** (that's 1 hour in seconds) to a smaller figure.

Changing display preferences

By default, CiviCRM displays a lot of data on the **contact summary** screen. Sometimes, this can lead to a cluttered display that is hard to use and slow to load.

How to do it...

CiviCRM components can add to the clutter on the screen. Here we can disable unwanted components and then fine-tune the display of other elements in the contact summary screen.

1. Navigate to **Administer | System Settings | Enable CiviCRM Components**, and disable any unused CiviCRM components.
2. Navigate to **Administer | Customize data and screens | Display preferences**.
3. Control which tabs are displayed in the detail screen (for each contact), using the checkboxes.

> Viewing Contacts ☑Activities ☑Relationships ☑Groups
> ☑Notes ☑Tags ☑Change Log
> ☑Contributions ☑Memberships ☑Events
> ☑Cases ☐Grants ☐Pledges

4. Control which sections you want to see when editing an individual contact, by checking the checkboxes in the **Editing Contacts** section.

Contact Details	Other Panes
‡ ☑ Email	‡ ☑ Custom Data
‡ ☑ Phone	‡ ☑ Address
‡ ☐ Instant Messenger	‡ ☑ Communication Preferences
‡ ☐ Open ID	‡ ☑ Notes
‡ ☑ Website	‡ ☑ Demographics
	‡ ☑ Tags and Groups

5. Drag the double-arrow icon to move the sections up and down the contact editing screen.

See also

▶ You can fully explore the display preferences at `http://book.civicrm.org/ user/current/initial-set-up/customizing-the-user-interface/`

Replacing words

This is useful for fine-tuning your website. For example, you could replace US spelling with UK spelling (thus avoiding installing the UK language translation). Or you might want to change the wording on parts of a standard form without having to make a custom template.

How to do it...

The words—or sentences—that we want to replace are called **strings**. In CiviCRM, we can enter the strings we don't want, and replace them with strings we do want.

1. Navigate to **Administer | System Settings | Customize Data and Screens | Word Replacement**.

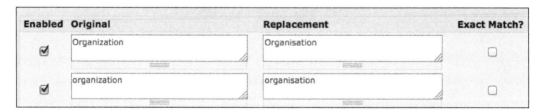

Enabled	Original	Replacement	Exact Match?
☑	Organization	Organisation	☐
☑	organization	organisation	☐

In this example, I am replacing the US spelling of "Organization" with the UK version, "Organisation".

2. Use the **Exact Match** checkbox to match words precisely. This would then exclude plurals of the word from being matched. All word replacements are case sensitive.

Setting up geocoding

Geocoding allows you to do location-based searching and to display the maps of contacts.

How to do it...

You need to set a mapping provider—that is a service that will provide you with the visual maps—and a geocoding provider, which will translate your contact addresses into latitude and longitude coordinates.

1. Navigate to **Administer | Localization | Address settings**. In **Address Display**, make sure that the **Street Address Parsing** checkbox is ticked.

2. Navigate to **Administer | System Settings | Mapping and Geocoding**. Set **Mapping Provider** to **Google** or **Openstreetmap**. Set **Geocoding Provider** to **Google**.

3. Navigate to **Administer | System Settings | Scheduled Jobs**. The **Geocode and Parse Addresses** scheduled job should now be enabled. You can set how regularly you want CiviCRM to geocode your address data.

How it works...

Geocoding Provider finds latitude and longitude coordinates for each contact address. **Mapping Provider** uses this information to draw a local map, with a pointer for the contact. **Geocode** and **Parse Addresses** do the geocoding work each day, though you can change this in the settings.

There's more...

Google currently limits geocoding requests to 2,500 per 24 hours. So, if you exceed this limit, Google may not process requests; it may even restrict access to their geocoding service should you continue to break this limit. This is a problem when you have thousands of addresses to process—for example, after a big import of address data.

CiviCRM does not have a tool to place a daily limit on the number of contacts that are processed each day. But you can put parameters into the Geocode and Parse Addresses scheduled job that provide a range of contact IDs to process. You would have to change this each day to work your way though all your contacts.

1. Navigate to **Administer | System Settings | Scheduled Jobs**, and edit the Geocode and Parse Addresses scheduled job.

2. In the **Command Parameters** box, enter:

```
start= 1
end=2500
```

1 would be the ID of your first contact. If you have access to your database tables, check the database table `civicrm_contact` to know what the first value for your contacts is.

See also

▶ Further details about geocoding in CiviCRM are available at `http://wiki.civicrm.org/confluence/display/CRMDOC43/Mapping+and+Geocoding`

Autofiling e-mails

Interactions between your contacts and your organization are many and complex. A lot of these interactions will involve exchanges of e-mail. You may want to keep a record of these exchanges for each of your contacts. This is particularly useful in situations where you are dealing with a contact and you need to see a history of correspondence relating to the contact and other members of your organization. CiviCRM lets you do this by filing e-mail correspondence as an activity on each contact record.

How to do it...

We will set up an e-mail account that will act as a "dropbox" for messages that we want to file, and link this to CiviCRM.

1. Set up an e-mail account. You can use Gmail or an account provided by your hosting provider. In this recipe we will use an account called `filing@mycivicrmsite.com`.

2. Navigate to **Administer | System Settings | Enable CiviCRM components**, and make sure that **CiviMail** is enabled.

3. Navigate to **Administer | CiviMail | Mail Accounts**.

4. Click on the **Add Mail Account** button and complete the details for each account you are adding. Getting this right can sometimes be a matter of trial and error. Leave the **Source** field blank.

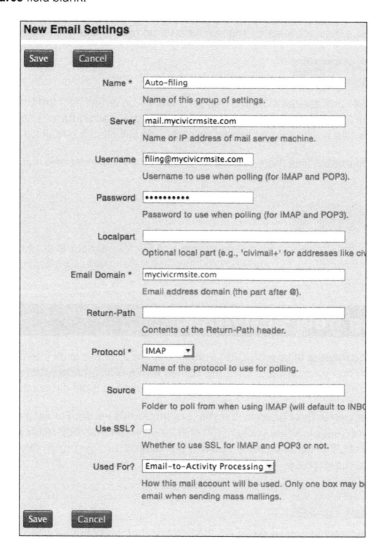

5. Create a test e-mail message in your e-mail client, and Bcc it to `filing@` `mycivicrmsite.com`.

6. Navigate to **Administer | System Settings | Scheduled Jobs**, and execute the job titled **Process Inbound Emails**.

7. Click on the **View Job Log** link to see the log entry. If the log error message is `Failure`, this is highly likely to be a connection problem, so you must go back to **Administer | CiviMail | Mail Accounts**, and make the necessary changes.

8. Navigate to **Reports | Contact Reports | Activities**. You will see that CiviCRM has recorded e-mail activities for the sender and the recipient of the e-mail.

How it works...

Each time CiviCRM processes inbound e-mails, it checks the e-mail account you had set up. It then processes each message. If the sender or recipient e-mail address is not held within CiviCRM, it will create a new contact record for each, and will file the e-mail activity.

If the contacts do exist, it files the e-mails as an activity for the sender and an activity for the receiver.

See also

▸ You can find detailed guidance on configuring CiviMail accounts at `http://wiki.civicrm.org/confluence/display/CRMDOC43/Autofiling+email+activities+via+EmailProcessor`

Creating new activities

Activities are fundamental to how CiviCRM works. They are a record of all interactions between your organization and your contacts. CiviCRM comes with a ready-made set of activity types, such as phone calls, meetings, and e-mails, that can be used in most circumstances.

You can add your own activity types to suit your organization's needs. For example, yours may be an organization that performs background checks on volunteers before they are allowed to work with its clients. You could create an activity type called `Background Check` that would help you manage this process.

How to do it...

You should consider what activity types you need as part of the planning stage of your CiviCRM deployment. Adding a new activity type in CiviCRM is easy.

1. Navigate to **Administer | Customize Data and Screens | Activity Types**. Click on the **Add activity type** button. In the **Label** field, enter your activity. In this case we will use **Background Check**.

2. In the **Component** field, we can choose to have the new activity set against **Contacts**.

3. Save the new activity type.

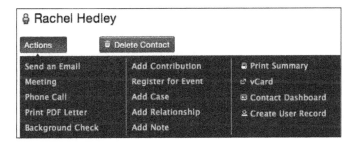

How it works...

Test your new activity type by going to a contact and clicking on the **Actions** button present at the top left of the contact screen. This will show a drop-down list of available actions. Activities are listed in the first column.

See also

▸ The *Adding custom fields* recipe in this chapter

▸ You can find further details about CiviCRM Activities at `http://book.civicrm.org/user/current/organising-your-data/activities/`

Adding custom fields

Custom fields are a great way of storing and organizing data in CiviCRM. Custom fields are contained in custom datasets, and you apply each set to an object in CiviCRM, such as a contact type, an activity, or an event. For example, if you were organizing soccer teams, you might want to have a custom fieldset called `Soccer Data` that contains custom fields for playing position, goals scored, games played, and so on. Custom fields are searchable using advanced search.

Getting ready...

Custom fields need a bit of planning because once you have created a custom fieldset and applied it to an object, you cannot re-edit it and apply it to a different object. For example, let's say you are organizing a boat race. You want to collect information on boat size and boat type. You could choose to collect this custom information for each individual who applies to race, or for each actual participant in the race, or for each team in the race. So if you applied it to an individual contact and then changed your mind and only wanted to collect it for each participant, you would have to recreate the whole custom set of fields.

So you need to think about the following questions:

▸ What sort of unique data do you want to collect?

▸ What object do you want to apply the custom data set to?

In this example, we will add a simple custom field to the `Phone Call` activity. So when a phone call activity is recorded with a contact, the custom field will record if the call was general, a membership enquiry, or an event enquiry.

How to do it...

First we will create a custom data set, and then we will add some custom fields to it. In this recipe, we will add some fields to get data about phone calls.

1. Navigate to **Administer | Customize Data and Screens | Custom Fields**. You will see a screen that contains the current listing of custom datasets.

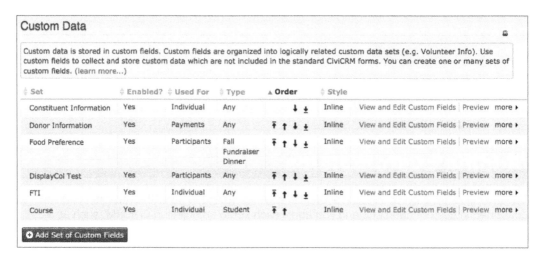

Custom Data

Custom data is stored in custom fields. Custom fields are organized into logically related custom data sets (e.g. Volunteer Info). Use custom fields to collect and store custom data which are not included in the standard CiviCRM forms. You can create one or many sets of custom fields. (learn more...)

⇕ Set	⇕ Enabled?	⇕ Used For	⇕ Type	▲ Order	⇕ Style			
Constituent Information	Yes	Individual	Any	↓ ⤓	Inline	View and Edit Custom Fields	Preview	more ▸
Donor Information	Yes	Payments	Any	⤒ ↑ ↓ ⤓	Inline	View and Edit Custom Fields	Preview	more ▸
Food Preference	Yes	Participants	Fall Fundraiser Dinner	⤒ ↑ ↓ ⤓	Inline	View and Edit Custom Fields	Preview	more ▸
DisplayCol Test	Yes	Participants	Any	⤒ ↑ ↓ ⤓	Inline	View and Edit Custom Fields	Preview	more ▸
FTI	Yes	Individual	Any	⤒ ↑ ↓ ⤓	Inline	View and Edit Custom Fields	Preview	more ▸
Course	Yes	Individual	Student	⤒ ↑	Inline	View and Edit Custom Fields	Preview	more ▸

⊕ Add Set of Custom Fields

2. Click on the **Add Set of Custom Fields** button.

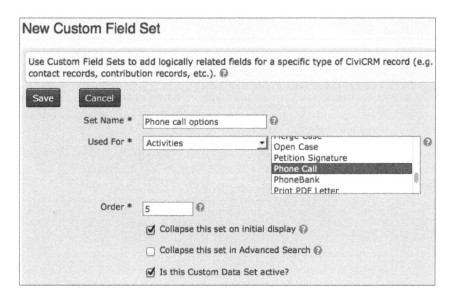

In this recipe, call the custom data set **Phone call options**, or substitute your own label.

3. In the **Used For** field, choose **Activities** and then choose **Phone Call**. This means that when a `Phone Call` activity is created, the fields will appear on the activity form for the user to complete.

4. The **Collapse this set on initial display** checkbox is checked by default. This means that when you look at the contact record, the custom fields will be hidden until you click on the custom fieldset title. Uncheck it.

5. Save the new custom fieldset and add custom fields.

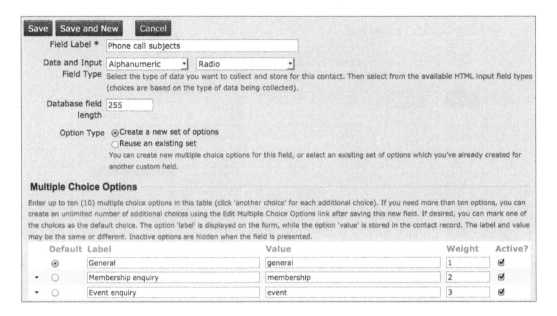

6. Add a set of three options to record the nature of the phone call. It is beyond the scope of this book to go into the details of the various field types available.

7. Save the custom fields.

8. Navigate to a contact and add the `Phone Call` activity. The custom field is available.

There's more...

If you add custom fieldsets to contacts, you will get more options. You can add a fieldset multiple times to the same record. This is useful for recording employment histories or academic achievements.

You can create a custom fieldset for cases, relationships, groups, events, and memberships.

- You can find further details about creating custom fields at `http://book.civicrm.org/user/current/organising-your-data/custom-fields/`

Using Scheduled Reminders for activities

Scheduled Reminders are a great new feature in CiviCRM. For example, you might have created an **Activity** for a colleague—perhaps a meeting that you have scheduled for next Friday. With Scheduled Reminders, you can send an e-mail reminder (say, the day before), reminding them to read the agenda for the meeting, and about the meeting itself.

You can also use Scheduled Reminders to accomplish the activity itself, if it involves e-mailing something. For example, you might schedule an activity, called `Welcome Information Pack`, for a new contact. `Welcome Information Pack` is an e-mail message that contains useful information and links back to your site for resources and so forth. You can configure a Scheduled Reminder as the `Welcome Information Pack` itself and have it sent to the contact at the scheduled time. This is how the Scheduled Reminder e-mail actually accomplishes the task.

Getting ready

You do not need to have cron running on your site to test this recipe. But, for this recipe to work on your live site, you must have cron running.

You will need to know how to set up and use mail templates within CiviCRM.

How to do it...

First we will set up the activities we want to schedule and then we will create the Scheduled Reminder for each activity. Every Scheduled Reminder uses a mail template. We will configure the mail template to accomplish the original activity.

1. Navigate to **Administer | Customized Data and Screens | Activity types**.

2. Set up two new activities, **Volunteer Pack 1** and **Volunteer Pack 2**. Make sure that the **Component** field is set to **Contact**. Now go to a test contact. Click on the **Actions** button and schedule the **Volunteer Pack 1** activity.

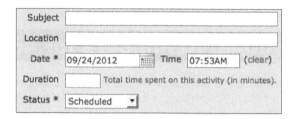

3. You do not need to fill in the **Subject** and **Location** fields. Fill in the **Date** field. For testing purposes set this to 10 minutes from the current time.

4. You do not need to fill in the **Duration** field. Make sure the **Status** field is set to **Scheduled**.

5. Now set up the **Volunteer Pack 2** activity in the same way. For testing purposes, set the date and time to 15 minutes from the current time.

6. Click on the **Activities** tab on the contact screen to check if your activities have been scheduled.

7. Navigate to **Communications | Schedule Reminders**, and click on **Add a reminder**.

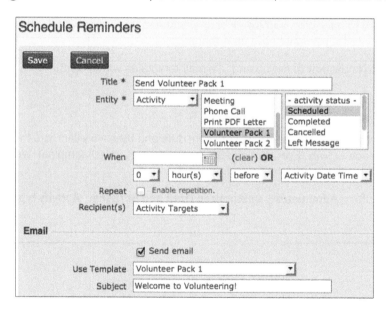

8. Give the reminder a title such as **Send Volunteer Pack 1**. Select the **Volunteer Pack 1** activity and select **Scheduled** for the **activity status** field.

9. For **When**, select the default values: **0, hour(s)**, **before**, **Activity Date Time**. For **Recipient(s)**, select **Activity Targets**. Make sure the **Send email** checkbox is checked.

10. Now select an e-mail template, or prepare an e-mail using the rich text editor. Save the schedule.

11. Now add another schedule for the **Volunteer Pack 2** activity.

12. Navigate to **Administer | System Settings | Scheduled Jobs**. Navigate to the **Send Scheduled Reminder** job.

13. Check that the job is enabled, and for testing purposes, set the interval to **every time cron is run**.

How it works...

CiviCRM will now send out your reminders at the scheduled test times. Check your test e-mail account for incoming mails at regular intervals.

There's more...

The Schedule Reminders system does not automate your workflow.

If you look at the **Activities** tab for your test contact, you will see that the status is still set to **Scheduled** even after the reminder has been sent. This is because Scheduled Reminder is sending out a reminder about the activity, not accomplishing the activity itself.

You may wish to investigate writing a module that switches the activity to the status **Completed** once the reminder is sent.

See also

▶ You can find further information about Scheduled Reminders at `http://book.civicrm.org/user/current/email/scheduled-reminders/`

Using CiviCase to create an HR system

CiviCase was developed to manage and track interactions between an organization and it's clients in case management situations. It can be adapted to suit any internal or external processes that have regular, predictable, and reasonably well-defined workflows or procedures. Many NGOs generally have human resource functions such as hiring and training staff. Using CiviCase to manage these processes provides consistency, compliancy, and accountability to our human resource procedures. In this recipe we will configure a CiviCase type that will enable us to create and manage the employment records of staff.

How to do it...

CiviCase does not have a user interface for configuring CiviCase types. Instead, we create all the activity types and relationships that we need, and then we create an XML file that generates and schedules these activities when a case is opened. The CiviCase type we are going to create will handle three activities:

- **Contract acceptance**: This activity happens when our new employee signs the employment contract

- **Annual appraisal**: This activity happens when our employee is appraised for performance each year

- **Exit interview**: This activity happens when our employee leaves employment with our organization

We will use the XML file to also generate the relationship types associated with the employment record. These are:

- Line Manager

- HR Officer

1. Enable CiviCase by navigating to **Administer | System Settings | Enable CiviCRM Components**.

2. Check that you have set up a **Custom Templates** path for CiviCRM. This is a directory on your server that stores custom files for CiviCRM. This is where you will store the CiviCase XML file. Create a directory on your web server for your custom CiviCRM files called `custom_civicrm`. You can give it any name you like. Navigate to **Administer | System Settings | Directories** to set the path to the directory you just created.

Custom Templates	/home/cookbook/custom_civicrm/
	Path where site specific templates are stored if any. This directory is searched first if set. Custo named *templateFile.extra.tpl*. (learn more...)
	CiviCase configuration files can also be stored in this custom path. (learn more...)

3. Create the following directory path in your `Custom Templates` directory:

    `custom_civicrm/CRM/Case/xml/configuration`

4. Create a text file called `StaffRecord.xml` in the `custom_civicrm/CRM/Case/xml/configuration` directory, so the path to the file will be `custom_civicrm/CRM/Case/xml/configuration/StaffRecord.xml`.

5. Using a suitable text editor, enter the following XML code:

```xml
<?xml version="1.0" encoding="iso-8859-1" ?>
<CaseType>
  <name>Staff Record</name>
  <ActivityTypes>
    <ActivityType>
      <name>Open Case</name>
      <max_instances>1</max_instances>
    </ActivityType>
    <ActivityType>
      <name>Contract acceptance</name>
        <max_instances>1</max_instances>
    </ActivityType>
    <ActivityType>
      <name>Annual appraisal</name>
    </ActivityType>
     <ActivityType>
      <name>Exit interview</name>
        <max_instances>1</max_instances>
    </ActivityType>
       <ActivityType>
      <name>Change Case Type</name>
    </ActivityType>
    <ActivityType>
      <name>Change Case Status</name>
    </ActivityType>
    <ActivityType>
      <name>Change Case Start Date</name>
    </ActivityType>
    <ActivityType>
      <name>Link Cases</name>
    </ActivityType>
  </ActivityTypes>
  <ActivitySets>
    <ActivitySet>
      <name>standard_timeline</name>
      <label>Standard Timeline</label>
      <timeline>true</timeline>
      <ActivityTypes>
        <ActivityType>
          <name>Open Case</name>
          <status>Completed</status>
        </ActivityType>
        <ActivityType>
```

```
            <name>Contract acceptance</name>
            <reference_activity>Open Case</reference_activity>
            <reference_offset>1</reference_offset>
         </ActivityType>
<ActivityType>
            <name>Annual appraisal</name>
            <reference_activity>Open Case</reference_activity>
            <reference_offset>365</reference_offset>
            <reference_select>newest</reference_select>
         </ActivityType>
      </ActivityTypes>
    </ActivitySet>
  </ActivitySets>
  <CaseRoles>
    <RelationshipType>
        <name>HR Manager</name>
        <creator>1</creator>
    </RelationshipType>
    <RelationshipType>
        <name>Line Manager</name>
    </RelationshipType>
  </CaseRoles>
</CaseType>
```

6. Save the XML file.

7. Navigate to **Administer | Customized Data and Screens |Activity types**, and create the three activity types described in the XML document:

    ❑ Contract acceptance

    ❑ Annual appraisal

    ❑ Exit interview

    Make sure the names of the activity types are exactly the same as shown in the XML document.

    Make sure that you select CiviCase as the component for each activity type.

8. Create the relationship types that are described in the XML document. Navigate to **Administer | Customize Data and Screens**, and create two relationship types, HR Officer and Line Manager. Make sure that these relationships have *exactly* the same names and capitalizations that you used in the XML file. Make sure you name the **Relationship Label** from **B** to **A**—exactly the same as the relationship type.

9. Navigate to this file on your web server: `sites/modules/civicrm/CRM/Case/xml/configuration.sample/settings.xml`, and copy it to the configuration directory, `custom_civicrm/CRM/Case/xml/configuration` you previously created.

   This is a global settings file for CiviCase. You do not need to alter it.

10. Navigate to **Administer | CiviCase**. Add a case type called `Staff Record`.

11. Navigate to a test contact, click on the **Actions** button and add a case, choosing **Staff Record**.

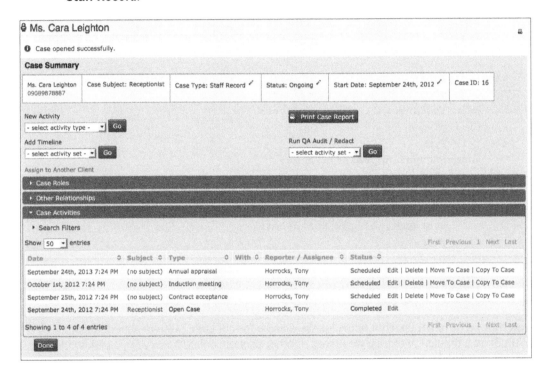

How it works...

The XML code does all the work for us once it is set up. Let's go through the structure. This provides the name of the case type that we will use:

```xml
<?xml version="1.0" encoding="iso-8859-1" ?>
<CaseType>
<name>Staff Record</name>
```

We have a section called `ActivityTypes` (note the plural!). It is a container for each activity type that is going to be associated with the `Staff Record` case.

```
<ActivityTypes>
<ActivityType>
      <name>Open Case</name>
      <max_instances>1</max_instances>
   </ActivityType>
</ActivityTypes>
```

CiviCase always starts with `<ActivityType>` named `Open Case`.

`<max_instances>` tells CiviCase how many instances of the activity to create. As a case is opened only once, there is only one instance.

```
<ActivityType>
      <name>Contract acceptance</name>
      <max_instances>1</max_instances>
   </ActivityType>
   <ActivityType>
      <name>Annual appraisal</name>
   </ActivityType>
   <ActivityType>
      <name>Exit interview</name>
      <max_instances>1</max_instances>
   </ActivityType>
```

The three activity types that we will use in our CiviCase are described next. You can see that the activity type named `Annual appraisal` does not have a `<max_instances>` tag. This is because annual appraisals take place each year and there is no defined maximum.

Now that we have set up what activities we will use for our case, we can schedule some of them on a timeline. For this, we create another section, called `ActivitySets`, in the XML file.

```
<ActivitySets>
<ActivitySet>
<name>standard_timeline</name>
<label>Standard Timeline</label>
<timeline>true</timeline>
<ActivityTypes>
<ActivityType>
<name>Open Case</name>
<status>Completed</status>
</ActivityType>
<ActivityType>
<name>Contract acceptance</name>
```

```
<reference_activity>Open Case</reference_activity>
<reference_offset>7</reference_offset>
<reference_select>newest</reference_select>
</ActivityType>
</ActivityTypes>
</ActivitySet>
</ActivitySets>
```

Here we have the section called `ActivitySets`. It is a container for one or more instances of `ActivitySet`.

`ActivitySet` is a set of scheduled activities that CiviCase will generate when our `Staff Record` case is opened. When the case is first generated, CiviCase uses the `<standard_timeline>` activity set to generate the initial set of activities. You can have additional `ActivitySet` instances that use a different timeline. This is used to create activity branches within a case. In our example it could be the case that if an employee has a poor annual appraisal, we need to generate another set of activities to deal with the outcome. We can do this by having it configured in our XML file and applying it in the `Add Timeline` section of the CiviCase screen.

Within each `<ActivitySet>` instance, we have `<ActivityType>` again, and we have some tags to schedule each type.

`<reference_offset>` is the time in days that the activity will be scheduled. The offset is measured from whatever activity is entered in the `<reference_activity>` tag.

If the referenced activity has multiple instances, such as a training course, then we use the `<reference_select>` tag to pick the newest instance of the activity. If we do not want an activity schedule, we do not include it in `<ActivitySet>`.

Finally, we have a `<status>` tag that allows us to see the initial status of the activity when it is scheduled.

In our previous example, we have set the `Contract acceptance` activity to be scheduled seven days after the `Open Case` activity.

```
<CaseRoles>
<RelationshipType>
<name>Human Resources Manager</name>
<creator>1</creator>
</RelationshipType>
<RelationshipType>
<name>Line Manager</name>
</RelationshipType>
</CaseRoles>
```

Finally, there is an XML section where we can create our relationships for each case. Each relationship we create becomes a role within the case.

There's more...

This is just a very simplified example of what can be achieved using CiviCase. There are other ways you could apply the same principles: training schedules, volunteer induction programs, membership induction programs, as well as traditional casework applications.

See also

- ▸ *Chapter 1, Creating Activity Types*
- ▸ You can find more about CiviCRM relationships at `http://book.civicrm.org/user/current/organising-your-data/relationships/`
- ▸ You can find more about CiviCase at `http://book.civicrm.org/user/current/case-management/what-is-civicase/`

Installing languages and localizing CiviCRM

You might want your users to be able to use CiviCRM in a different language than US English. The CiviCRM user interface is available in many languages. This recipe shows you how to install these languages and localize your CiviCRM installation.

How to do it...

There are two stages to localizing CiviCRM. First we will download and install an interface translation and then we will configure CiviCRM using the **Localization admin** screens.

1. Go to `http://sourceforge.net/projects/civicrm/files/civicrm-stable` and open the latest stable version of CiviCRM. There you will see an archive that contains the translation files. It is called `civicrm-<version number>-l10n.tar.gz`. If you uncompress this archive you will see there are two folders, `l10n` and `sql`.

2. Copy the `l10n` folder into the CiviCRM module folder.

3. Copy the contents of the `sql` folder into the `sql` directory that already exists in your CiviCRM module folder. You can now explore what is in the `l10n` folder. It contains subdirectories for each language that CiviCRM supports. The name of each subdirectory is a locale code for the translation. These are reasonably easy to understand. For example, `es_ES` is mainland Spanish, `es_MX` is Mexican Spanish.

4. Remove languages that you do not wish to use from the `l10n` folder. Do the same for unused languages in the `sql` folder.

5. Navigate to **Administer | Localization | Languages, Currency, Location**.

6. At the top of the screen, select a new **Default Language**. In this case we will use French.

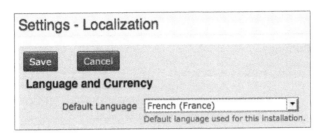

7. Complete the other settings on this page for currency, date formats, and addressing. Save your settings. The site is now displayed in French and supports the date, currency, and addressing formats that were configured.

8. Optionally under **Multiple Languages Support** you can check the **Enable Multiple Languages** checkbox. This allows the CiviCRM user to switch between two or more languages using the CiviCRM **Language Switcher** block available in your CMS. It also enables data entry in a different language.

9. If you have checked **Enable Multiple Languages**, save your settings and then at the top of the screen add in the extra languages that you require.

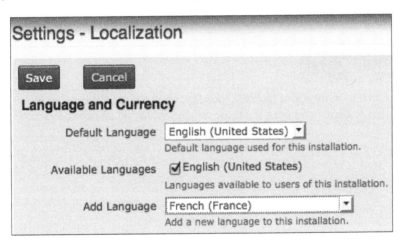

Here we are adding French. We can add extra ones by checking the checkboxes under **Available Languages**.

10. Save the settings.

11. In your CMS—in this case Drupal—navigate to **Structure | Blocks** and enable the CiviCRM Language Switcher block. The user can now switch between languages within CiviCRM.

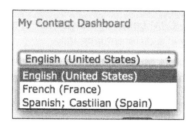

<h1>See also</h1>

▸ You can find more about CiviCRM localization at `http://book.civicrm.org/ user/current/the-civicrm-community/localising-civicrm/`

2
Organizing Data Efficiently

In this chapter we will cover:

- ▶ Adding contact types
- ▶ Adding a time-limited relationship
- ▶ Using tag sets to quickly organize data
- ▶ Using tags and groups to segment data
- ▶ Changing option lists
- ▶ Creating and updating a smart group
- ▶ Using Google Refine to prepare data
- ▶ Importing into CiviCRM using an import script
- ▶ Using external identifier deduping rules to import contacts
- ▶ Using Google Refine to create a unique ID
- ▶ Importing relationship data
- ▶ Exporting related data
- ▶ Batch updating using profiles

Introduction

Organizing data is a critical planning step in your transition to CiviCRM. What sort of contacts will you be managing and what are your data needs? How will your contacts be grouped and tagged? What relationships will they have between each other and you? What information will you want to get out of CiviCRM? Once you have a plan in place, you will want to get your existing data into CiviCRM the way you want. This often exposes the poor quality of your data, and the effort required to clean it up and get it into shape. This can sometimes take longer than the data planning stage. This chapter shows you some recipes that don't even use CiviCRM but will help get your data in shape. In other recipes we'll explore some of the techniques of organizing your data once you get it into CiviCRM.

Adding contact types

Imagine you are managing a soccer club using CiviCRM. For some contacts—players—you would want to record the goals scored, attendance, age, playing position, injuries, and other data. For other contacts such as coaches, you would want to collect different data: first aid qualifications, coaching qualifications, and so on. Having both these sets of data showing up on every contact summary screen does not make sense. What you need is to have two different sorts of contacts; contacts who are players and contacts who are coaches so that they both hold separate data. CiviCRM makes this easy to accomplish.

How to do it...

CiviCRM comes with three main contact types: **individuals**, **households**, and **organizations**. As we are dealing with individuals, we will create two subtypes of the the individual contact type, teachers and students. These subtypes inherit all the information you can collect from their parent contact type and can be extended to collect more information using custom field sets. This allows you to segregate your contact data more efficiently and makes data input easier. Perform the following steps to add different contact types:

1. Navigate to **Administer | Customize Data and Screens | Contact Types** and click on **Add a Contact Type**. You will then find the edit screen that looks like this:

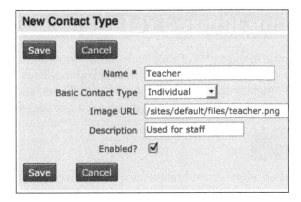

2. Give your new contact type a name and pick the parent contact type. You can also provide a link to an icon for your contact type.

How it works...

Contact subtypes are most useful in situations where you want to collect specific and unique data for each type.

Contact subtypes are useful in building CiviCRM relationships. For example, you can build a relationship between a teacher and a student where the teacher has to be a teacher subcontact and the student a student subcontact.

There's more...

You can create custom field sets targeted at each subcontact you create.

Navigate to **Administer | Customized Data and Screens | Custom data** to do this.

 Contact subtypes become available for use in CiviCRM core functions such as importing, exporting, and searching data.

See also

▸ The *Adding custom fields* recipe in *Chapter 1, Setting Up CiviCRM*

▸ Find out more about contact types at `http://book.civicrm.org/user/current/organising-your-data/contacts/`

Adding a time-limited relationship

Relationships are a central feature of CiviCRM. For example, you may run an organization that has contacts related to it because they are volunteers, or you may have individual contacts that are the children of other contacts who are their parents. Some relationships are time-limited. For example, the chair of an organization may have a one year fixed term of office.

How to do it...

In this recipe we will set up a time-limited relationship between two contacts using the following steps:

1. Navigate to **Administer | Customize Data and Screens | Relationship Types** and click on **Add relationship**:

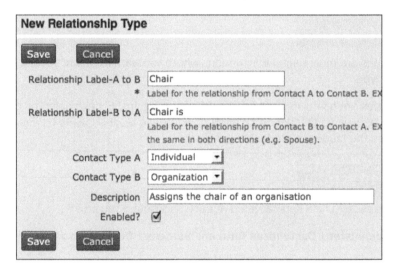

2. Set **Relationship Label-A to B** to Chair.
3. Set **Relationship Label-B to A** to Chair is.
4. Set **Contact Type A** to **Individual**.
5. Set **Contact Type B** to **Organization**.
6. Set a suitable description in the **Description** field.
7. Check if the relationship is enabled.
8. Save the relationship.

9. Navigate to an individual contact, click on the **Relationship** tab, and add the relationship.

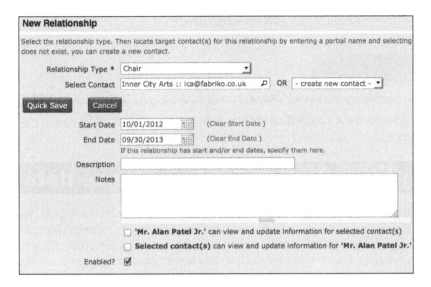

10. Select the relationship type **Chair** and select the contact to relate to. CiviCRM autocompletes your entry from the organizations available in the database.

11. Enter a start date and an end date for the relationship and add a description.

12. Navigate to **Administer | System Settings | Scheduled Jobs** and enable and set the **Disable Expired Relationships** job.

How it works...

Contact Type A is set to **Individual**. **Contact Type B** is set to **Organization**. This means that only individuals can be chairs of organizations.

The Disable Expired Relationship job checks the dates on relationships and disables them if they have expired. This requires cron in order to function properly.

There's more...

You can allow the two related contacts to be able to view and edit each other's records by using the checkboxes below the **Notes** field. For example, you could allow the chair to be able to edit the organization record. This would also require the individual contact to have an active account on your CMS and permission to access their CiviCRM contact dashboard.

[Relationships become available for use in CiviCRM core functions such as importing, exporting, and searching data. They are also used in creating membership types.]

See also

▸ The *Setting up cron using cPanel* recipe in *Chapter 1, Setting Up CiviCRM*

▸ Find more about CiviCRM relationships at `http://book.civicrm.org/user/current/organising-your-data/relationships/`

Using tag sets to quickly organize data

Tags are a way of organizing your contacts, activities, and cases within CiviCRM. You can regard a tag as a way of *describing* data and as a powerful way to *segment* your contacts. Any tags you create are visible on the contact edit screen so they are great with getting summary information about a contact quickly. You need to include tags in your data plan for CiviCRM, otherwise your screens can get overrun by redundant tags.

How to do it...

Tag sets allow you to add tags on the fly without going to the **Manage Tags** screen. Here are the following steps to do so:

1. Navigate to **Contacts | Manage tags** and click on **Add a Tag Set**.

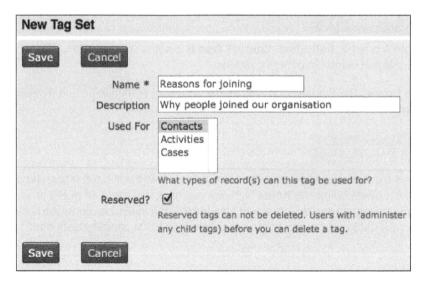

2. Enter the name and description for your tag set, and apply it to **Contacts**, **Activities**, **Cases**, or any combination of these.

3. Navigate to a contact record and click on the **Tags** tab.

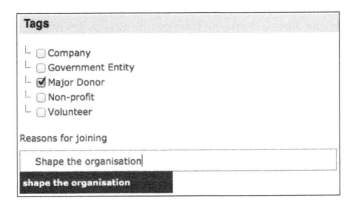

4. Now start typing in new tags into the **Reasons for joining** box on the edit screen.

5. CiviCRM turns this into a tag option (in black). Click on the tag option to add it.

6. You can add as many tags as you like. CiviCRM will autocomplete any existing tags to reduce duplication.

7. Navigate to **Search | Advanced search**. You will see a screen like this:

8. Here you can enter one or more of the tags contained within the tag set.

 We could also enter the word Shape into the **All Tags** field. This would pick up any items that have tags that contain the word "Shape".

See also

▶ Find out more about CiviCRM groups and tags at http://book.civicrm.org/user/current/organising-your-data/groups-and-tags/

Using tags and groups to segment data

Tags are ways of describing your contacts. When you look at a contact summary screen, all the tags applied to the contact are visible, providing at-a-glance information without having to drill down. Contacts can also be segmented into groups. Groups are not visible on the contact summary screen so they are not useful for getting instant information. They come into their own when they are used for other actions within CiviCRM. For example, they can be used to control permissions, or as mailing lists. Once you get to a group listing there are a wide range of actions you can apply to contacts within the group.

How to do it...

This recipe shows you how to combine group and tag data in a search to target newsletter readers.

1. Create a group in CiviCRM and allocate contacts to it. In this example we have a group called **Newsletter Subscribers**.

2. Create a tag or a tag set and apply tags to some of the contacts within the group.

3. Now navigate to **Search | Advanced Search**.

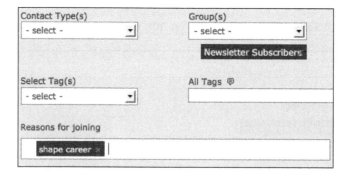

4. Here you can see that we are searching within the **Newsletter Subscribers** group to see which ones are tagged with **shape career**.

From the result set you could make a decision on whether to write an article about careers in the next edition of the newsletter.

Changing option lists

Option lists are used throughout CiviCRM to ensure data integrity and to make CiviCRM core functions work. Some of these are not available from the menu system.

How to do it...

The option lists available through the menu system are limited. There is a main screen where you can edit all option lists:

Here there are only a few drop-down options available to edit.

1. Navigate to **Administer | Administration Console**.

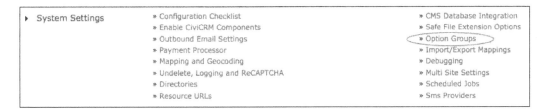

2. In **System Settings** you will see the **Option Groups** link in the second column. This provides you with the full list. Many of these option lists are generated internally by CiviCRM so you need to be very careful about which ones you alter.

Creating and updating a smart group

Searching for contacts and doing something with the set of results is a day-to-day task in CiviCRM. For example, you might want to find all your contacts that live in Alaska and send them a mail shot. This is pretty easy to do in Advanced Search, and you can add all the contacts you find into a group called Alaska. This means that you can always go back to the group and find the contacts you added. The group represents a snapshot of your data that you took when you did the search and added contacts to the group.

The problem is that if new contacts are added into CiviCRM who live in Alaska, you will have to remember to add them to the group, and you will have to remove them from the group if they move from Alaska.

To overcome this problem, CiviCRM has smart groups. Smart groups automatically contain any contacts that match your search criteria. So, if the data in your contacts changes, or contacts are added or removed, this is reflected dynamically in the smart group without you having to do anything.

How to do it...

Creating a smart group is easy. We just perform a search and create the smart group directly from the search results screen:

1. Navigate to **Search | Advanced Search**.

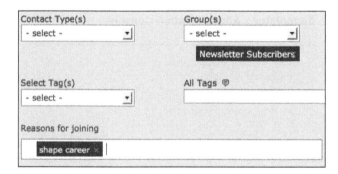

2. In this example we are looking inside an existing group called **Newsletter Subscribers** for contacts tagged with "shape career".

3. From the search results, use the **actions** drop-down menu and add these contacts to a new smart group and call it **Newsletter Shapers**.

4. You can access the smart group by navigating to **Contacts | Manage Groups**.

5. Now let's suppose we want to change the criteria. Locate the smart group you created and click on the **Contacts** link. This will list the contacts in the smart group.

6. Click on the **Edit Search Criteria** button at the top of the group screen. This will display the **Advanced Search** pane with the existing criteria loaded.

7. Amend the search criteria to get a different result set.

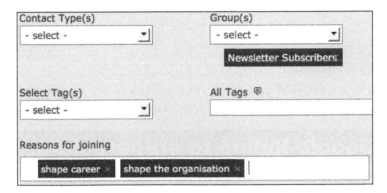

Here we added an extra tag to our search criteria. Now click on **Search** to see the new set of results.

8. If the search results are what you want, you must use the **actions** drop-down menu to update the smart group as shown in the following screenshot:

How it works...

Smart groups are based on search criteria. They are effectively saved searches. So if you find yourself repeatedly doing the same search, save the results as a smart group to save yourself time.

See also

▸   Find more about CiviCRM groups and tags at `http://book.civicrm.org/user/current/organising-your-data/groups-and-tags/`

Using Google Refine to prepare data

Preparing data for CiviCRM import can be a time-consuming, frustrating, and traumatic experience. But it is a job that has to be done. CiviCRM does an enormous amount of error checking on data import and will not import records with errors it spots.

Consider this data:

Preesall	Poulton Le Fylde	Lancashire
Preesall	Poulton Le Fylde	Lancashire
	Poulton-le-Flyde	Lancashire
Carlton	Poulton-Le-Fylde	Lancashire
Furness Driv	Poulton-le-fylde	Lancashire

Here you can see that there are data inconsistencies in the center column. The town Poulton-le-Fylde has five different ways of spelling and presenting the data. This is quite a common problem in legacy systems that were designed to hold addressing data for label printing rather than for searching or geocoding. Another common problem is having data in the wrong columns. Towns, cities, and postcodes are often spread across many columns. The result is you cannot guarantee accurate search results or do any geocoding.

How to do it...

Google Refine is an excellent tool for cleaning your data, which is free and easy to use. This recipe shows you some of the basics of Google Refine.

1.   Download and install Google Refine from `http://code.google.com/p/google-refine/wiki/Downloads?tm=2`.

2. You can import data from CSV, Excel, or a variety of other files into Google Refine to see how the import mechanism works. It is incredibly easy. Here we have launched Google Refine and have imported this data:

▼ Street	▼ Area	▼ Town/City	▼ County	▼ Country	▼ Post Code
6 Longton Grove Road		Weston Super Mare	Somerset	England	BS23 1LT
437 Beechdale Road		Nottingham	Nottinghamshire	England	NG3 3LF
439 Beechdale Road			Nottingham	England	NG8 3LF
61 Hatfield Road		St Albans	Hertfordshire	England	AL1 4JE [edit]
11 Church Street	Harston	Cambridge	Cambridgeshire	England	CB2 5NP

Here you can see that the **Area** column is mostly empty. The **County** column contains a city, **Nottingham**, which should be in the city column. If you were importing thousands of addresses it would be very time-consuming to try and fix the data using a spreadsheet or a database. Google Refine makes it easy.

3. At the top of the **Town/City** column we can choose **Text Facet** as shown in the following screenshot:

This creates a list in the left-hand pane of the Google Refine screen:

The list contains the unique values in the **Town/City** column and how many rows contain each unique value. So in this example we can see there are 1482 different town/city choices, and that for the choice **Aberdeen** there are 13 rows that have that value.

4. Click on the **Cluster** button in the top-right of our list; we can group these values based on algorithms that Google Refine provides:

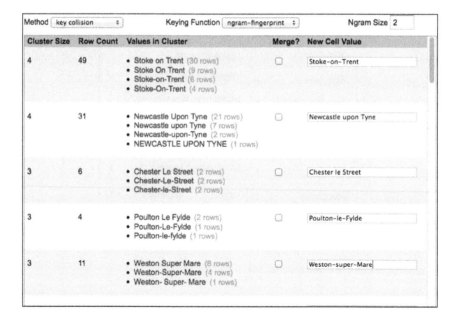

You can play around with the **Method** and **Keying Function** values to see which values in the cluster suit you best. In the preceding screenshot you can see that each cluster contains spelling and formatting errors in the address data.

For each cluster you can then enter a value in **New Cell Value** and then update the data. You can work through your data in this way and clear up errors very quickly.

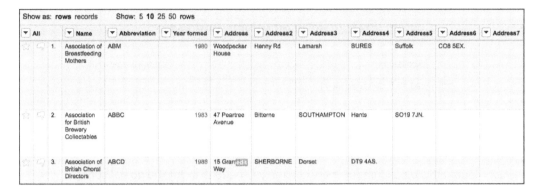

5. In the preceding data, some postal codes contain a "period", and both postal code and city data are scattered in different columns, so if you wanted to use this to geocode data it would not work.

6. Select the **Address2** column and pick up postal code data and store a copy in the **Address6** column.

7. From the drop-down menu on the **Address4** column, select **Text Filter**. If you look at the postal codes, you can see that there is a pattern within them. The postal code prefix ends with a number, then there is a whitespace, then the postal code suffix begins with a number. So you can search for that pattern using a regular expression. You can find out more about regular expressions at http://www.regular-expressions.info.

   The expression for any digit is \d, and for a space it is \s.

8. Search on \d\s\d. That is the same as saying "find cells in this column that contain the pattern of a number followed by a space followed by another number."

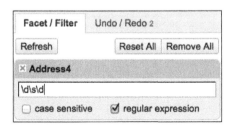

9. Tick the **regular expression** box.

10. As you type in the filter, Google Refine automatically refreshes the data to meet the filter criteria. You will see that this filters the postal code data properly.

11. Copy your found postal code values to the **Address6** column. Go to **Edit Cells | Transform** from the **Address6** drop-down menu and copy the data from the **Address4** column using Google Refine's syntax, as shown in the following screenshot:

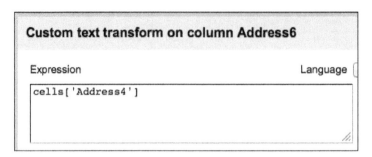

12. Repeat this procedure for every column you need to fix for the postal codes.

13. Once you have them all in the **Address6:** we can rename the column. We go to the **Address6** column menu and select **Edit Column** and rename the column to `Postal Code`.

14. Finally we can remove the period from the data. We will have to go to **Edit Cells | Transform** to do so. And the resultant page is shown in the following screenshot:

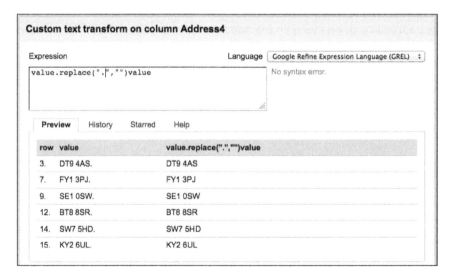

How it works...

Google Refine gives you a dynamic view of your data directly as you transform it.

Google Refine stores all of your transformations. This means they can be reapplied to data again. In situations where the same data needs to be imported several times during the course of a development project, this is a godsend.

See more

- ▶ Find more about Google Refine at `http://code.google.com/p/google-refine/`
- ▶ Find the Google Refine documentation at `http://code.google.com/p/google-refine/wiki/DocumentationForUsers`

Importing into CiviCRM using an import script

There are occasions where you want to get some data into CiviCRM but there is no quick way of doing it. For example, your existing contacts may all be tagged. You want to get these tag values into CiviCRM so that when you import your contacts your tags work properly.

The CiviCRM interface only allows you to add one tag at a time. So this could be very time-consuming if you have hundreds of tags. This recipe introduces the use of the command-line interface to rapidly add data to CiviCRM.

The recipe can be used to migrate data into most CiviCRM tables. It's not as terrifying as it sounds.

Getting ready

First, you must have a local testing environment.

A local testing environment is a CiviCRM installation that runs on your own computer rather than the Internet.

In this recipe our local testing environment was set up on a Mac using the MAMP software. There are similar setups for Windows-based machines.

Once your local testing environment is set up you need to be able to execute PHP from the command line. PHP is the scripting language that powers CiviCRM. We want to be able to type in a command that will run a PHP file that will control our data import.

Navigate to where MAMP stores the PHP executable file, normally `/Applications/MAMP/bin/php/php5.3.14/bin/php`. Make a note of this path.

Now let's open the Terminal application and enter the following command:

```
open -a TextEdit .bash_profile
```

Hit the *Enter* key.

This makes the **TextEdit** application open the `.bash_profile` file, which is normally a hidden file. Now let's add the following line to `.bash_profile`.

```
alias phpmamp="<path> "
```

Here, `path` is the path to the PHP executable file.

In this example the line reads:

```
alias phpmamp="/Applications/MAMP/bin/php/php5.3.14/bin/php"
```

Now save the file.

What this means is that when you type `phpmamp` into the Terminal application it will execute the version of PHP held in the MAMP installation.

Test it by going to the Terminal application and typing `phpmamp -help`.

If all is well, it will return a list of help options for PHP.

How to do it...

We will prepare a CSV file for import, and call the `import.php` CiviCRM file using a command-line interface.

1. Prepare tag data as a `.csv` file. Each tag must have a name and a description. Your file might look like this:

```
name,description
Learner, People who join to learn things
Influencer, People who want to influence our organization
Participator, People who want to attend our events
Status booster, People who gain professional status
Like minders, People who agree with our politics
Passives, People who just want our resources
```

2. Open the Terminal application and navigate to the `site module` folder that contains your CiviCRM installation in your local testing environment. This is easy.

3. Navigate to the CiviCRM module folder using the Finder and make sure it is visible when you use Terminal. Then type `cd` into the Terminal application window. Then drag the `civicrm` folder onto the Terminal window. This accomplishes the navigation with the minimum of work:

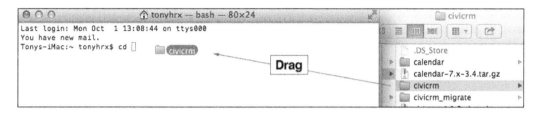

4. Enter the command to import the data. In the Terminal application, enter:

```
phpmamp bin/csv/import.php -e Tag --file <path_to_file>
```

Here, `path_to_file` is the place where you stored your CSV file. You can grab this path by dragging the file from the Finder into the Terminal window.

In this example the finished text will be:

```
phpmamp bin/csv/import.php -e Tag -file /Users/tonyhrx/Sites/book/
tmp/tags.csv
```

5. Copy and paste this into the Terminal window and press *return*. You should get the following result:

```
Last login: Sun Sep 30 16:27:34 on ttys000
You have new mail.
Tonys-iMac:~ tonyhrx$ cd /Users/tonyhrx/Sites/book/sites/all/modules/civicrm
Tonys-iMac:civicrm tonyhrx$ phpmamp bin/csv/import.php -e Tag --file /Users/tony
hrx/Sites/book/tmp/tags.csv

line 2: created Tag id: 50

line 3: created Tag id: 51

line 4: created Tag id: 52

line 5: created Tag id: 53

line 6: created Tag id: 54

line 7: created Tag id: 55

line 8: created Tag id: 56

line 9: created Tag id: 57

line 10: created Tag id: 58
```

How it works...

`phpmamp` invokes PHP to run `bin/csv/import.php`.

`-e` tells the import script what CiviCRM entity we are going to target, in this case **Tag**.

`--file` is the absolute path to the file of data we are going to import, in this case `/Users/tonyhrx/Sites/book/tmp/tags.csv`.

Then the CiviCRM API does the rest.

There's more...

This simple but powerful technique can take hours off import times and accomplish most of your import routines.

You can explore the CiviCRM API on your own installation. Just type in `civicrm/api/explorer` after your domain URL:

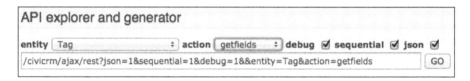

If we look at the Tag entity we can see what fields it contains by selecting **getfields** from the **actions** drop-down menu.

You can do this for any entity that is listed.

For example, let's look at the Relationships entity and see what the fields are:

```
"id":"1",
"name_a_b":"Child of",
"label_a_b":"Child of",
"name_b_a":"Parent of",
"label_b_a":"Parent of",
"description":"Parent\/child relationship.",
"contact_type_a":"Individual",
"contact_type_b":"Individual",
"is_reserved":"0",
"is_active":"1"
```

Using this, we could construct another CSV file and add relationship data to it such as:

```
name_a_b,label_a_b,name_b_a,label_b_a,description,contact_
type_a,contact_type_b,is_reserved,is_active
Secretary,Secretary,Secretary is,Secretary is,Used for Organization
secretaries,Individual,Organization,0,1
```

And then run the import using Terminal:

```
phpmamp bin/csv/import.php -e RelationshipType --file /Users/tonyhrx/
Desktop/relationships.csv
```

See more

▶ Refer to *Chapter 11, Developing for CiviCRM* for more information

▶ Find out more about this technique at `http://civicrm.org/blogs/xavier/api_batch_tools`

Using external identifier deduping rules to update contacts

When data is imported to update contacts, CiviCRM has a set of rules to match contacts already in the database. By default, CiviCRM uses the e-mail address. If it finds a matching e-mail address it will update the matching contact. A problem will arise because not all of your contacts will have an e-mail address. So if we try to import some updates, only those contacts with an e-mail address will be updated.

In these situations we need to have a different unique identifier that we can let CiviCRM use to match records.

How to do it...

We will use the **External Identifier** field in CiviCRM as our unique identifier. This field has to have a unique value for each contact. This will provide us with a good alternative to e-mail addresses to match contact data.

1. Navigate to **Contacts | Find and Merge Duplicate Contacts**.

The screenshot shows the deduping rules that are available to use for each contact type:

If we were importing data for individuals then CiviCRM would use the **Email (reserved)** rule that matches on e-mail addresses. So we need a different unique identifier for each contact that we can use instead of the e-mail address.

Quite often legacy data will already have a unique identifier, such as a client ID or membership number. If you already have an existing unique identifier then it is a good idea to have mapped this to CiviCRM's **External Identifier** field when your data is first imported.

If you do not have a unique identifier, then you can construct one using Google Refine.

2. Click on **Add Rule**. The following screenshot is what you will find:

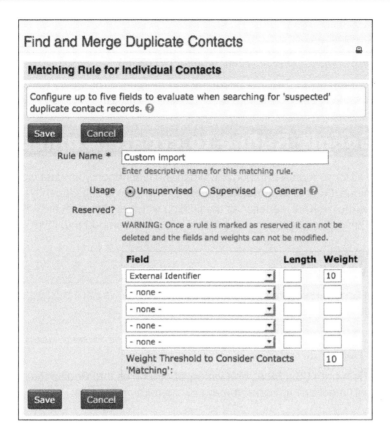

3. Give the rule a name. Here we used **Custom import**.

4. Select **Unsupervised** for **Usage**. Unsupervised rules are used for imports and entries through online forms such as event signups or contact information using profiles. Supervised rules are used when user information is added manually through the contact screen.

5. Enter the external identifier as the first matching field with a weight of 10. Make the weight threshold to trigger the rule at 10. That's it. You can now use this rule to match contacts when you are importing data.

See also

▸ The *Using Google Refine to create a unique ID* recipe

▸ Find out more about CiviCRM deduping and merging at `http://book.civicrm.org/user/current/common-workflows/deduping-and-merging/`

Using Google Refine to create a unique ID

Having a unique ID for your data is important. When you first import your data into CiviCRM you can store this unique ID in the **External Identifier** field. When you subsequently update this data, you can use the external identifier as the field on which to match records. But sometimes you simply don't have a unique ID for contact data you want to import into CiviCRM.

How to do it...

Here we will use Google Refine to create our unique ID. Once we have this, we can use it to match contact data during CiviCRM import operations:

1. Download Google Refine from `http://code.google.com/p/google-refine/wiki/Downloads?tm=2`.

2. Import data from CSV, Excel, or a variety of other files into Google Refine to see how the import mechanism works. It may look something like this:

▼ First Name	▼ Last Name	▼ Postal Code
Peter	Adams	86545
Chris	Adams	33359
Peter	Adams	63034
Greg	Adams	56502
Bruce	Grant	87825
Andrew	Jameson	85378
Charles	Jameson	14812
Walter edit	Jameson	1540
John	Jameson	60012
Rebecca	Jones	86545
Henry	Jones	12915

You can see that we cannot use **Last Name** values as a unique identifier as it is not unique. If we did an import using the last names, CiviCRM would only update the first matching record it found.

A combination of **First Name** and **Last Name** values is not unique either. There are two people called Peter Adams. But if we combine all three columns then we can get a unique identifier as the value is unique for each record.

3. In the **Postal Code** column, click on the drop-down menu and select **Edit Column | Add column based on this column**.

4. In the edit window enter the following:

Add column based on column Postal Code

New column name `Key`

On error   ⦿ set to blank   ◯ store error   ◯ copy value from original column

Expression   Language   `Google Refine Expression Language (GREL)  ⬍`

```
cells["First Name"].value + "_" + cells["Last
Name"].value + "_" + cells["Postal Code"].value
```
No syntax error.

| **Preview** | History | Starred | Help |

row	value	cells["First Name"].value + "_" + cells["Last Name"].value + "_" + cells["Postal Code"].value
1.	86545	Rebecca_Jones_86545
2.	12588	Jason_Williamson_12588
3.	50255	Justin_Smith_50255
4.	86545	Peter_Adams_86545
5.	43056	Richard_Williamson_43056
6.	12915	Henry_Jones_12915

OK   Cancel

The data will now look like this:

First Name	Last Name	Postal Code	Key
Peter	Adams	86545	Peter_Adams_86545
Chris	Adams	33359	Chris_Adams_33359
Peter	Adams	63034	Peter_Adams_63034
Greg	Adams	56502	Greg_Adams_56502
Bruce	Grant	87825	Bruce_Grant_87825
Andrew	Jameson	85378	Andrew_Jameson_85378
Charles	Jameson	14812	Charles_Jameson_14812
Walter	Jameson	1540	Walter_Jameson_1540
John	Jameson	60012	John_Jameson_60012
Rebecca	Jones	86545	Rebecca_Jones_86545
Henry	Jones	12915	Henry_Jones_12915

5. You can now use the data in the **Key** column as a unique identifier that CiviCRM can store in the **External Identifier** field.

How it works...

Google Refine has joined together the data in three columns to create a unique identifier for each record in the **Key** column.

For this to work properly, each of the fields in use needs to contain a value. With big datasets, it would be possible that even this key would not be unique. You may also have data such as date of birth to improve the uniqueness.

Importing relationship data

A relationship is a connection between two or more contacts. For example, some contacts may be children of other contacts, who are the parents. Some contacts will be employers of other contacts—employees.

How to do it...

This recipe will show you how to import relationships properly. We will use the built-in employer-employee relationship.

1. Navigate to **Administer | Customize Data and Screens | Relationship Types** and check that the employer relationship exists and is enabled.

2. Import all the contacts that will be employers. These will generally be organization contacts.

3. Now import all the contacts that will be employees. Make sure you have a unique identifier for each contact.

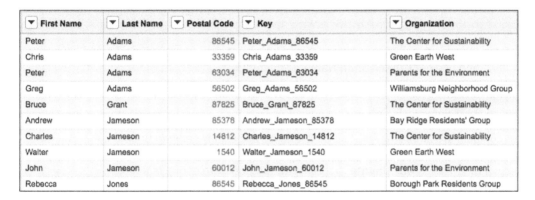

▼ First Name	▼ Last Name	▼ Postal Code	▼ Key	▼ Organization
Peter	Adams	86545	Peter_Adams_86545	The Center for Sustainability
Chris	Adams	33359	Chris_Adams_33359	Green Earth West
Peter	Adams	63034	Peter_Adams_63034	Parents for the Environment
Greg	Adams	56502	Greg_Adams_56502	Williamsburg Neighborhood Group
Bruce	Grant	87825	Bruce_Grant_87825	The Center for Sustainability
Andrew	Jameson	85378	Andrew_Jameson_85378	Bay Ridge Residents' Group
Charles	Jameson	14812	Charles_Jameson_14812	The Center for Sustainability
Walter	Jameson	1540	Walter_Jameson_1540	Green Earth West
John	Jameson	60012	John_Jameson_60012	Parents for the Environment
Rebecca	Jones	86545	Rebecca_Jones_86545	Borough Park Residents Group

In the preceding data, the **Key** column contains a unique identifier. The **Organization** column contains the name of the employer.

4. Now import the individual contact data again, but this time we will import the relationship.

5. Navigate to **Contacts | Import contacts** and set your import.

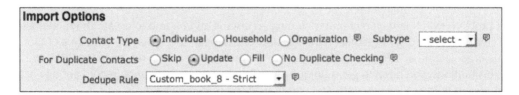

Import Options

Contact Type	⦿ Individual ◯ Household ◯ Organization 🗩 Subtype [- select - ▾] 🗩
For Duplicate Contacts	◯ Skip ⦿ Update ◯ Fill ◯ No Duplicate Checking 🗩
Dedupe Rule	[Custom_book_8 - Strict ▾] 🗩

6. Note we are *updating* our original individual contacts and are using the external identifier as the matching field. In the following screenshot, the options should look like this:

Column Names	Import Data (row 1)	Import Data (row 2)	Matching CiviCRM Field
First Name	Rebecca	Jason	- do not import -
Last Name	Jones	Williamson	- do not import -
Postal Code	86545	12588	- do not import -
Key	Rebecca_Jones_86545	Jason_Williamson_12588	External Identifier (match to contact) *
Organization	Borough Park Residents Group	Organization	Employee of Organization Name (match to contact) *

7. Map the **Organization** field for your import with the relationship type **Employee of**, and use the **Organization Name** as the match.

How it works...

Our contacts are already in the database and we are simply going to update them. So when CiviCRM encounters a matching contact for the **External Identifier** field, we want it to update that contact. That is why **Update** is chosen for the duplicate contacts action.

When it updates, it will create an "Employee of" relationship between the individual contact and the organization that has a name that matches the data in the organization field in the CSV file.

There's more...

Only import one piece of relationship data at a time. Trying to import more than one simply does not work.

One problem with this recipe is that matching an organization name to create the relationship will create errors if organizations share names. For example, there may be branches of the same organization at different addresses, each with its own contact record in CiviCRM. In these situations, you need to get a unique identifier for each organization record set against each record in the individual data and use that as the matching field.

See also

▸ Find out more about CiviCRM importing at `http://book.civicrm.org/user/current/common-workflows/importing-data/`

Exporting related data

This recipe shows you how export data that is accessible through a relationship. For example, you might have contacts that are employees of other contacts and you want to send all the employees a mail shot at their workplace address. Or you might want to send all members of the same household a mail shot.

How to do it...

In this recipe we will merge the individual contact data with household contact data to create a CSV file that we can use in a mail merge.

1. Search for the individuals you wish to target and select **Export contacts** from the **actions** drop-down menu at the top of the search results listing.

2. Click on the **Select fields for export** button and then set up your export fields as follows:

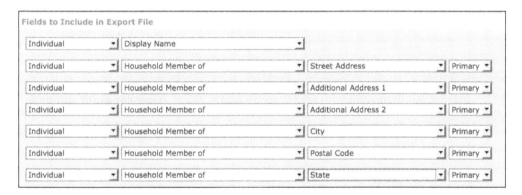

3. Save your field mapping and click on **Export**.

How it works...

CiviCRM uses the "Household member of" relationship to grab the address data from the house contact record.

This is a good way of preserving data integrity as there is no need to record an address for the individual contact record.

See also

▶ Find out more about CiviCRM exporting at http://book.civicrm.org/user/current/common-workflows/exporting-data/

Batch updating using profiles

CiviCRM has a useful feature called **batch updating**. For example, you might have a group of contacts where you want to update the value in a custom field. You could go to each contact and update them one at a time, but this would be time consuming. This is where you can use batch updating.

How to do it...

In this recipe we will update some participant information from a recent event.

1. Here, prepare a set of custom fields for use with individuals and have them added to a profile that we will use for our batch update. Batch updating works with any contact fields.

In this example we created a custom field called **Event outcome** with some checkbox options. We then added the field to a new profile called **Volunteer event outcome**.

2. Navigate to **Search | Find Participants** and search for contacts that attended a volunteer meeting.

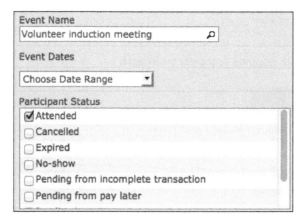

3. Use the **actions** drop-down menu to create a smart group.

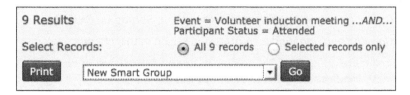

4. Navigate to **Contacts | Manage groups** and select the smart group you just created.
5. From the **actions** menu at the top of the listing, select **Batch Update via Profile**:

6. Select the profile prepared previously and enter the appropriate options for each contact in the list:

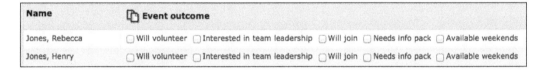

How it works...

CiviCRM loops through each contact and updates each one with the options you have chosen.

Batch updating via profiles has a limit: if there are more than 100 contacts to update then you will need to use an import file instead. You cannot mix contact types in a batch profile. They must all be the same type; for example, individuals or organizations.

There's more...

In this recipe we have been batch updating contacts. CiviCRM contains other batch data entry systems for contributions and memberships.

See also

- The *Creating Custom Fields* recipe in *Chapter 1, Setting Up CiviCRM*
- The *Creating and updating a smart group* recipe in this chapter
- Find out more about CiviCRM profiles at `http://book.civicrm.org/user/current/the-user-interface/profiles/`

3
Using the Power of Profiles

In this chapter we will cover:

- ▸ Speeding up data entry
- ▸ Using URLs to change profile displays
- ▸ Creating a membership directory
- ▸ Controlling the search result columns using profiles
- ▸ Using the Profile Pages and Listings setting to improve usability
- ▸ Setting up reCAPTCHA for user profiles

Introduction

You will find yourself using profiles a lot in CiviCRM. A profile is a custom-made collection of contact fields made for a specific purpose. Profiles can be used throughout CiviCRM to display and collect information.

Speeding up data entry

You can use profiles to speed up data entry and to control access to contact data. For example, you might have a set of volunteers who are responsible for maintaining specific data about contacts. You will want to give them access to the data they require but not other sensitive data.

How to do it...

In this recipe we will use a profile to enter some data for potential new members for our organization.

1. Create a group that will store all the new contacts you are going to add.

2. Navigate to **Contacts | New Group** and create a new group. Call it Quick add membership prospects.

3. Navigate to **Administer | Customize Data and Screens | Profiles** and create a new profile. Give the profile a sensible name that reflects its purpose. Call it Quick add member prospects.

4. In the **Used For** field select **Standalone Form or Directory**.

5. Add in some guidance to the top and the bottom of the profile to help the people who are going to be doing the data entry.

6. Click on the **Advanced** field set at the foot of the profile entry screen.

7. In **Add Contact to a Group** select the group we created as shown in the following screenshot:

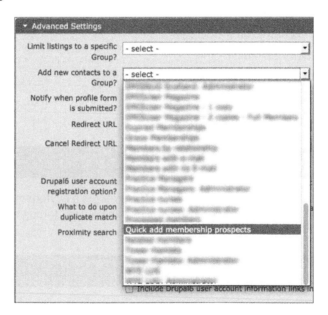

8. Save the profile and begin to add fields to it.

9. For this recipe we are going to add some fields for an **Organization** contact type. We will also include a couple of custom fields. See the *Creating custom fields* recipe in *Chapter 1, Setting Up CiviCRM*. From the **Organization** option list, choose **Organization Name**.

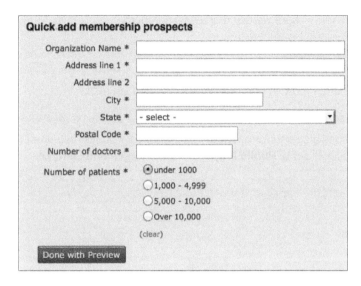

10. From the **Contact** option list, choose a few address fields for the organization.

11. Here we have added in a couple of custom fields, **Number of doctors** and **Number of patients**.

12. For each field added, tick the **Required** checkbox for data that *must* be entered; the organization name is a must, as well as the **City**, **State**, and **Postal Code** fields.

13. Click on the **Preview All Fields** button to check the fields and play around with them to get the order right.

14. Now click on the **Use Create mode** button to create a contact entry.

15. Copy the create mode URL from your browser navigation bar (`civicrm/profile/create?gid=N&reset=1`, where `N` is the ID of your profile). Use it to create a menu entry in your CiviCRM navigation menu.

See also

▸ The *Adding items to the CiviCRM navigation menu* recipe in *Chapter 1, Setting Up CiviCRM*

▸ Find more about CiviCRM profiles at `http://book.civicrm.org/user/current/the-user-interface/profiles/`

Using URLs to change profile displays

In the previous recipe we used a URL to access the profile we created, that is, `civicrm/profile/create?gid=N&reset=1`, where `N` was the ID of our profile. This URL made the profile appear as a form where we could create a contact.

How to do it...

By using different URLs you can create search forms and listings:

1. Create a search form with this URL: `civicrm/profile?gid=N&reset=1`.

   This provides a search form. When you create your profile, you must make sure that field visibility is set to **Public Pages** or **Public Pages and Listings**.

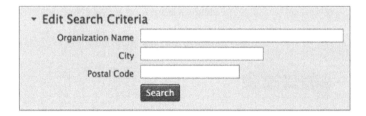

2. Create a listing with an editable search with this URL: `civicrm/profile?gid=N&reset=1&force=1`.

   This provides a listing with editable search criteria at the top. When creating the profile for this, under the **Advanced** settings, you can restrict the contacts listed using **Limit listings to a specific Group**.

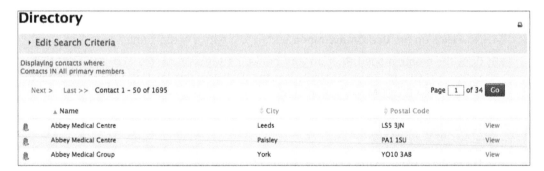

3. Create a listing without a search with this URL: `civicrm/profile?gid=17&reset =1&force=1&search=0`.

This provides a listing with no editable search criteria.

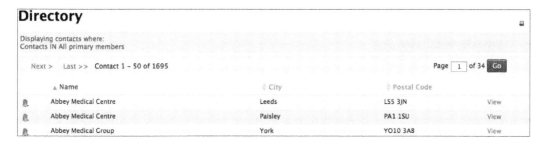

4. Create a contact map with this URL: `civicrm/profile/ map?map=1&gid=N&reset=1`.

This provides a map of contacts. You must have geocoded your contacts and you must have **Enable mapping for this profile?** selected in the **Advanced** settings for the profile.

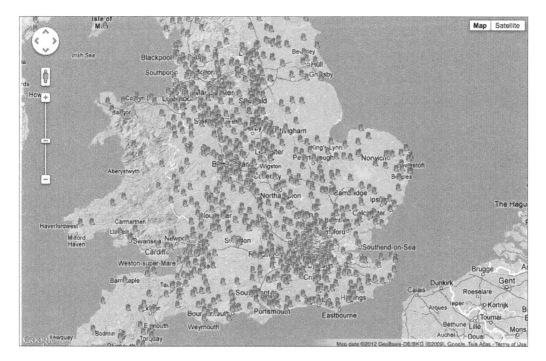

Creating a membership directory

Profiles can be used to create listings of contacts. You can display these lists publicly on your website so it's a quick way to show a membership directory.

How to do it...

Setting up a membership directory is easy. We just create a smart group to list our contacts and then create a profile that lists contacts within the group.

1. Set up a group that will contain the contacts that you want to list. It's a good idea to make this a **smart group**. This means any contact that matches the smart group criteria will automatically be added to your group and thus to your listing. When you create your smart group, make sure that **Visibility** is set to **public pages**.

2. Navigate to **Administer | Customize Data and Screens | Profiles** and add a new profile that will contain the fields you wish to display on your directory.

3. For the **Used for:** field, select **Standalone Form or Directory**.

4. Navigate to the **Advanced** settings. In the **Limit listings to a specific Group?** field, select the smart group that you created previously as shown in the following screenshot:

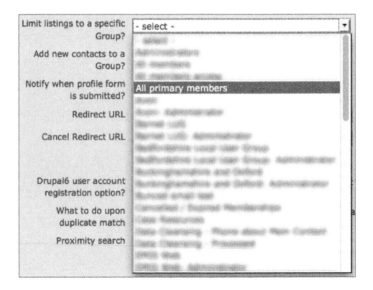

5. Click on **Save** and begin adding fields to your profile. For this recipe we will list the organizations that are members with their city and postal code:

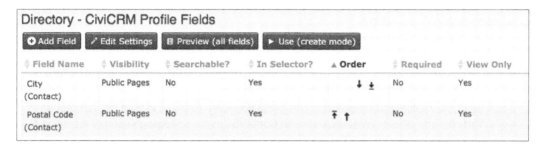

The fields have been set for public pages. Note that you do not have to include the name of the organization itself. CiviCRM puts the contact display name in the search result set by default.

6. Create a profile URL, such as `civicrm/profile?gid=17&reset=1&force=1&search=0`, to display the directory.

Here GID is the ID of the profile we created. This will display the directory as a list.

There's more...

You might want to control permissions for profiles. For example, you may only want members to be able to see the member directory.

See also

▶ The *Creating and updating a smart group* recipe in *Chapter 2, Organizing Data Efficiently*

▶ *Chapter 4, Controlling Permissions*

Controlling the search result columns using profiles

CiviCRM uses a default template to display search results. There are columns for the contact name, addressing, and other contact data. What if you want it to display other data instead, such as custom data fields you have created? We can use CiviCRM profiles to achieve this.

How to do it...

In this recipe we couple the power of CiviCRM profiles with Advanced Search to create customized search result pages.

1. Navigate to **Administer | Customize Data and Screens | Profiles** and add a new profile.

2. Select **Search Views** in the **Used For** field.

3. Save the profile and then add in the fields you want to show in your search results. You can only add in fields available to Contacts. In the following example we added in some custom data fields for organization contacts.

4. Make sure that each field set for **Public Pages** is included in the results table. You only need to set them to **View Only** for the **Search Views** profiles:

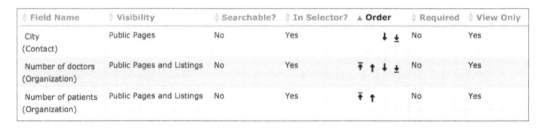

Field Name	Visibility	Searchable?	In Selector?	Order	Required	View Only
City (Contact)	Public Pages	No	Yes	↓ ↧	No	Yes
Number of doctors (Organization)	Public Pages and Listings	No	Yes	⤒ ↑ ↓ ↧	No	Yes
Number of patients (Organization)	Public Pages and Listings	No	Yes	⤒ ↑	No	Yes

5. Navigate to **Search | Advanced Search**. You can now perform a search and choose the profile you created to display the search results.

How it works...

Here we use the **Search members** profile to display search results:

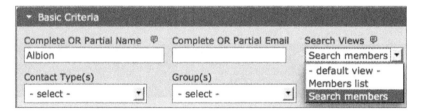

The search result set looks like the following screenshot:

		▲ Name	⇕ City	⇕ Number of doctors	⇕ Number of patients
☐	🐾	Albion			
☐	🐾	Albion House	Dudley	6	Over 10,000
☐	🐾	Albion Street Group Practice	London	0	under 1000
☐	🐾	The Albion Road Surgery	Broadstairs	1	1,000 - 4,999

CiviCRM only displays the fields we added to the profile.

Using the Profile Pages and Listings setting to improve usability

CiviCRM has great search facilities. By using Advanced Search or Search Builder you can find pretty much anything within your database. You can use profiles to provide useful links to list your data without having to go back and forth between searches.

How to do it...

We will use a setting in profiles that creates more search links to explore data further.

1. Navigate to **Administer | Customize Data and Screens | Profiles** and add a new profile.

2. Save your profile and add the fields that interest you.

3. In the **Used For** field, select **Standalone Form or Directory**.

4. When you add fields to your profile make sure that the fields are set to:

   ❏ **Public Pages and Listings**

   ❏ **Show in Results Column**

❑ **Searchable**

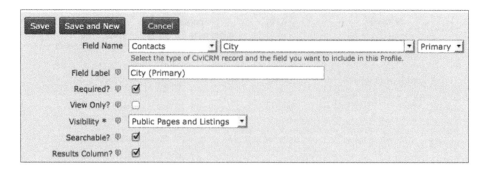

In the following example we have added three fields:

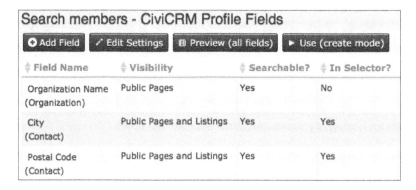

5. Once you have done this, use the search URL `civicrm/profile?gid=N&reset=1`, where `N` is the ID of your profile, and perform a search. From the result set, you will see there is a column containing the **View** links.

6. Click on **View** on any of the contacts.

How it works...

You can now see there are links to search for the fields you set to **Public Pages and Listings**. In this case, they are **City** and **Postal Code**:

Search members - Abbey Medical Centre

Organization Name	Abbey Medical Centre
City	Leeds
Postal Code	LS5 3JN

These allow you to explore the result set further without having to navigate back and change your search criteria.

Setting up reCAPTCHA for user profiles

reCAPTCHA is a useful tool to reduce spam submissions to your site.

How to do it...

You will need to register your website with Google and obtain **public** and **private** keys for reCAPTCHA.

1. Navigate to **Administer | System Settings | Undelete, Logging and ReCaptcha**.

2. Get your public and private reCAPTCHA keys from `http://www.google.com/recaptcha`.

3. Enter them into the settings fields:

4. You can also add in theme settings.

5. You can then enable reCAPTCHA by editing the **Advanced** settings for any profile where you wish to use it.

See also

▶ Find more about reCAPTCHA customization at `https://developers.google.com/recaptcha/docs/customization`

4

Controlling Permissions

In this chapter, we will cover the following recipes:

- ▸ Integrating profiles into Drupal user accounts
- ▸ Restricting access to custom fields
- ▸ Using CRM profile permissions correctly
- ▸ Creating permissions for administrators
- ▸ Managing event registrations using CiviCRM Access Control Lists

Introduction

CiviCRM provides two levels of permission control. At the CMS level, for example, Drupal, there are global CiviCRM permissions that can be applied to your users. If you disable these permissions, you can use CiviCRM's **Access Control Lists** (**ACLs**) to achieve fine-grained permissions for viewing and editing your database. These recipes explore how to get the best out of both permissioning systems, using Drupal as a CMS.

Integrating profiles into Drupal user accounts

It's quite easy to add a CiviCRM profile to Drupal's user account page. In the **Settings** page for your profile, you can choose to have the profile used for **View** and **Edit Drupal User Account**. This means that when the user logs in to Drupal and visits their user page, the CiviCRM profile is exposed. This is a great way to allow users to edit their CiviCRM data without giving full access to CiviCRM. The trouble comes when you want to make different profiles available to different sorts of users. For example, in CiviCRM, you could have two different sorts of individual contacts, students and teachers. You would not want to expose the teacher profile to the student and vice–versa.

How to do it...

In this recipe, we are going to have two individual contact subtypes, namely Boat Skippers and Boat Crew.

Boat Skippers will have custom fields that hold information about what sort of boats they have. **Boat Crews** will have custom fields about what sailing skills they have. When they log in to our website, they will have the correct profiles exposed on their user page.

1. Make sure that the **CiviGroup Roles Sync** module is enabled.

2. Navigate to **Administer | Customize Data and Screens | Contact Types**, and create an **Individual contact** subtype for **Skipper** and for **Crew**.

3. Create custom datasets for each content type. For **Skippers**, you can create **Boat Name**, **Boat Type**, and **Sail Number** fields. For **Crew**, you can create a competence multiple choice field and enter a few choices.

4. Navigate to **Administer | Customize Data and Screens | Profiles**, and add a new profile.

5. Name the profile `Skipper`.

6. In the **Used For** field, select **View/Edit Drupal User Account**.

7. Save the profile and add in custom fields for **Skippers**.

8. Create another profile for **Crew**. Name it `Crew`.

9. In the **Used For** field, select **View/Edit Drupal User Account**.

10. Save the profile and add in custom fields for **Crew**.

▲ Profile Title	⇕ Type	⇕ ID	Used For
Crew	Crew	16	Standalone Form or Directory, View/Edit Drupal User Account
Skipper	Skipper	15	Standalone Form or Directory, View/Edit Drupal User Account

You now have two profiles, with custom fields added for the two contact types.

11. Navigate to a **Drupal User Page**, and edit the account. You will now see both profiles available as tabs on the user profile.

12. In Drupal, navigate to `admin/people/permissions/roles`, and create a **Skipper** role and a **Crew** role. Allocate users to each role to test the recipe.

13. In CiviCRM, navigate to **Contacts | New Group**, and create a group for **Skippers** and a **Group for Crew**. Make sure that the checkbox for **Access Control** is checked. Make sure that visibility is set to **User** and **User Admin** only.

14. In Drupal, navigate to `admin/config/civicrm/civicrm_group_roles`. You want to match the Drupal roles to the CiviCRM groups you set up:

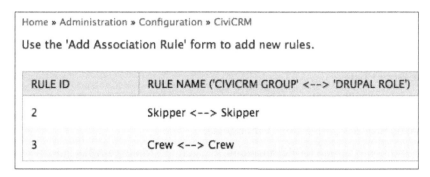

Home » Administration » Configuration » CiviCRM

Use the 'Add Association Rule' form to add new rules.

RULE ID	RULE NAME ('CIVICRM GROUP' <--> 'DRUPAL ROLE')
2	Skipper <--> Skipper
3	Crew <--> Crew

15. Select the **Manually Synchronize** tab and synchronize the contacts. Check the CiviCRM groups to see if the Drupal users have been added. Now, when a Drupal user is allocated to the role **Skipper**, they are automatically added to the CiviCRM group. The same goes for the crew. You can now use the CiviCRM group to control access to the CiviCRM profiles you created.

16. In Drupal, navigate to `admin/people/permissions`. Drupal permissions overrule any permissions that we set up in CiviCRM. CiviCRM assigns a default set of Drupal permissions on installation, so we need to remove these first.

CiviCRM: profile listings and forms	☐	☐
CiviCRM: profile listings	☐	☐
CiviCRM: profile create	☐	☐
CiviCRM: profile edit	☐	☐
CiviCRM: profile view	☐	☐
CiviCRM: access all custom data	☑	☑

17. Remove the permissions to create, edit, and review profiles. This means the profiles you created will no longer appear on the user account edit form. We left the CiviCRM access to all custom data permissions checked for the **Anonymous** and **Authenticated** roles. In your own situation, you can also remove these global permissions to have a further layer of control. We can now refine and reinstate these permissions in CiviCRM.

18. Navigate to **Administer | Users and permissions | Permissions (Access Control)**, and add an ACL role. This is not the same as a Drupal role. An ACL role acts as a container to hold groups of contacts.

19. Create an ACL role for **Skippers** and an ACL role for **Crew**.

20. Now, click on **Assign Users to ACL Roles**. For each ACL role, we can add one or more CiviCRM groups of users. These groups must have **Access Control** set as the **Group Type**.

21. Add the **Skippers** group to the **Skippers ACL** role, and add the **Crew Group** to the **Crew ACL** role. In your situation, you can add extra groups to these roles. This makes CiviCRM permissions very flexible.

22. On the home screen for **Permissions**, click on the **Manage ACLs** link and then **Add ACL**.

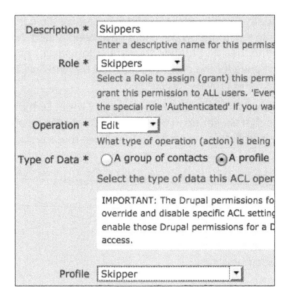

23. Make the ACL description `Skippers`.

24. Add the ACL role `Skipper` that you created in step 16.

25. Set **Operation** as `Edit`.

26. Make the type of data **A profile**. This will now automatically provide you with a drop-down list of CiviCRM profiles.

27. Set **Profile** as **Skipper**.

28. Repeat the procedure for the **Crew** profile.

How it works

If you now edit a Drupal user account, for each role, you will see the tab for **Skippers** is only available for users in the **Skipper** role and similarly for the crew role.

The CiviCRM **Civi Group Roles Sync** module synchronizes Drupal roles to CiviCRM Groups. So, when a user is given the **Skipper** role in Drupal, they are added to the CiviCRM Group called **Skipper**.

The CiviCRM **Skipper** group is set to be used for access control. We created an ACL role called **Skippers** and added all the contacts in the CiviCRM skipper group to it. We then gave the ACL role permissions to edit the skipper profile.

 Do not use the Drupal Masquerade module to test CiviCRM profile visibility. Masquerade only takes into account Drupal permissions.

See also

▸ The *Adding custom fields* recipe in *Chapter 1, Setting Up CiviCRM*

▸ The *Adding contact types* recipe in *Chapter 2, Organizing Data Efficiently*

Restricting access to custom fields

There may be situations where you will want to restrict sensitive confidential data to certain roles. For example, in a drug rehabilitation center it would be critical to ensure that any client confidential data is only viewable and editable by client caseworkers and other authorized people.

How to do it...

In this recipe, we will have a group of volunteer managers who will be able to edit custom fields for volunteer information. We will remove any overriding CMS permissions and use CiviCRM ACLs to provide permissions for custom data.

1. In Drupal, navigate to **People | Permissions | Roles**. Create a role called CiviCRM Admin.

2. In Drupal, navigate to **People | Permissions**, and remove the **Access all custom data** permission for all roles. Removing the **Access all custom data** permission is not without it's difficulties. It means that every time you add a new custom field, you will have to add permissions using CiviCRM, rather than globally in your CMS. This is why data planning is such a critical step when planning your CiviCRM deployment.

3. Add the permissions **Access CiviCRM**, **View All Contacts**, and **Edit all contacts** to the **CiviCRM Admin** role.

4. Add some Drupal users to the role **CiviCRM Admin** to test the recipe.

5. In CiviCRM, navigate to **Administer | Customize Data and Screens**, and add a custom field set. In this case, we have added a custom field set called **Volunteer Information** and some custom fields to hold volunteering data.

6. Navigate to **Contacts | New Group**, and create a **Volunteer Admin** group, making sure that the **Access Control** checkbox is ticked.

7. Navigate to **Administer | Users and permissions | Permissions (Access Control)**, and add an ACL role called Volunteer Managers.

8. From the **Permissions** home screen, click on **Assign Users to Roles**.

9. Add the **CiviCRM Volunteer Admin** group to the CiviCRM ACL role Volunteer Managers.

10. On the **Permissions** home screen, click on the **Manage ACLs** link and **Add ACL**.

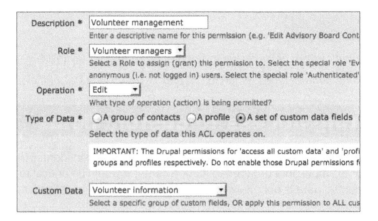

11. Make the ACL description **Volunteer Management**.

12. Set **Role** as **Volunteer Managers**.

13. Make the operation **Edit**.

14. Make the type of data **A set of custom data fields**.

15. Make the custom data **Volunteer Information**.

16. Add some contacts to the **CiviCRM Volunteer Manager** group. They must also have the Drupal role **CiviCRM Admin**.

17. Log in as a user that has the Drupal CiviCRM admin role and is in the CiviCRM group **Volunteer Manager**. You will see that the **Volunteer information** custom field set is editable, where it appears on the contact summary screen:

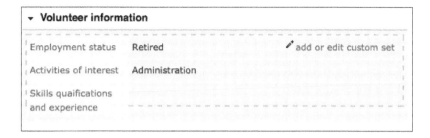

How it works

The Drupal permissions system is used to check whether the user has the correct admin rights for CiviCRM. We removed the permissions to view all custom fields. So, we then used CiviCRM's permissions to see if the user can access the **Volunteer information** custom field set.

See also

▸ The *Adding custom fields* recipe in *Chapter 1, Setting Up CiviCRM*

Using CRM profile permissions correctly

When CiviCRM is installed for the first time, it provides a standard set of permissions with the CMS. The biggest source of security problems with CiviCRM is permissioning, so it is critical that you visit your CMS permissions and check them.

How to do it...

Setting permissions is an important part of the CiviCRM planning process. From the outset, you should understand what each permission does so that you can configure your installation properly.

1. Navigate in Drupal to **People | Permissions**, and scroll down to **CiviCRM Profile permissions**.

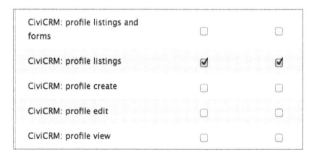

CiviCRM: profiles listings is used in situations where you provide listings of contacts on your website, for example, a membership directory. If you want everyone to be able to search for and see the lists of contacts on your site, you can give the anonymous user and the authenticated user this permission. Note that these permissions are global. If you want only some lists to be available, then you can remove this permission and control the access by using CiviCRM access control lists.

CiviCRM grants this permission to anonymous and authenticated users by default, and one of the most common errors in a CiviCRM site is that sensitive data is exposed to anonymous users because this permission has not been removed.

CiviCRM: profile view is used in situations where you want to display profile information on a page. For example, you may have a site where you want to allow users to view other users' Drupal user pages, which also contain CiviCRM data. You can expose it using this permission.

CiviCRM: profile edit is used when you want users to be able to search for and edit profile fields that are not a part of an event registration form. A typical example might be a short survey. Anonymous users can be given this permission but cannot actually edit the information if it were just presented on a screen. They would need to navigate to the survey by using a URL that contains a checksum token, which gives them a unique URL, so they can edit this information.

CiviCRM: profile create is used when you want users to be able to complete a profile as part of an event registration.

CiviCRM: profile listings and forms is a powerful permission that you should only assign with care. It gives global permissions to all the online forms and listings.

See also

> ▸ http://book.civicrm.org/user/current/initial-set-up/access-control/

Creating permissions for administrators

If you look at the CMS permissions for CiviCRM, there are 60 or so permissions that you can control, depending upon what CiviCRM components you have enabled. If you are new to CiviCRM, it can be quite a daunting proposition to allocate these permissions correctly. For example, you might want to create a role in your CMS for CiviCRM Admin and let those users the admin CiviCRM. What permissions do you give them in the CMS?

How to do it...

CiviCRM has a preconfigured ACL role called **Administrators** linked to a CiviCRM group called **Administrators**. It is already set up with the main permissions to administer CiviCRM. All we need to do is to hook our users up to it and use it for our admin permissions rather than using CMS permissions.

1. In Drupal, create a role called `CiviCRM Admin`.

2. In your Drupal, disable the **CiviCRM: access CiviCRM** permission for everyone except the **CIVICRM ADMIN** role.

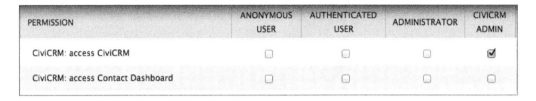

PERMISSION	ANONYMOUS USER	AUTHENTICATED USER	ADMINISTRATOR	CIVICRM ADMIN
CiviCRM: access CiviCRM	☐	☐	☐	☑
CiviCRM: access Contact Dashboard	☐	☐	☐	☐

3. In Drupal, ensure that the **CiviCRM Group Roles Sync** module is enabled.

4. In Drupal, navigate to `admin/config/civicrm/civicrm_group_roles`, and set up a new association rule:

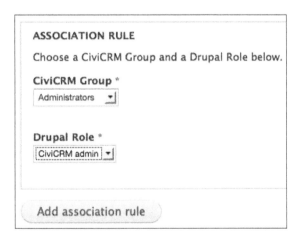

5. Match the CiviCRM **Administrators** group to the Drupal **CiviCRM admin** role.

How it works...

The **Administrator** group in CiviCRM is already set up with CiviCRM access control permissions to administer CiviCRM. Anyone who has the Drupal CiviCRM admin role now has CiviCRM administrative rights to the site.

There's more...

You can set up extra roles in Drupal to refine your CiviCRM administration. For example, you can set up an **Events Administration** role in Drupal and synchronize it with an events manager group in CiviCRM. You can then give the members of that group CiviCRM ACL permissions to manage CiviCRM events.

Managing event registrations using CiviCRM Access Control Lists

This recipe is used for situations where you want to restrict access to event registrations to a group of contacts. For example you might be holding an event that is exclusive to members.

How to do it...

Here, we remove the global permissions set by the CMS—in this case Drupal—and replace them with CiviCRM access control list permissions.

1. Navigate to **Drupal | Administer | People | Permissions**, and look at the permissions for **Events**. You need to remove global permissions for **CiviEvent: Register for Events**.

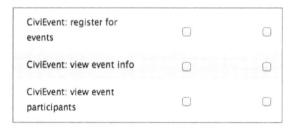

2. Navigate to **Administer | Events | New Event**, and create an event.

Note that events can include profile fields and a contribution. Both these can also be controlled by permissioning.

3. Navigate to **Search | Advanced Search**, and search for a group of contacts that are to be targeted for invitations. Save these contacts to a group. For example, you can do a search for current members of your organization and add them into a group called **Members**. You might want to create other groups such as **Staff**, **Press Contacts**, and **Donors**. Each group that you create needs to have **Access Control** checked. Note also that you cannot use smart groups for access control.

4. Navigate to **Administer | Users and Permissions |ACL(Access Control)**, and create a new ACL role called Fall Dinner.

5. Navigate to **Administer | Users and Permissions | ACL (Access Control)**, and click on **Assign Users to CiviCRM ACL Roles**.

6. Add the CiviCRM groups you created to the **Fall Dinner** role:

Fall Dinner	ACL Members	Yes	Edit	Disable	Delete
Fall Dinner	Staff	Yes	Edit	Disable	Delete
Fall Dinner	Donors	Yes	Edit	Disable	Delete
Fall Dinner	Press contacts	Yes	Edit	Disable	Delete

Now, we can apply permissions to register for our event to the **Fall Dinner** role:

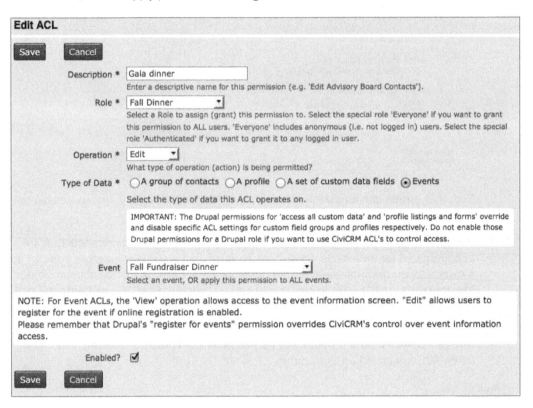

7. Make the description `Gala dinner`.
8. Make the role `Fall Dinner`.
9. Make the operation **Edit**.
10. Set **Type of Data** to `Events`.
11. Make the event the **Fall Fundraiser Dinner** event.

How it works

By removing the CiviCRM global permissions in the CMS, we are able to fine-tune permissions to register for the event by using CiviCRM's ACL permissioning.

5
Managing Communications

In this chapter, we will cover:

- ▸ Setting up a bounced e-mail account using Gmail
- ▸ Creating mail templates for CiviMail
- ▸ Creating mail templates for CiviMail in Drupal
- ▸ Using tokens in templates
- ▸ Creating custom date tokens
- ▸ Scheduling CiviMail
- ▸ Throttling mailings to comply with hosting restrictions
- ▸ Creating newsletter subscription services using profiles
- ▸ Creating newsletter subscriptions using URLs
- ▸ Creating a standalone newsletter subscription form
- ▸ Getting a CiviMail report
- ▸ Mailing attachments in e-mails and CiviMail
- ▸ Allowing users to update information without logging in

Introduction

CiviCRM comes with very sophisticated mail services that will form the basis of how you communicate with your contacts. It is vital that you provide consistent, personalized, and high quality communications—and this chapter shows you how.

Setting up a bounced e-mail account using Gmail

CiviCRM comes with two flavors of mail. You can choose to send mail to your contacts using the **Send email** action available for every set of contact search results. Or for a lot of contacts you can choose to use CiviMail, which provides additional tracking, notifications for bounced e-mail, and subscription features not available in ordinary mail. If you plan to use CiviMail to communicate with your contacts, then having a **bounced e-mail account** is essential. Contact e-mail addresses are constantly changing and become out of date very quickly. A bounced e-mail account is required so that CiviMail can disable contact e-mails that reply with bounced e-mail messages. Getting this set up can be quite frustrating, but this recipe works every time.

Getting ready...

Ensure that CiviMail is enabled in CiviCRM components, and ensure that you have set up cron to manage **Fetch Bounces**.

How to do it...

We will set up an e-mail account to capture bounced e-mails and then configure CiviCRM to check the account periodically.

1. Set up an account in Gmail to manage the bounced e-mails. Give it a name such as `mysite.bounce@gmail.com`.

2. Log in to the Gmail account and navigate to the settings page.

3. Click on the **Filter** tab. You do not want Gmail to filter any bounced messages into the **Spam** folder, otherwise CiviCRM will not have access to them. Create filters for phrases such as **The e-mail address you entered couldn't be found**, or from accounts containing `mailer-daemon` or `postmaster`.

4. For each filter you create, ensure that the **Never send it to spam** checkbox is checked so that messages are never sent to the **Spam** folder.

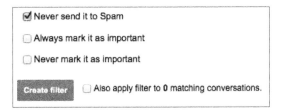

5. Navigate to **Administer | CiviMail | Mail accounts**.

6. Add a new account and complete the details as shown in the following screenshot, entering the information from the Gmail account you created.

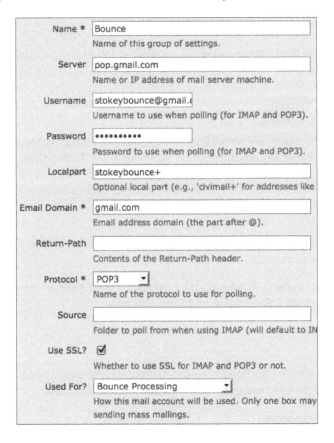

7. Test the setup by navigating to **Administer | System Settings | Scheduled Jobs** and run the **Fetch Bounces** scheduled job.

Fetch Bounces (Hourly)	no parameters	November	Yes	View Job Log | Edit more ▸
Fetches bounces from mailings and writes them to mailing statistics API Prefix: civicrm_api3 API Entity: Job API Action: **fetch_bounces**		3rd, 2012 5:35 PM		**Execute Now** **Disable** Delete

8. Click on the **View Job Log** link and see if bounce processing was successful.

2012-11-03 17:35:05	Fetch Bounces	0 **Summary** Finished execution of Fetch Bounces with result: Success (a:0:{})

9. Configure the **Fetch Bounced mails scheduled job** settings to check the account regularly.

How it works...

The bounced e-mail system only works for mailings sent out using CiviMail, so it does not work if you use the **Send Email to Contacts** option available in the **Action** drop-down list when viewing contact search results.

If your mailing is bounced from a particular e-mail account, the bounced message is sent to the Gmail account you set up.

CiviCRM checks this account. It will put on hold any e-mail accounts that bounce messages and provides you with a report.

You can access these reports at **Administer | Reports | Mail bounce report**, or by navigating to **Administer | Mailings | Scheduled and Sent Mailings**.

The report shows the contacts' e-mail addresses affected, and gives an explanation of why the bounce occurred.

It is worth going back to the bounced e-mail messages in your Gmail account to check why they are getting rejected and make edits to your contacts accordingly.

See also

▸ http://book.civicrm.org/user/current/initial-set-up/email-system-configuration/

Creating mail templates for CiviMail

Developing e-mail templates for anything used to be a long, hard, and frustrating process because not all e-mail clients work in the same way. With the growth of mobile platforms, this became even more difficult. Now there are freely available services that will let you create a tested e-mail template that you can use in CiviCRM.

How to do it...

There are freely available, tested templates that you can use with CiviCRM.

1. Navigate to `http://www.campaignmonitor.com`; this website provides a free templating service with a visual editor. Other mail templates are available, such as MailChimp templates at `http://mailchimp.com/resources/html-email-templates/`. Using the Campaign Monitor service you can create an excellent e-mail template that can be downloaded as an HTML file. Alternatively, you can simply choose one from the MailChimp collection.

2. Open the HTML file in a text editor.

3. Navigate to **Administer | CiviMail | Message templates** and create a new template.

4. Paste in this template the HTML code from your downloaded file and you have an instant tested template that you can now edit.

5. Make sure that you include CiviCRM's **Unsubscribe and Domain** tokens in your template.

 When you compose your message, it's always better to create and test the plain text message first. Once you have perfected your message it's easy to copy and paste the basics into the HTML version. It's much harder to do it the other way round.

Creating mail templates for CiviMail in Drupal

CiviCRM's mailing system is excellent, but the templating system demands a certain degree of skills and knowledge of HTML, particularly if things go wrong.

Add to that the complexity of modern mail templates and it can become very challenging. When planning your CiviCRM deployment, you should consider the skill set of the users who are going to be responsible for sending out mailings. If the HTML-savvy skill set is not there, this recipe shows a different technique for creating perfect e-mail newsletters that use the CMS to create the e-mail. As a developer you will need to know a little about creating templates within your CMS system. In this example we will use Drupal.

How to do it...

Here we will create a new content type in our CMS to handle the composition of each mailing. Users will then be able to cut and paste the HTML into CiviMail.

1. Create a new Drupal content type. Call it `email news` or something similar.

2. Plan your e-mail newsletter content. What are the maximum number of stories you will want to publish at any time? Which ones will have pictures? For each story, create a `text area` field and an `image` field on your `e-mail news` content type. So if you have 10 stories, you will have 10 `text area` fields and 10 `image` fields.

 For usability, you can contain the fields for each story inside a fieldset.

3. Create a node using your new content type. The edit screen may look something like this:

Here we have included only three stories and have collapsed the **STORY 2** and **STORY 3** fields.

4. Add the text and image for each story. Notice that you do not have to size the images at all, and you can use a Rich Text Editor such as CKEditor to style your text, so adding a story is a snap because you do not have to worry about design.

5. Download freely available templates from the Mailchimp website `http://mailchimp.com/resources/html-email-templates/` or Campaign Monitor, `http://www.campaignmonitor.com`.

6. Edit these in a suitable editor such as Dreamweaver and add into your design the number of stories that you have planned for in your `email news` content type. So if you have 10 stories, then you need to plan and place the 10 stories in your e-mail template.

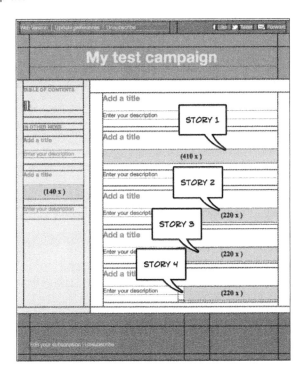

Here we have a very simplified plan for four stories. You can see that you have to add the title, image, and story text for each story at specific places within the templates.

7. This e-mail template conveniently gives you the width for the images you need to use. So for **STORY 1** you need to use images that are 410 pixels wide. In Drupal, navigate to `admin/config/media/image-styles` and create the image styles for each width.

8. In Drupal, navigate to `admin/structure/types/manage/email-news/display` and allocate the image styles to the images for each story. So now you have an e-mail newsletter that displays the headlines, stories, and images in the right size with no fiddling around. But we have not added in the design we created in step 6.

9. In Drupal, follow the template-naming conventions and create a node template for the e-mail newsletter. In this case it would be `node—email_news.tpl.php`. Store it in your theme's `templates` folder.

10. In Dreamweaver, you have your e-mail template designed to hold the stories you are going to create with the `email news` content type. The template is composed of complex nested tables that have placeholders for your stories. In Dreamweaver it is easy to highlight a table that contains a content placeholder and then look at the underlying code.

Here is its screenshot:

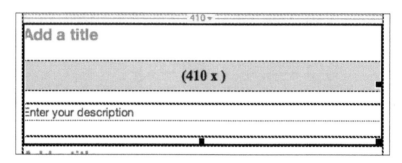

And here is the underlying code:

```
<layout label="Text with full-width image">
  <table class="w410" border="0" cellpadding="0"
    cellspacing="0" width="410">
    <tbody>
      <tr><td class="w410" width="410"><p class=
        "article-title" align="left"><singleline
        repeatertitle="true" label="Article Title">
        Add a title</singleline></p></td></tr>
      <tr><td class="w410" width="410"><img
        editable="true" label="Image"
        class="w410" border="0" width="410">
        Place image</td></tr>
      <tr><td class="w410" height="15"
        width="410"></td></tr>
      <tr><td class="w410" width="410">
      <div class="article-content" align="left">
        <multiline label="Description">
        Enter your description</multiline></div></td></tr>
```

```
   <tr><td class="w410" height="10"
      width="410"></td></tr>
  </tbody>
 </table>
</layout>
```

The placeholders are highlighted.

11. Substitute your Drupal fields into the placeholders. This one is for the first story.

 Using the **Devel** module in Drupal you can isolate all the field values you want.

For the first story the substitutions would look as follows:

```
<layout label="Text with full-width image">
  <table class="w410" border="0" cellpadding="0" cellspacing="0"
width="410">
    <tbody>
      <tr><td class="w410" width="410"><p class="article-title"
align="left"><singleline repeatertitle="true" label="Article
Title"> <php print $node->title;?> </singleline></p></td></tr>
      <tr><td class="w410" width="410">
        <?php print theme('image_style',
        array('style_name' => '410', 'path' =>
        $base_path. $node->field_image_1
        ['und'][0]['filename'], 'alt' =>$node-
        >field_image_1['und'][0]['alt']  ));?> </td></tr>
      <tr><td class="w410" height="15" width="410"></td></tr>
      <tr><td class="w410" width="410">
        <div class="article-content"
        align="left"><multiline label="Description">
        <?php print  $node->field_story_1
        ['und'][0]['safe_value'];?>
        </multiline></div></td></tr>
      <tr><td class="w410" height="10"
        width="410"></td></tr>
    </tbody>
  </table>
</layout>
```

For the images you need to add in the $base_path variable, otherwise our image src values will only show local paths.

12. Repeat this for each story placeholder.

13. Check that your code is working by removing the print render (`$content`) line from `node—email_news.tpl.php`. Copy the code between the body tags of your now-edited e-mail template and paste it into the `node—email_news.tpl.php` template. There may be some style problems, but the important thing is to make sure the field values are showing.

14. Once you are satisfied that the code is working correctly, add some form tags to `node—email_news.tpl.php`. Then, add in a `textarea` tag and paste the full code, including the opening and closing HTML tags from your e-mail template. Your code should look something like this:

```
<form action="none" method="get">
  <textarea id="pasteup" rows="5" cols="60"
    readonly>
    <!--All the email template code goes here-->
  </textarea>
</form>
```

15. Now complete all the stories in your `email news` node. The HTML text can now be copied from the text area of the form and pasted directly into a CiviMail mailing.

```
┌──────────────────────────────────────────────────┐
│   View      Edit      Track      Devel            │
│ ┌────────────────────────────────────────────┐   │
│ │<table bgcolor="#f4fff4" cellpadding="0" cellspacing="0" │
│ │width="612">|                                  │
│ │        <tbody>                                │
│ │                <tr>                           │
│ │                        <td bgcolor="#ffffff" colspan="2"│
│ │valign="middle">                               │
│ └────────────────────────────────────────────┘   │
│   47 reads                                         │
└──────────────────────────────────────────────────┘
```

How it works...

This recipe exploits the content management features of the CMS to produce e-mail newsletters easily. It is quite an effort to set up and test, but the payoff is that users responsible for newsletter production require no HTML or design skills; yet they can produce very high quality mailings.

There's more...

You can add further code in your node template to account for **plain text** mailings—again a major reduction in the time and effort required to create mailings.

This recipe also stores the newsletter as content in your CMS. This means you can maintain a newsletter archive for website visitors. You can theme the content for use on the website and link back to it from your newsletter.

By adding some permission checks you can stop the form element from being visible to ordinary users.

Using tokens in templates

In CiviMail you can substitute tokens for contact data so that your recipients get a personalized message.

How to do it...

CiviCRM has a comprehensive collection of tokens that you can use to personalize mailings.

1. Navigate to **Mailings | New Mailings** and create a new mailing.
2. Place your cursor in the main edit screen and click where you wish to place a token.
3. At the top right corner of the main edit screen, click on the **Insert Tokens** link. A pop-up box appears containing all the tokens that are available.
4. Click on the token you wish to use. This is now inserted into your message.

There's more...

You can also mail contacts by doing a search and selecting **Send Email to Contacts** in the **Actions** menu. You can put tokens into these mails too. CiviCRM restricts you to 50 contacts or less using this method.

Creating custom date tokens

Sometimes there is a token that is not available to you, so you will have to create it programmatically. This recipe shows a very simple example of adding a date token for the current date. It uses **plugin code**, which means you can substitute different token values.

Getting ready...

You don't really need to know much PHP but it helps if you know the basics of how to set up a basic Drupal module.

How to do it...

In this recipe we will create our own Drupal module to do the work. This is not too intimidating, particularly as our code is readily available online.

1. Create a folder in `/sites/all/modules` and give it a suitable name. Let's call this one `Cookbook`.

2. Inside this folder create a file called `cookbook.info`.

3. Open `cookbook.info` and add in the basic code that Drupal needs to identify the module:

   ```
   name = Cookbook
   description = Custom CiviCRM functions
   core = 7.x
   files[] = cookbook.module
   ```
   Easy!

4. Create a file called `cookbook.module` and add in this code:

   ```php
   <?php
   function cookbook_civicrm_tokens(&$tokens) {
     $tokens['date'] = array(
       'date.date_short' => 'Today\'s Date: mm/dd/yyyy',
       'date.date_med' => 'Today\'s Date: Mon d yyyy',
       'date.date_long' => 'Today\'s Date: Month dth, yyyy',
     );
   }

   function cookbook_civicrm_tokenValues(&$values, $cids, $job =
   null, $tokens = array(), $context = null) {
     // Date tokens
     if (!empty($tokens['date'])) {
       $date = array(
   ```

```
        'date.date_short' => date('m/d/Y'),
        'date.date_med' => date('M j Y'),
        'date.date_long' => date('F jS, Y'),
      );
      foreach ($cids as $cid) {
        $values[$cid] = empty($values[$cid]) ? $date : $values[$cid]
  + $date;
      }
    }
  }
```

5. Enable the module and test it by seeing if the tokens are available for placing into a test message.

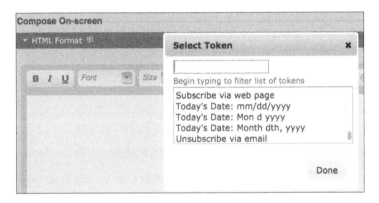

How it works...

CiviCRM has a range of **hooks**. When CiviCRM runs a process such as getting a list of tokens, you can "hook" into that process with your own function and alter what CiviCRM does.

The first hook used here is as follows:

```
function cookbook_civicrm_tokens(&$tokens)
```

Here's the function in full:

```
function cookbook_civicrm_tokens(&$tokens) {
  $tokens['date'] = array(
    'date.date_short' => 'Today\'s Date: mm/dd/yyyy',
    'date.date_med' => 'Today\'s Date: Mon d yyyy',
    'date.date_long' => 'Today\'s Date: Month dth, yyyy',
  );
}
```

All this function is doing is adding the names of our tokens into the list of available tokens. We have three tokens for the current date, available in different formats, so adding token names is really easy.

The second hook used in our module is shown here:

```
function cookbook_civicrm_tokenValues(&$values,
  $cids, $job = null, $tokens = array(), $context = null)
```

Here is the first part of the function:

```
function cookbook_civicrm_tokenValues(&$values, $cids, $job = null,
$tokens = array(), $context = null) {
  // Date tokens
  if (!empty($tokens['date'])) {
    $date = array(
      'date.date_short' => date('m/d/Y'),
      'date.date_med' => date('M j Y'),
      'date.date_long' => date('F jS, Y'),
    );
```

Here we fill the date token with an array of three date formats for the current date.

Here is the second part of the function:

```
    foreach ($cids as $cid) {
      $values[$cid] = empty($values[$cid]) ? $date : $values[$cid] +
$date;
    }
  }
}
```

Here, for each contact ID that we cycle through during the mail process, we check if `$values[$cid]` has anything in it. If it is empty, we put in our date token. If it is not empty, we add our date token.

See also

▸ http://civicrm.org/blogs/colemanw/create-your-own-tokens-fun-and-profit

Scheduling CiviMail

You should consider scheduling mail particularly if you mail out to thousands of addresses. Mailings hog server resources, so it is always best to schedule them to your server when your server is least busy.

How to do it...

CiviCRM has an easy-to-configure scheduling system for CiviMail.

1. Ensure that you have set up a cron job on your web server.

2. Navigate to **Administer | System Settings | Scheduled Jobs** and make sure that the **Mailings Scheduler** option is set to run at regular intervals.

3. Navigate to **Mailings | New mailing** and create your new mailing.

4. In the last screen, ensure the **Send Immediately** box is unchecked. Then schedule your mail.

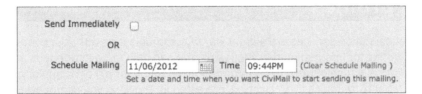

See also

▸ The *Setting up cron using cPanel* recipe in *Chapter 1, Setting Up CiviCRM*

Throttling mailings to comply with hosting restrictions

Many hosting companies put a limit on how many e-mails you can send out per hour. If you exceed this total then your hosting company will bounce all your e-mails and it rapidly becomes impossible to manage your system.

How to do it...

CiviCRM can set limits to how many mailings are sent out per hour.

1. Navigate to **Administer | System Settings | Scheduled Jobs** and make sure that the **Mailings Scheduler** option is set to run at hourly intervals.

2. Navigate to **Administer | CiviMail | Mail settings**.

3. Configure the **Mailer Batch Limit** option to a figure slightly below the hourly limit allowed by your hosting provider.

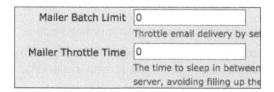

Creating newsletter subscription services using profiles

Newsletter subscription services are a great way of communicating with your contacts, as your audience is opting for information that they want. You can gain more information about your users if you add a couple of extra fields into your subscription form. For example, you might want to see what extra topics they might be interested in. Provided you do not overdo it, users will be willing to transact this information in return for the subscription service.

How to do it...

You can exploit the power of CiviCRM profiles to collect the extra data you want and combine it with the subscription checkbox.

1. Navigate to **Contacts | New Group** and create a group for each newsletter you wish to publish. You must ensure that the **Group Type** is a **Mailing List** and that **Visibility** is set to **Public Pages**.

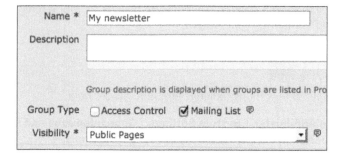

2. Navigate to **Administer | Customize Data and Screens | Profiles** and add a new profile. Give the profile the title **Newsletter subscriptions**.

3. Add the **Contact email** field and the **Contact Group(s)** field.

4. Add **Contact fields** for **First Name**, **Last Name**, and any other extra fields you need. Try and limit the amount of extra information you want to gather otherwise it will put subscribers off.

5. Navigate to **Administer | CiviMail | CiviMail Component Settings**. Tick the **Enable Double Opt-in for Profile Group(s)** field if you wish subscribers to confirm their group subscriptions by e-mail. Your profile may look something like this:

How it works...

CiviCRM adds contacts to the group that have been selected. If you configured **Enable Double Opt-in for Profile Group(s)** then it will send out a confirmation e-mail for the subscriptions. You must have an e-mail field included in the profile to account for **Anonymous user** subscriptions.

There's more...

Navigate to **Administer | Customize Data and Screens | Profiles**. Click on the **More** link against the **Newsletter Management** profile and you will get an HTML snippet that you can paste into any web page and use straight away for your subscription service.

Creating newsletter subscriptions using URLs

You may want to provide your users with a central location where they can manage their CiviCRM subscriptions.

How to do it...

CiviCRM uses different URLs so that you can target some or all of your users' subscription services. You simply need to provide a link to this on your CMS user page.

1. `civicrm/mailing/subscribe` will provide a page to manage all group subscriptions.

2. `civicrm/mailing/subscribe?reset=1&gid=N` will provide a subscription link to a specific group where `N` is the group ID.

How it works...

Users have to be logged in to your website for these links to work. When they click on the links they are taken to a CiviCRM page where they can choose to subscribe or unsubscribe from groups set up as mailing lists.

Creating a standalone newsletter subscription form

You may want to provide a standalone form that allows your users to subscribe to a CiviCRM mailing group rather than providing a URL as in the previous recipe.

How to do it...

It's easy to set up a bit of HTML code that can be pasted into your CMS. In this example we will use Drupal. All you need to know are your group IDs.

1. Navigate to **Contacts** | **Manage Groups** and make a note of any group ID that you wish to use. The groups must be configured for use as mailing lists.

2. Open up a text editor, create a text file, and enter the following code:

```
<form action="http://book.dev/civicrm/mailing/
  subscribe" method="post">
<p>Email: <input name="email" type="text"
  id="email" /></p>
<table> <tr> <td><input name="groupID1"
  type="checkbox" value="1" /></td>
  <td>Advisory Board</td></tr>
  <tr><td><input name="groupID2" type="checkbox"
    value="1" /></td><td>Newsletter Subscribers</td></tr>
  <tr><td><input name="groupID3" type=
    "checkbox" value="1" /></td><td>Summer Program
    Volunteers</td></tr>
```

```
</table><p>
<input name="_qf_Subscribe_next" value="Subscribe"
  type="submit" /></p></form>
```

3. Substitute your own domain for `http://book.dev`.

4. Substitute your own group IDs for `groupID1`, `groupID2`, and `groupID3`.

5. Cut and paste the text into your website. In Drupal you could create a custom block to hold the text. This works well, but anonymous users are not sent to the confirmation page because Drupal does not create a session ID. You can fix this by adding a function into a custom module.

6. Create a folder in `/sites/all/modules` and give it a suitable name. Call it `Cookbook`.

7. Inside the folder create a file called `cookbook.info`.

8. Open `cookbook.info` and add in the basic code that Drupal needs to identify the module:

```
name = Cookbook
description = Custom CiviCRM functions
core = 7.x
files[] = cookbook.module
```

9. Create a file called `cookbook.module` and add in this code:

```php
<?php
function cookbook_base_init() {
  if (!isset($_SESSION['cookbook'])) {
    $_SESSION['cookbook'] = 'session_initialized';
  }
}
```

10. Enable the module.

How it works...

If the user is already logged in the form works well but will fail for the anonymous user. This is why we create a simple function to provide a session ID for the anonymous user.

See also

▶ `http://drupal.org/developing/modules`

Getting a CiviMail report

Getting useful information about your users' interests is critical if you wish to communicate effectively and keep them interested in what you are offering on your website. Some of these techniques involve forms, surveys, quizzes, and polls. All these methods rely on the user taking the trouble to actively complete forms and become less effective when there is a lot to fill in or when time is not available to the user.

CiviMail reports an indirect way of assessing what interests your contacts.

How to do it...

CiviCRM has an extensive and sophisticated reporting system. By setting up your mailings properly you can get CiviCRM to record what users click on in your mailings and provide a report.

1. Navigate to **Mailings | New mailing**. On the second screen of the mailing wizard, **Track and Respond**, make sure that **Track Click-throughs?** and **Track Opens?** are checked.

2. Once your mailing has been sent, navigate to **Mailings | Scheduled and Sent Mailings** and check the **mailing report** checkbox. Or you can navigate to **Reports** and select the various **Mail report** options that are available.

3. On the **Click Through Summary** tab on the report you can see what links the recipients clicked on when they read the mailing. In this way you can see what they are interested in.

How it works...

CiviCRM routes all links in your e-mail back to itself so that it can register what your contacts are looking at. From these reports you can see what sort of content is popular. Combine this information with some intelligent profiling and you can begin to segment and target your contacts much more effectively.

Mailing attachments in e-mails and CiviMail

Generally it is not a good idea to add attachments to mass e-mails in CiviCRM. Delivering each attachment consumes your bandwidth. If you have 1,000 contacts and you deliver each one a 1 MB attachment then you will have used 1 GB of bandwidth.

How to do it...

CiviCRM has controls that allow you to limit attachments in e-mail messages.

1. Navigate to **Administer | System Settings | Undelete, Logging and ReCAPTCHA** and set the e-mail attachment limits.

2. You can set the number of files and the maximum file size.

3. A less bandwidth-intensive method is to use the **Link** tool in the rich text editor to upload large files to your server and simply put links to them in your mail.

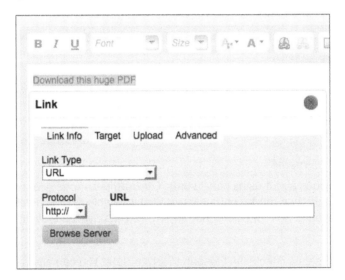

Allowing users to update information without logging in

Your users are busy people. Time is a commodity. You might be in a situation where you want to get users to provide you with data but they have to log in to your site to do it. The act of having to log in is a huge barrier to interaction. Luckily CiviCRM provides a way around this.

How to do it...

Using the CiviCRM checksum token in combination with a profile allows you to bypass the requirement to log in.

1. Create a profile you wish to use. The profile contains all the fields of information that you want the user to complete.

2. Make a note of the profile ID.

3. Enable **Profile Listings and Forms access** for **anonymous** and **authenticated** users in your CMS.

4. Now create a CiviMail mailing in the normal way.

5. You now need to use the `{contact.checksum}` token and the `{contact.contact_id}` token to construct a link back to edit the profile you created:

   ```
   http://www.myorganization.org/civicrm/profile/
   edit?reset=1&gid=N&id={contact.contact_id}&{contact.checksum}
   ```

6. Substitute your website for `http://www.myorganization.org`.

How it works...

When your contacts click on the link from within your mailing, they can update the profile without logging in. CiviCRM uses the checksums to link the profile to the contact ID for each user receiving the mailing.

There's more...

You need to be cautious about using checksums. For example, if one user forwards the e-mail to another user, then the second user would still be able to use the checksum and alter the first user's data. So make sure that any profile data available using a checksum is non-sensitive.

By default, CiviCRM sets a checksum lifespan to seven days. You can alter this by navigating to **Administer | System Settings | Undelete, Logging and reCaptcha** and changing the **Checksum Lifespan** setting.

See also

▸ `http://book.civicrm.org/user/current/common-workflows/tokens-and-mail-merge/`

6
Searching and Reporting

In this chapter, we will cover:

- ▶ Creating a membership mailing list using Advanced Search
- ▶ Using Search Builder to create a smart group
- ▶ Adding the external identifier to full-text searching
- ▶ Adding custom fields to a report
- ▶ Adding an extra display field to a report template
- ▶ Creating a dynamic relationship report using Drupal Views

Introduction

CiviCRM has powerful search features. **Advanced Search** provides the interface to accomplish most searches. **Search Builder** is slightly more technical and is useful when you cannot use Advanced Search. **CiviReports** is a component that adds reporting features to CiviCRM. The reports are in themselves excellent, and you can use them as templates to build your own, more customized versions.

Creating a membership mailing list using Advanced Search

Advanced Search is a powerful tool that allows you to search across all CiviCRM components for useful information about your contacts. These searches can be saved as a smart group.

How to do it...

This recipe will show you how to create a smart group for a newsletter mailing and will provide extra hints for searching using Advanced Search.

1. Navigate to **Search | Advanced Search**. The main window shows the basic search interface:

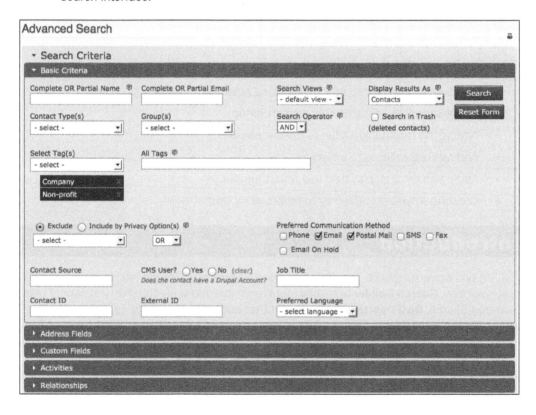

The **Search Operator** option in the second row is, by default, set to **AND**. This means that contacts will have to fulfil | any search criteria you select here *and* any criteria that we select in any of the other search sections, for example, Relationships. You can change this to **OR** if you want to. That would mean contacts would have to fulfill either criteria that you select in search sections.

For the **Select Tag(s)** option in the third row, you can select more than one tag. When you do this, you are creating an OR selection for the tags. In this example, contacts will show if they are tagged **Company** OR **Non-profit**.

The **Preferred Communication Method** checkboxes, in the fourth row, is an AND search for the criteria selected. So, in this example, contacts would have to have e-mail AND postal mail as preferred communication methods to be shown in the results list. Once you decide your search criteria, we can perform the search.

2. Use the **Advanced Search Membership** search section to find primary members who have the status of **New**:

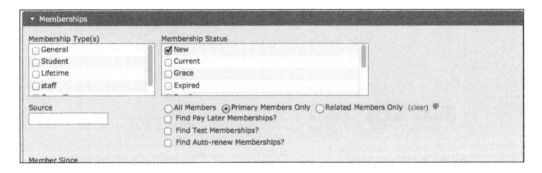

3. From the **actions** drop-down menu, select **New Smart Group** and save your contacts:

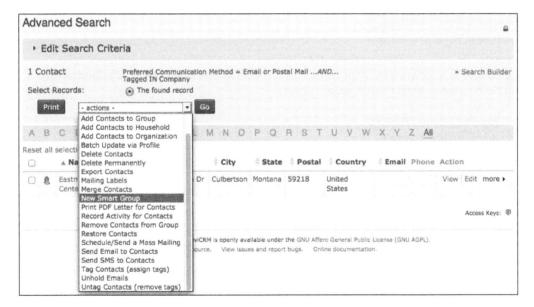

4. Give the smart group a name.

5. Give the smart group a description.

6. If you want to use it for mailings, check the group type **Mailing list** checkbox as shown in the following screenshot:

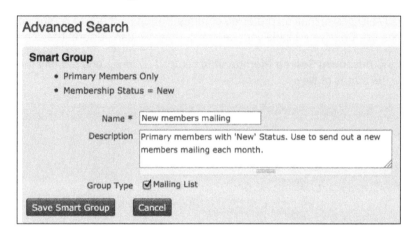

This means you can send new members a mailing. They will be automatically removed from the group when their membership status changes to **Current** or another value that is not new.

How it works...

Advanced Search is pretty awesome. It combines core CiviCRM contact searches with search sections provided by other components, such as **CiviMember** and **CiviContribute**, and accomplishes most of your search tasks.

There's more...

If you create custom field sets, these become available in Advanced Search, provided you set each custom field as searchable.

See also

▸ The *Adding custom fields* recipe in *Chapter 1, Setting Up CiviCRM*

▸ Find out more about Advanced Search at http://book.civicrm.org/user/current/the-user-interface/searching/

Using Search Builder to create a smart group

Search Builder is an alternative method of creating smart groups in CiviCRM. It differs from Advanced Search in that you can search for NULL values: for example, finding contacts with no e-mail address. It also allows OR searching with groups and tags.

How to do it...

Search Builder also has a slightly different syntax, which means you have to look up some values by visiting other administrative pages within CiviCRM. This recipe explores the Search Builder interface to create a smart group.

1. Navigate to **Search | Search Builder**.

2. Under **Include contacts where**, select **Contact** from the drop-down menu. CiviCRM now dynamically changes the search options available.

3. Select **Email** from the first drop-down menu.

4. Select **Primary** from the next drop-down menu.

5. Select **IS NULL** from the last drop-down menu.

This is a search for all contacts with no e-mail address.

6. Do an AND search. Click on the **Another search field** link.

7. Under **Include contacts where**, select **Contact** from the drop-down menu.

8. Select **City** from the first drop-down menu.

9. Select **Primary** from the second drop-down menu.

10. Select **=** as the operator.

11. Enter London as the search value.

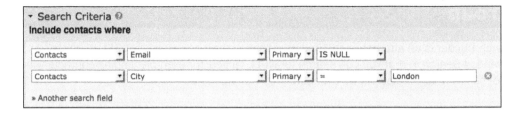

Now you have searched for contacts with no e-mail address *and* who live in London.

12. Do an OR search. Click on the **Also include contacts where** link.

13. Under **Include contacts where**, select **Contacts** from the drop-down menu.

14. Select **City** from the first drop-down menu.

15. Select **Primary** from the second drop-down menu.

16. Select **=** as the operator.

17. Enter Manchester as the search value.

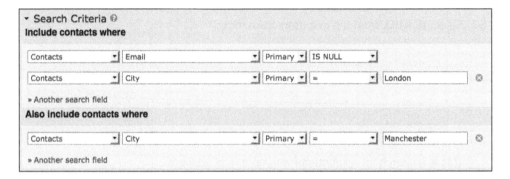

Now you have searched for contacts with no e-mail address *and* who live in London *or* contacts that live in Manchester.

 You can combine AND and OR searches to create very complex queries and save them as smart groups.

18. Once you are happy with your search results, you can save them to a smart group.

There's more...

The **operator** drop-down menu has some options that may seem unfamiliar:

The **IN** operator allows you to test whether a value is contained in a list of other values. For example, you might want to find contacts that are in one or more groups in a list of groups.

You can enter these group IDs into a search as follows:

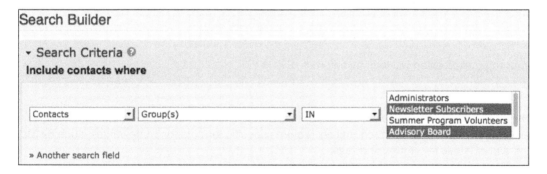

This would return a list of contacts that are in **Newsletter Subscribers** or **Advisory Board**.

The **LIKE** operator allows you to use wildcards and perform **fuzzy searching**. The symbol for the wildcard in CiviCRM is %:

Here you would be looking for contacts with last names that contain the letters "it".

RLIKE is similar to **LIKE** but allows you to search using more complex patterns, using the regular expression syntax REGEX.

A regular expression is a pattern that provides a means of matching text.

In this example, you want to search for contacts with UK postcodes of N16 or N17 or N19:

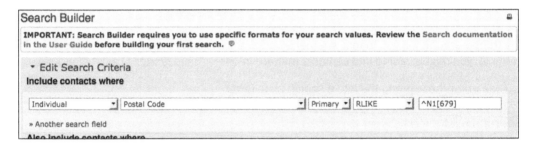

Your regex expression will look as follows:

    ^N1[679]

Option values in Search Builder are not the same as in Advanced Search as we saw in the IN example in this chapter. Search Builder requires specific formats for some values, such as IDs, instead of labels for groups and tags.

See also

> ▸ Find more about regex at http://en.wikipedia.org/wiki/Regular_
>   expression for details about Regex/
>
> ▸ Find more about searching in CiviCRM at http://book.civicrm.org/user/
>   current/the-user-interface/searching/

Adding the external identifier to full-text searching

Many CiviCRM installations contain legacy data that has different unique identifiers than CiviCRM's contact ID. For example, you might have a membership system that identifies contacts with a membership number. Your staff will be used to using this identifier to locate data quickly. CiviCRM provides the external identifier field to hold this information and you can continue to use it to find your contacts.

CiviCRM also has a custom full-text search that allows you to search multiple contact fields at the same time. It is available as a block in Drupal. Unfortunately the custom search does not include the external identifier as a searchable field.

How to do it...

We will navigate to and open up the custom search PHP file and make a small edit to include the external identifier field in searches.

1. Make sure that the **Full-text Search** block is visible in Drupal:

2. Navigate to `/sites/all/modules/civicrm/CRM/Contact/Form/Search/Custom/FullText.php`.

3. Find the `fillContactIDs()` function. Inside this function look for the `$tables` array around line 421 as shown in the following screenshot:

```
421  ▼     $tables = array(
422  ▼       'civicrm_contact' => array(
423           'id' => 'id',
424  ▼         'fields' => array(
425             'sort_name' => NULL,
426             'nick_name' => NULL,
427             'display_name' => NULL,
428  ⌐       ),
429  ⌐     ),
```

4. Add in the external identifier field:

```
421  ▼     $tables = array(
422  ▼       'civicrm_contact' => array(
423           'id' => 'id',
424  ▼         'fields' => array(
425             'sort_name' => NULL,
426             'nick_name' => NULL,
427             'display_name' => NULL,
428             'external_identifier' => NULL,
429  ⌐       ),
430  ⌐     ),
```

5. Save the file. The external identifier is now available to search. Note that this is a change to a core file in CiviCRM, so it will be overwritten by any updates.

Adding custom fields to a report

CiviCRM comes with an excellent suite of reports. If we navigate to **Reports | Membership Report (Detail)** and click on the report criteria, we can see CiviCRM divides the report criteria into sections. In the following screenshot you can see that there is a main section (for contact data) and then a section for membership. In the membership section there are a couple of custom fields:

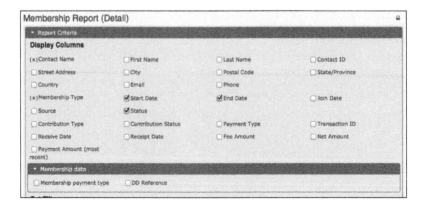

What the report does not allow you to do is to display any custom fields that you created for contacts. For example, you might use CiviCRM to manage a Health IT Association, where the membership consists of health centers. For each health center, you want to know how many patients they have and how many doctors they have. You want to display this data on a membership report but it is not available from the default template.

Getting ready

Create a custom field set for an organization and add in some custom fields for number of doctors, and number of patients.

How to do it...

We need to set up and tell CiviCRM where to find any custom files that we create. We will copy an existing CiviCRM membership detail report template and customize it to display the data we need.

1. On your web server, explore the filesystem structure. It varies from host to host. For example, if we look for where the Drupal `index.php` file is held, in some servers it will be `/var/www/vhosts/example.com/httpdocs/`. In others it might be `/home/siteaccount/public_html/`.

2. Create a directory within this structure that is going to hold CiviCRM customized template files. Make sure that the directory is writeable. Name it `custom_civicrm`. You can choose any name that suits you.

3. Create a directory within this structure that is going to hold CiviCRM customized PHP files. Make sure that the directory is writeable. Name it `custom_php`. You can choose any name that suits you.

4. Navigate to **Administer | System Settings | Directories**.

5. Set the **Custom Templates** path to the directory you created for templates.

6. Set the **Custom PHP Path Directory** field to the directory you created for PHP.

Custom Templates	/home/book/custom_civicrm/
	Path where site specific templates are stored if any. This directory is searched first if set. Cust to templates by creating files named *templateFile.extra.tpl*. (learn more...) CiviCase configuration files can also be stored in this custom path. (learn more...)
Custom PHP Path Directory	/home/book/custom_php/
	Path where site specific PHP code files are stored if any. This directory is searched first if set.

7. Navigate to **Reports | Membership Report (detail)** and run the report.

8. In your browser, view the page source and search it for the text "Report class":

```
328
329  <!-- Report class: [CRM_Report_Form_Member_Detail] --><div class="clear"></div>
330
```

This gives you a clue as to where to find the form that is used for the membership detail report. The Report class is `[CRM_Report_Form_Member_Detail]`. This is the directory structure within the CiviCRM module. The underscore (_) represents a backslash (\).

9. Navigate to your CiviCRM module and then `crm/report/form/member/detail.php`.

10. Copy `detail.php` and rename it `special.php`.

11. Store it in the custom PHP directory you created, recreating the exact directory structure used in the CiviCRM module.

   ❑ CiviCRM module path: `/sites/all/modules/member/CRM/Report/Form/Member /detail.php`

   ❑ Custom path: `/custom_php/ CRM/Report/Form/Member/special.php`

12. Return to the page source for the membership detail report.

13. Now search for ".tpl". The results show you directly where to find the report template file.

```
<!-- .tpl file invoked: CRM/Report/Form/Member/Detail.tpl.
    <form  action="/civicrm/report/instance/20" method="po
```

14. Navigate to your CiviCRM module and then the `templates` directory.

15. Within the templates directory navigate to `CRM/Report/Form/Member/detail.tpl`.

16. Copy `detail.tpl`.

17. Store it in the custom templates directory you created, recreating the exact directory structure used in the CiviCRM module. Rename it `special.tpl`.

   ❑ Original path: `/sites/all/modules/civicrm/templates/CRM/Report/Form/Member/Detail.tpl`

   ❑ Custom path: `/custom_civicrm/CRM/Report/Form/Member/Special.tpl`

18. Edit `special.php` and change the opening line from:

    `class CRM_Report_Form_Member_Detail extends CRM_Report_Form {`

    To:

    `class CRM_Report_Form_Member_Special extends CRM_Report_Form {`

    Note that "class" in this sense is not a class that you might use in CSS. In this case the PHP class is your blueprint for our special report.

19. Navigate to **Administer | CiviReport | Register Report**.
20. Set **Title** to **Special Report**.
21. Set **Description** to **Display Organizational Fields**.
22. Set the **URL** field for the report to **membership/special**.
23. Set the **Class** field for the report to **CRM_Report_Member_Special**.
24. Set **Component** to **CiviMember**.
25. Enable the report.

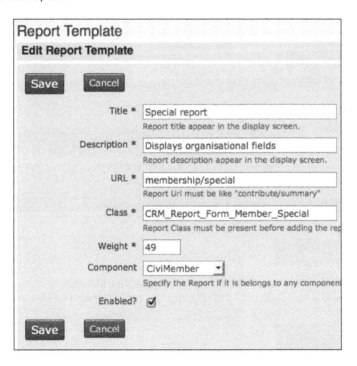

26. Save the template and now go to the URL `special/report/membership/special`. You will notice that it looks exactly the same except it has the title we gave it when we registered it as a report template.

27. Open `special.php` and navigate to the following line:

```
protected $_customGroupExtends = array('Membership',
'Contribution');
```

28. Add `Organization` into the array as follows:

```
protected $_customGroupExtends = array('Membership',
'Contribution', 'Organization');
```

29. Refresh the URL. The custom fields are now available.

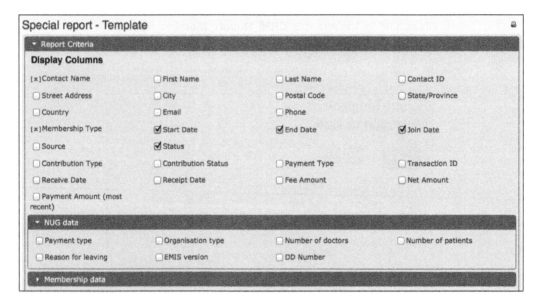

How it works...

CiviCRM looks at the class you created when you registered the report. This in effect tells it where to look for the template and PHP files for the report when the URL is run.

See also

▶ Find more about report customization and report extensions at `http://book.civicrm.org/developer/version/4.1/the-extensions-framework/reports`

Adding an extra display field to a report template

There may be instances when you wish to add display fields to a CiviCRM report that is not available on the report template. For example, you might want to add the external identifier field.

How to do it...

In this example we will add the external identifier as a display option for a report.

1. Set up a custom report template and register it with CiviCRM.

2. Open the report PHP file. In this example we will use the `special.php` template created in the *Adding custom fields to a report* recipe in this chapter.

   Around line 49 we can see the code that generates the Contact checkboxes.

```php
protected $_customGroupGroupBy = FALSE; function __construct() {
    $this->_columns = array(
        'civicrm_contact' =>
        array(
            'dao' => 'CRM_Contact_DAO_Contact',
            'fields' =>
            array(
                'sort_name' =>
                array('title' => ts('Contact Name'),
                    'required' => TRUE,
                    'default' => TRUE,
                    'no_repeat' => TRUE,
                ),
                'id' =>
                array(
                    'no_display' => TRUE,
                    'required' => TRUE,
                ),
                'first_name' =>
                array('title' => ts('First Name'),
                    'no_repeat' => TRUE,
                ),
                'id' =>
                array(
                    'no_display' => TRUE,
                    'required' => TRUE,
                ),
```

You can see that the code has a pattern: an array for the name of the field followed by an array for ID.

3. Copy one in for the external identifier.

```
'external_identifier' =>
          array('title' => ts('External Identifier'),
            'no_repeat' => TRUE,
          ),
          'id' =>
          array(
            'no_display' => TRUE,
            'required' => TRUE,
          ),
```

4. Save the file and reload the report.

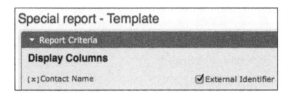

The external identifier now shows in display columns and shows in our report.

Contact Name	External Identifier	Membership Type
Aarons, M_F	Aarons_1746	Full
Abbas, M_F	Abbas_3397	Full
Abbey Medical Centre	xxxx124	Full
	SNUG002	SNUG
Abbey Medical Group	xxx6227	Full

There's more...

Have a good look at the form for your report. In this example you can see that under CRM_ Contact_DAO_Contact—effectively the Contacts table—you could have added any field that is defined in the table, for example, the birth date.

In other parts of report forms you can see other tables that reaccessed, for example, the membership table. So all you need to do is identify what extra fields you want to put in by looking at the database table fields and then add them in.

▸ The *Adding custom fields to a report* recipe

Creating a dynamic relationship report using Drupal Views

There are some limitations to the CiviCRM searching and reporting. For example, you might have a set of organizations that are tagged "Not For Profit" and you want to list all the employees of those organizations, grouped by each organization.

Such a search or report is not possible in CiviCRM without customization.

How to do it...

We will use the power of Drupal Views to create a relationship report. We will also expose the tag and relationship filter so that our report is dynamic.

1. In Drupal, navigate to **Structure | Views** and add a view. Call it `Relationship and Tag report`.

2. Set **Show** to CiviCRM contacts.

3. Click on **Continue and Edit** to continue and edit the view.

4. Set the view to display 100 items, paged.

5. Remove the CiviCRM **Contact ID** field.

6. Add the **CiviCRM Contact: Display Name** field. The view is now showing a list of contact display names.

7. Add a relationship. Select **CiviCRM Relationships: Contact ID A** as shown in the following screenshot:

CiviCRM Contacts: Contribution Records
   The numeric ID of the Contact

CiviCRM Contacts: Drupal ID
   Relates a CiviCRM Contact to the Druapl User Record

CiviCRM Phone Details: Contact ID
   Contact phone number belongs to

☑ CiviCRM Relationships: Contact ID A
   The contact A

8. Select **Limit results only to active relationships**.

9. Apply the relationship.

10. Add the **CiviCRM Contact: Display Name** field, but this time set it to display using the relationship.

11. Exclude the field from the display.

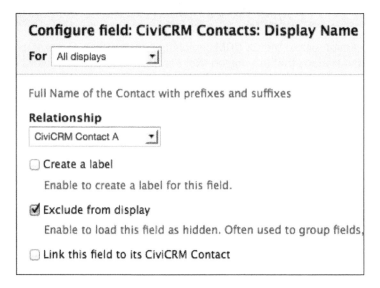

12. Add a filter. Choose **CiviCRM Tags** and select **Tag Name**.

13. Expose the tag filter.

14. Set the relationship for the filter to **CiviCRM Contact A**.

15. Add another filter. Choose **CiviCRM Relationships**.

16. Select **CiviCRM Relationships: Relationship Type A-to-B**.

17. Expose the filter. Do not set a relationship on this filter.

18. In **Format**, choose **Settings**.

19. For **Grouping Field**, select the *second* **CiviCRM Contact: Display Name** value that has the relationship.

20. Test the view and the filters.

How it works...

When we create the relationship in Drupal we do not specify what the relationship is. We do this in the exposed relationship filter.

We do not display the **CiviCRM Contact: Display Name** field that is linked to the relationship, as it would repeat for every record in the view.

Instead we use it as a grouping field. This makes it appear once in the display. So if we choose the employee relationship, the display name linked to the relationship, that is, the employer, is shown only once in summary with the display names of the employees beneath it. The tags filter adds an extra refinement.

7
Integrating CiviCRM with Drupal

In this chapter we will cover:

- ▶ Enabling Drupal Views
- ▶ Creating user accounts from contacts in CiviCRM
- ▶ Mapping contact data
- ▶ Creating user accounts on the fly with CiviCRM entities
- ▶ Using Webform CiviCRM to update relationship data
- ▶ Combining CiviCRM contacts with Drupal content using CiviCRM entities

Introduction

This chapter explores how to present and integrate CiviCRM data into your content management system. The recipes make extensive use of Drupal modules, some of which are still in development.

Enabling Drupal Views

Sometimes it is convenient to display CiviCRM data through Drupal. For example, you might want to display a list of contacts without giving the user access to CiviCRM. You might also want to combine data from CiviCRM with data from Drupal. For example, you have collected custom data about your contacts stored in CiviCRM that you want to display on the Drupal user page.

How to do it...

The key to integrating CiviCRM data is to install the **Drupal Views** module and to give Drupal access to the CiviCRM database tables.

1. Download the Drupal Views module from `http://drupal.org/project/views`.
2. Install and enable the module in the normal way.
3. Navigate to **Administer | System Settings | CMS Database integration**. Here you will see a page of code that you need to put into the Drupal `settings.php` file.

Views integration settings

To enable CiviCRM Views integration, add the following to the site `settings.php` file:

```
$databases['default']['default']['prefix']= array(

  'civicrm_acl'                          => '`emis_civicrm`.',
  'civicrm_acl_cache'                    => '`emis_civicrm`.',
  'civicrm_acl_contact_cache'            => '`emis_civicrm`.',
  'civicrm_acl_entity_role'              => '`emis_civicrm`.',
  'civicrm_action_log'                   => '`emis_civicrm`.',
  [...]
  'civicrm_value_membership_data_2'      => '`emis_civicrm`.',
  'civicrm_value_nug_dasta_1'            => '`emis_civicrm`.',
  'civicrm_value_test_sub_activity_3'    => '`emis_civicrm`.',
  'civicrm_value_workshop_options_6'     => '`emis_civicrm`.',
  'civicrm_website'                      => '`emis_civicrm`.',
  'civicrm_worldregion'                  => '`emis_civicrm`.',
);
```

We have shortened this table for the illustration.

4. Copy the code.
5. Navigate to `sites/default/settings.php`. You may have to change permissions on the `default directory` and on the `settings.php` file so that you can change it.
6. Edit `/site/default/settings.php` and paste the code at the end of the `settings.php` file.
7. Reset the permissions on `/site/default/settings.php` and `/site/default`.
8. Go to your MySQL manager. You need to give the Drupal database user "Select" permission on the CiviCRM database.

In Drupal 6, replace the line `$databases['default']['default']` `['prefix']= array(` with `$db_prefix = array(`.

Each time you add a set of custom fields, CiviCRM creates a new table. These fields will not be available to Drupal Views unless you add the table into `settings.php`.

How it works...

When you install and enable the Drupal Views module, it activates the database integration settings at **Administer | System Settings | CMS Database integration**.

Pasting the code into `settings.php` allows Drupal Views to access the CiviCRM tables. Giving the Drupal database user "Select" permission to the CiviCRM database tables is important for linking CiviCRM contact data with Drupal user accounts.

See also

▸ Find out more information about Drupal integration at `http://book.civicrm.org/user/current/website-integration/integrating-with-drupal/`

Creating user accounts from contacts in CiviCRM

It's pretty easy to bulk create CiviCRM contacts from your Drupal users, but not so easy to bulk create Drupal users from CiviCRM contacts. For example, you can migrate a membership-based website into CiviCRM and Drupal, and you can create login accounts for your members.

How to do it...

We can use another useful Drupal module, **User Import**, to create our user accounts.

1. Install and enable the Drupal User Import module available at `http://drupal.org/project/user_import`.
2. In CiviCRM, navigate to **Search** and perform a search for the contacts you wish to add.
3. On the result set, select **Export Contacts** from the **actions** drop-down menu.

4. Select **export primary fields** and export your records. The exported file will be sent to your browser's `Downloads` folder.

5. Navigate to **Contacts | Find and Merge Duplicate Contacts**.

6. Select the **Individual Strict In-built** rule.

7. Ensure that this is set as the **Default** rule.

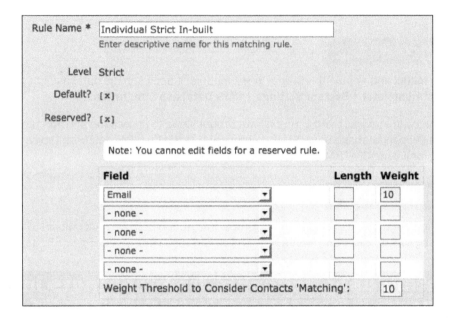

8. In Drupal, navigate to **People | Import**.

9. Use the CiviCRM export file and match its fields to the Drupal **Username** and **Email** fields.

10. Map the CiviCRM **Display Name** field to the Drupal **Username** field.

11. Map the CiviCRM **Email** field to the Drupal **Email** field.

 There are various other settings for your import that are beyond the scope of this book, such as setting roles, sending e-mails, and so on. Read the Drupal documentation carefully so that you set the rest of your imports correctly.

12. Import the users.

How it works...

CiviCRM combines the first name and last name Individual contact fields into the **Display Name** field, making it convenient to use as a Drupal username.

When each username is added, CiviCRM will use the **Individual Strict In-built** default rule to match contacts using just the **email** field. This means your CiviCRM contacts will be updated and no duplicates will be created.

See also

> ▶ Find more about the Drupal User Import module at `http://drupal.org/project/user_import`

Mapping contact data

CiviCRM has excellent geolocation features. This means that you can map contact address data. For example, you could create a profile to hold data on voting intention, or political allegiance that you can then map. This means you can *visualize* the voting data.

How to do it...

CiviCRM's mapping features are very rudimentary, but, when linked to Drupal Views, they become very powerful. In this recipe we will use **Drupal Views** and **Drupal Open Layers** modules to produce a dynamic map that filters the display of contacts. In this example we will simply use the contact's last name as our filter.

1. Navigate to **Administer | System Settings | Geocoding** and ensure that geocoding is set up correctly.

2. Navigate to **Administer | System Settings | Scheduled Jobs** and ensure **Address geocoder** is enabled and scheduled.

3. Install and enable the following modules:

   - Views (`http://drupal.org/project/views`)
   - OpenLayers (`http://drupal.org/project/openlayers`)
   - Libraries (`http://drupal.org/project/libraries`)
   - Proj4js (`http://drupal.org/project/proj4js`)
   - geoPHP (`http://drupal.org/project/geophp`)
   - CTools (`http://drupal.org/project/ctools`)

4. Make sure that you have integrated CiviCRM with Drupal Views.

5. In Drupal, navigate to **Administration | Structure | Views** and add a new view. Name it `Contacts by Last name`.

6. Show the CiviCRM contacts and save the view.

7. Add CiviCRM address fields for latitude and longitude.

8. Add the **CiviCRM Display Name** field as shown in the following screenshot:

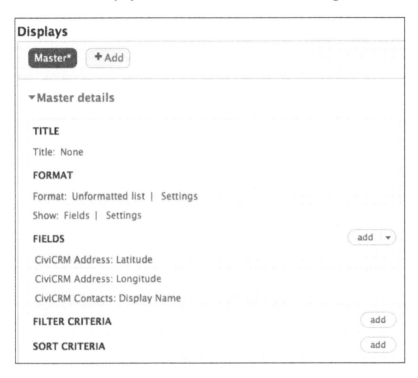

9. Add an **OpenLayers Data Overlay** display to the view.

10. Name the overlay `Contact Map` and make the title `Contact Map`.

11. Change the format of the view from **Unformatted List** to **OpenLayers Data Overlay**.

12. Click on the **Format | Settings**.

13. Set **Map Data Sources** to **Lat/Lon Pair**.

14. Set **Latitude Field** to **CiviCRM Address: Latitude**.

15. Set **Longitude Field** to **CiviCRM Address: Longitude**.

16. Set **Title field** to **CiviCRM Contact: Display Name**.

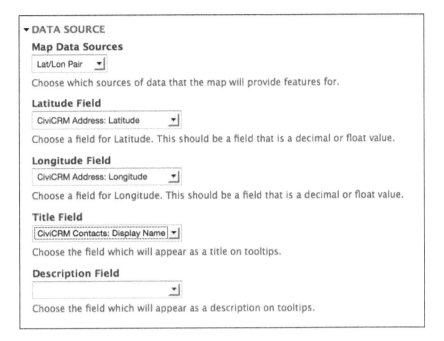

 You can add more fields to the display from CiviCRM and use Drupal Views re-write to combine field values together. All of these can be styled to present a rich source of information in the pop up.

17. Save the view. What you have created is called an **overlay**. Imagine it as a transparent film with your CiviCRM contacts marked on it.

18. Navigate to **Drupal | Structure | OpenLayers** and click on the **Layers** tab. The OpenLayer Data Overlay you created in the view is now listed.

19. Click on the **Maps** tab. This lists all available maps.

20. Select the **Default** map and in the **Operations** menu, select **Clone**.

21. Give the clone a name, a title, and a description.

22. Click on the **Centers** and **Bounds** tab. Scroll and zoom to set an initial view of the map.

23. Click on the **Layers** and **Styles** tab. In **Base Layers**, select the **MapQuest OSM** default layer.

24. In **Overlay Layers**, enable and activate the overlay you created in Drupal Views.

25. Set the map marker to **Red**.

26. Click on the **Behaviors** tab. In the pop up for features, select **Popup for Features**.

27. Save your clone.

28. Navigate to **Structure | Views** and edit the CiviCRM contacts by the **CiviCRM Last Name** view you created.

29. Add a **Page** display.

30. Set the format to **OpenLayersMap**, making sure that you apply the format only to this display.

31. Click on **Format | Settings**.

32. Give the page a URL, `contacts-name`.

33. Remove the page and display all records. Apply this to all displays. Check both displays to ensure that the page has been changed.

34. Add a **starts with** filter for the **CiviCRM Last Name** field and expose it on the view. Check and make sure the filter is applied to all displays.

35. Save the view and test it.

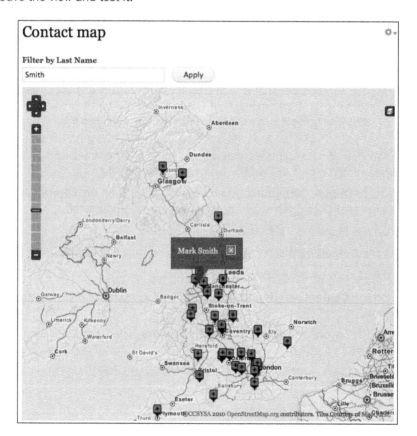

There's more...

These views can also be filtered by CiviCRM Group ID or by custom field values transforming CiviCRM into a powerful data visualization tool.

Using Webform CiviCRM to update relationship data

Updating related contact information is not very straightforward in CiviCRM. Let's imagine you are using CiviCRM to organize a soccer league. You would have three types of contacts: an organization contact type representing a soccer team, an individual contact type representing the team manager, and another individual contact type representing players. You would create a "manager" relationship between the team and the manager and a "player" relationship between the team and the players. Suppose you want to allow the manager to be able to update the team contact? You can do this by allowing managers to update teams by checking the permissions box on the relationship. But the update interface is through the user CiviCRM dashboard, and custom fields are not available through this technique. Enter `CiviCRM Webforms for Drupal`.

This powerful module exposes CiviCRM contact fields to the Drupal Webform module. CiviCRM Webforms can create and update information about contacts, relationships, cases, activities, event participants, group subscriptions, tags, and custom data.

How to do it...

In this recipe we will create a simple form that allows you to update individual contact details and organizational contact details where the relationship between the two is Employee-Employer. We will use the CiviCRM Webform and Drupal Webform modules to achieve this.

1. Install and enable the Webform module from `http://drupal.org/project/webform`.

2. Install and enable the dependent Libraries module (`http://drupal.org/project/libraries`).

3. Install and enable the Webform CiviCRM module (`http://drupal.org/project/webform_civicrm`).

4. Create a Webform node and call it `Update your details`.

5. Select the **CiviCRM** tab. Tick the **Enable CiviCRM processing** checkbox, and set the number of contacts on the form to **2**. The first contact will contain fields to update an individual contact record and the second will be to update the individual's employer contact record.

6. Click on the **Contact 1** tab. This is going to be set to **Individual**. Webform CiviCRM has prechecked the **Existing Contact**, **First Name**, and **Last Name** fields from CiviCRM. The **Existing Contact** checkbox is used to prefill the form with the logged in user's CiviCRM data.

7. Select the **Contact 2** tab. You need to set this contact to **Organization**.

8. Include the organization name.

9. Add an address field.

10. Add in a custom field set. Here we added in one called **Employer**.

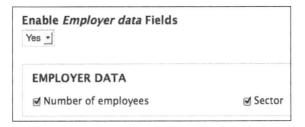

11. Enable **Relationship Fields**.
12. Set the **Relationship to Contact 1** to **Employer of**.

13. Set the **Relationship to Contact 1 Is Active** to **Yes**, as shown in the following screenshot:

14. Save your work so far.

15. Click on the **Webform** tab.

16. Change the label for the **Contact 1 Field set** to **Your details**.

17. Change the label for the **Contact 2 Field set** to **Your employer details**.

18. Click on the **Edit** link on the **Existing Contact Field for Contact 2**, the organization.

19. In the **Default Value** section, select **Relationship to Contact 1** in **Set default contact from**.

20. Set **Specify relationship(s)** to **Employer of Contact 1**:

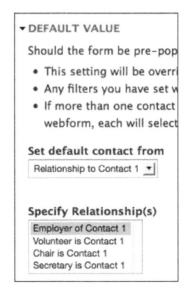

21. In the **Display** section, set the **form widget** to **Static**.
22. Set **Display Contact Name** to **No**.
23. Save everything and test the form.

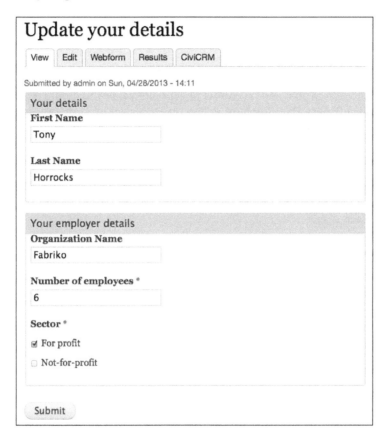

How it works...

Setting the **Existing Contact** checkbox for Contact 1 ensures Contact 1 is prepopulated with the logged in user.

Setting the default value for Contact 2 to **Employer relationship to Contact 1** ensures Contact 2 is prepopulated with any employer details related to Contact 1.

This makes the form behavior work for the logged in user.

Enabling **Employer relationship** between Contact 1 and Contact 2 ensures that, if an anonymous user completes the form, both contact details and the relationship are saved to CiviCRM.

See also

▶ Find out more about Webform CiviCRM at `http://drupal.org/node/1615380`

Creating user accounts on the fly with CiviCRM entities

You might want to add Drupal user accounts to your site when you create a CiviCRM contact. There is a **Create User Account** action on each contact summary screen on the **Actions** button menu. This allows you to create the account once the contact is created. However, this means completing information in an additional screen. Furthermore, Drupal does not send the user a notification that the account has been created. To overcome this, there is a new module by Eileen McNaughton still under development called **civicrm_entity**. This exposes CiviCRM entities to Drupal, which means that they can be recognized by the Drupal Rules module. CiviCRM entities include contacts, activities, memberships, cases, events, and contributions.

How to do it...

We will create a CiviCRM tag called "Create User Account". When we add a contact with this tag, it will trigger a rule that creates the user account:

1. Download, install, and enable the civicrm_entity module (`https://github.com/eileenmcnaughton/civicrm_entity`). Note that it is an experimental module and thus subject to change without notice.

2. Download, install, and enable the Drupal Rules module (`http://drupal.org/project/rules`).

3. Download, install, and enable the Drupal Entity API module (`http://drupal.org/project/entity`).

4. In CiviCRM, navigate to **Contacts | New tag** and create a new tag called **Create User Account**.

5. Set **Used For** to **Contacts**.

6. Save the tag.

7. On the **Tag Management** screen, make a note of the tag ID.

8. In Drupal, navigate to **Components | Workflow | Rules**.

9. Add a new rule. Name it `Create User Record from Civi Contact`.

10. Set **React on Event** to **CiviEntity Tag has been created**.

11. Save the new rule.

12. In the **Conditions** section, add a **Data comparison** condition.

13. Set the data selector to **civicrm-entity-tag:tag-id** (which is currently the last selector in the data selector list).

14. Set the operator to **equals**. Set the value to the tag ID. In this example the tag ID was **15**:

> **Conditions**
>
> ELEMENTS
>
> ✛ Data comparison
>   Parameter: *Data to compare:* [civicrm–entity–tag:tag-id], *Data value:* 15
>
> ✚ Add condition   ✚ Add or   ✚ Add and

15. Add an action. Select **Create or Load Linked Drupal User Account.**

16. On the action configuration screen, select **Activate account** and **Send account notification email**.

17. Save the action.

18. In CiviCRM, test the rule by adding a new contact with the **Create User Account** tag.

How it works...

The CiviCRM contact is exposed to Drupal Rules and you can configure actions to be undertaken when the tag is created. CiviCRM actions are currently limited, but the whole scope of Drupal actions are available. So, you could add roles for the contact, send them custom e-mails, and so on. This module and others like it make it easy for the nondeveloper to create valuable functionality with no coding skills.

Combining CiviCRM contacts with Drupal content using CiviCRM entities

Linking CiviCRM contact data with Drupal data has until now not been possible directly. For example, imagine you run a cycling club. You have some members who are interested in mountain bikes, some in road bikes, and some in BMX bikes. You want to create "category" pages on your website that link users and content together in a community. In other words, if you could tag contacts and content with "Mountain bike", you could create a page that displays the two together.

Before now, you would have to create a user account on your website for each contact and link them both using a tag. Now you can do it directly. This makes it possible to produce category pages that list linked contacts without the requirement for a user account.

How to do it...

This recipe takes advantage of a module called **civicrmentity**, by Benjamin Doherty. This is not to be confused with the **civicrm_entity** module by Eileen McNaughton. These modules are currently incompatible. civicrmentity exposes CiviCRM entities to Drupal entities. This means that you can add Drupal fields to a CiviCRM contact, or, for this recipe, add taxonomy terms. Here, we will create a taxonomy term to link together CiviCRM contacts and content, and create an online community based around it.

1. Download, install, and enable the following modules:

    - civicrmentity module at `https://github.com/bangpound/civicrmentity/`

    - Entity API module (`http://drupal.org/project/entity`)

    - Views module (`http://drupal.org/project/views`)

    - CTools module (`http://drupal.org/project/ctools`)

    - Panels module (`http://drupal.org/project/panels`)

2. In Drupal, navigate to **Structure | Taxonomy** and add a new vocabulary called `Topics`.

3. Add the following terms to the `Topics` vocabulary: `Mountain bikes`, `Road bikes`, and `BMX`.

4. Navigate to **Configuration | CiviCRM | Entities**. The current version of the module does not label each content type. We have shown these in the following screenshot:

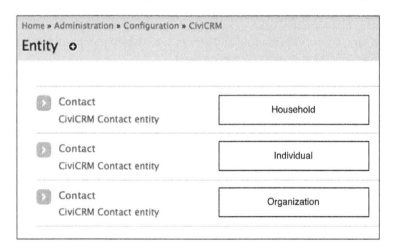

5. Click on the second Contact link for individuals and add a new field to the contact entity, and name it `Topics`.

6. Set the field type to **Term reference**.

7. Set the widget to **Checkboxes/Radio buttons**.

8. Save the field.

9. In the field settings, set **Vocabulary** to **Topics**.

10. Navigate to any CiviCRM contact and edit it. You will see a link to **Edit Drupal fields** at the foot of the page as shown in the following screenshot:

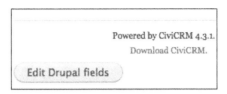

11. Click on the link, check the **Mountain Bike** box and save.

12. Navigate to **Structure | Views** and add a CiviCRM Contact view.

13. Add the **CiviCRM Contacts: Display Name** field to the view.

14. Add a contextual filter to the view. Select the **Contact: Topics** filter.

15. Preview the view using the **term ID** for Mountain bike. The contact with the term will appear.

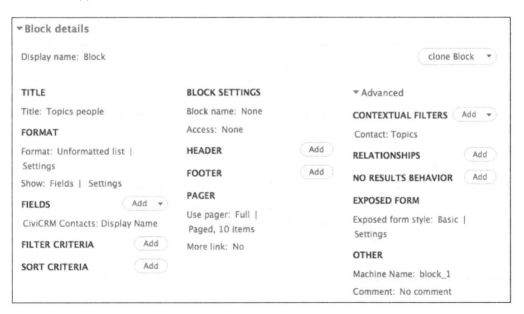

How it works...

The civicrmentity module allows us to apply terms to CiviCRM contacts. This means we can use these terms as arguments in a Drupal view, so that if we filter the view for a term ID, all the CiviCRM contacts with that term will be listed.

There's more...

You can add the same term fields to CiviCRM events and Drupal content types. You could then create views for CiviCRM events and Drupal content that use the term IDs as arguments.

You could then use **Drupal Panels** to gather these views together so that you get a page that displays events, CiviCRM contacts, and Drupal content together. This in effect would be a community of users and content based on a topic of interest.

8

Managing Events Effectively

In this chapter, we will cover:

- ▶ Using jQuery to control form elements
- ▶ Using jQuery to show and hide form elements by user choices
- ▶ Using CiviDiscount with CiviEvents
- ▶ Collecting data for a paid event registration with Webform CiviCRM
- ▶ Using a shopping cart and Drupal views for event registration

Introduction

CiviCRM documentation for CiviEvents is comprehensive, so in these recipes we will use CiviEvents as a vehicle to explore how we can alter forms and introduce a couple of techniques using jQuery. We will also look at a relative newcomer to CiviCRM, **CiviDiscounts**, and the use of Drupal modules with CiviEvents.

Using jQuery to control form elements

jQuery is a versatile method used to alter any HTML page. In CiviCRM, we can use it to accomplish tasks that are impossible using custom templates or CSS. A common problem is how to expose different price sets on an event registration form.

Getting ready

In this example we have a membership organization called Inner City Arts. We have enabled the **CiviMember Roles Sync** module. This module synchronizes membership status to a Drupal role. In this case, if an individual is a current member of Inner City Arts, CiviMember Role Sync automatically assigns them the role of Member in Drupal. This means that when a member logs in, we can tell that they are a member of Inner City Arts because they have the Member role in Drupal.

If you want to play around with jQuery and see how the components work, you can use Firefox as your browser and install the Firebug extension, or use Google Chrome.

How to do it...

In this recipe, we will use jQuery to show different price sets to users depending on whether the logged-in user is a member of your organization:

1. Set up a price set for an event and include prices for members and non-members.

Desert landscapes: a Cara Leighton retrospective

Event Fee(s) * ○ Inner City Arts Members - $ 8.00
⦿ General Public - $ 10.00

Your Registration Info

Email Address * _____

Continue >>

Note that two price set items are showing. You want the **General Public** price to show to the anonymous user and the **Inner City Arts Members** price to show to logged-in users who are Inner City Arts members. You accomplish this using jQuery.

2. Create a Drupal block and copy and paste in the following piece of jQuery:

```
<script type="text/javascript">
(function($) {
  $(document).ready(function() {

//This is our custom jQuery code
```

```
   $("#priceset").find("label:not(:contains('Members'))").
each(function() {
       var id = $(this).attr('for');
           if (id) {
             $(this).prev().remove();
                $(this).remove();
             }
          });
//This is the end of our custom jQuery code
   });
   }) (jQuery);
</script>
```

3. Set the block's **Text Format** to **Full HTML**.

4. Set the block's visibility to only show on specific CiviCRM event pages *and* only to users who have the **Member** role.

5. Create another block and copy and paste in the following jQuery:

```
<script type="text/javascript">
   cj(function($) {
   $(document).ready(function() {

//This is our custom jQuery code

   $("#priceset").find("label:contains('Members')").each(function(){
       var id = $(this).attr('for');
       if (id) {
         $(this).prev().remove();
         $(this).remove();
           }
       });
   $("#priceset").prepend("<h3>If you are an Inner City member, log
in for reduced ticket prices</h3>");
//This is the end of our custom jQuery code
   });
   }) (jQuery);
</script>
```

6. Set the block's visibility so it only shows on specific CiviCRM event pages *and* only to the **anonymous** user.

7. Test the event registration.

How it works...

`cj(function($)` is used to tell CiviCRM to use the jQuery version that comes with the CiviCRM installation rather than the jQuery that comes with your CMS. If the user is anonymous, the second block jQuery runs and the **General Public** price is displayed with the message for Inner City Arts members to log in, as shown in the following screenshot:

Desert landscapes: a Cara Leighton retrospective

If you are an Inner City member, log in for reduced ticket prices

Event Fee(s) * ⦿ General Public - $ 10.00

Your Registration Info

Email Address *

Continue >>

If the user is logged in *and* is a member, the first block jQuery runs and only the member price is displayed.

This technique requires that the price set label for the members' price contains the word "Members".

The first block of jQuery only runs if the user is logged in and has the Drupal "Member" role. jQuery looks at the price set and finds all the items with a `label` element that does not contain the word "Members". It checks that the label is attached to a form input and then removes the input and the label. The effect of this is to remove the **General Public** price set item.

The second block does the reverse. It only runs for the anonymous user. jQuery finds all the items with a label that does contain the word "Members" and removes the price set items. The effect of this is to remove the member price set item. It also adds in a reminder for members to log in to get reduced ticket prices.

 Note that this technique is not secure and that your page can be manipulated so that the member prices could become available.

See also

▸ Find out more about this technique at `http://civicrm.org/blogs/stoob/using-only-jquery-and-civicrm-create-members-only-pricing`

Using jQuery to show and hide form elements by user choices

Sometimes, you may want to expose form elements depending on what previous choices a user has made. For example, you might run a conference over two days. If people only want to attend one day, you will only want to show them further options for that day.

How to do it...

This recipe shows you how to gain control of your event registration forms using jQuery.

1. Set up a pricelist for your event. Navigate to **Administer | CiviContribute | New Price sets** and create a new set.

2. In the new set, create a checkbox field so users can choose what days they want to attend:

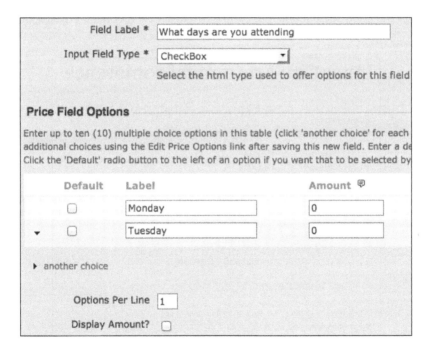

3. Provide two choices: **Monday** and **Tuesday**.

4. Make the **Amount** column for each choice to be free.

5. Uncheck **Display Amount**. This presents the user with two checkboxes with no price display.

6. Add another checkbox field for further choices for Monday, to be used if the user selects **Monday** in the first field.

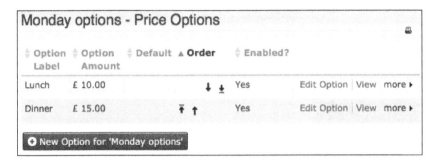

7. Provide the **Lunch** and **Dinner** options for **Monday**.

8. Repeat this for **Tuesday**.

9. Create an event.

10. Apply the price set to it and make the event available for online registration. It will look something like this:

All the options are now displayed. When a user checks the boxes in **Which days will you attend?**, you will want the following behavior:

❑ If the user chooses **Monday**, display the Monday options, otherwise hide them

❑ If the user chooses **Tuesday**, display the Tuesday options, otherwise hide them

11. Get the ID for each of the checkboxes in **Which days will you attend?**.

   Use Firefox and Firebug to get these values. In your own situation, the values will be different from the ones shown in the following screenshot:

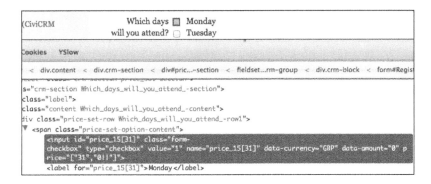

Here you can see that the **Monday** checkbox has an ID of `price_15[31]`. We can find the value for the **Tuesday** checkbox as well.

12. Get the class for each price set.

Here you can see that the **Monday options** field is contained in a `div tag` with a class of `Monday_options_section`.

13. Next, in a text editor, create the following code:

```
<script>
(function($) {
  $(document).ready(function() {
    $('.Tuesday_options-section').hide();
    $('.Monday_options-section').hide();
    $("#price_15\\[31\\]").change(function() {
      if($(this).is(':checked')){
        $('#priceset').find('.Monday_options-section').show();
      }
      else {
        $('#priceset').find('.Monday_options-section').hide();
      }
    });
    $("#price_15\\[32\\]").change(function() {
      if($(this).is(':checked')){
        $('#priceset').find('.Tuesday_options-section').show();
      }
      else {
        $('#priceset').find('.Tuesday_options-section').hide();
      }
    });
  });
}) (jQuery);
</script>
```

14. Add the code to a Drupal block.

15. Set the block's **Text Format** to **Full HTML**.

16. Set the block's visibility to show on your CiviCRM event.

17. Now test the event registration page.

How it works...

The following code is called a **wrapper**. It just ensures that the code works in Drupal:

```
<script>
(function($) {
$(document).ready(function() {
```

The following code looks for the classes that contain the **Monday** and **Tuesday** options and hides them when the event is loaded:

```
$('.Tuesday_options-section').hide();
$('.Monday_options-section').hide();
```

The following function looks for the **Monday** checkbox ID and tests whether it has been checked. If it has, the price set with the `Monday_options-section` class is displayed. If not, it is hidden:

```
$("#price_15\\[31\\]").change(function() {
if($(this).is(':checked')){
$('#priceset').find('.Monday_options-section').show();
}
else {
$('#priceset').find('.Monday_options-section').hide();
}
});
```

The following function does the same for the **Tuesday** checkbox. If it is checked, the Tuesday price set is shown, if not, it is hidden:

```
$("#price_15\\[32\\]").change(function() {
if($(this).is(':checked')){
$('#priceset').find('.Tuesday_options-section').show();
}
else {
$('#priceset').find('.Tuesday_options-section').hide();
}
```

This code closes the wrapper for the jQuery:

```
});
  });
  }) (jQuery);
</script>
```

There's more...

jQuery is very versatile and powerful for all sorts of development tasks, not just CiviCRM. It is really quite easy to learn the basics and go on from there.

See also

▶ Find out more about customizing CiviCRM with jQuery at `http://civicrm.org/blogs/hershel/how-customize-civicrm-pages-jquery`

Using CiviDiscount with CiviEvents

CiviDiscount is an example of an agnostic CiviCRM extension, which means that it works in both Drupal and Joomla!. You can use the extension to create discount codes or to provide consistent discounts to your members.

How to do it...

CiviDiscount is an example of a CiviCRM extension. You will have to configure an **extensions directory** for your CiviCRM installation and download the extension before you can use it.

1. Navigate to **Administer | System Settings | Directories** and set a directory to hold CiviCRM extensions. The directory must exist on the server:

CiviCRM Extensions Directory	/Users/tonyhrx/Sites/book/sites/default/files/civicrm/extensions/
	Path where CiviCRM extensions are stored.

2. Navigate to **Administer | System Settings | Resource URLs** and set a URL for your CiviCRM extensions:

Extension Resource URL	http://book.dev/sites/default/files/civicrm/extensions/

[Note that the URL has to match the path you created for the extensions directory.]

3. Navigate to **Administer | Customize Data and Screens | Manage extensions**.

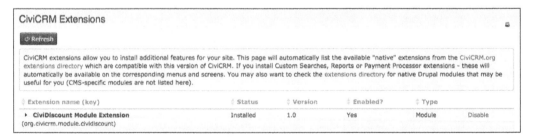

CiviCRM Extensions

↻ Refresh

CiviCRM extensions allow you to install additional features for your site. This page will automatically list the available "native" extensions from the CiviCRM.org extensions directory which are compatible with this version of CiviCRM. If you install Custom Searches, Reports or Payment Processor extensions - these will automatically be available on the corresponding menus and screens. You may also want to check the extensions directory for native Drupal modules that may be useful for you (CMS-specific modules are not listed here).

Extension name (key)	Status	Version	Enabled?	Type	
▸ **CiviDiscount Module Extension** (org.civicrm.module.cividiscount)	Installed	1.0	Yes	Module	Disable

4. Download the CiviDiscount extension.
5. Add a navigation menu item for CiviDiscount. The URL is `civicrm/cividiscount/discount?&reset=1`.

6. Add a discount.

7. Add a 50 percent discount through the use of a discount code.

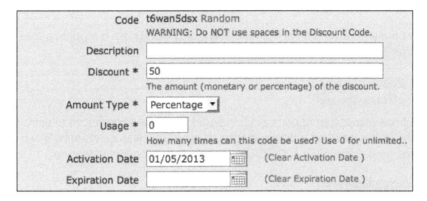

8. Apply this to an event.

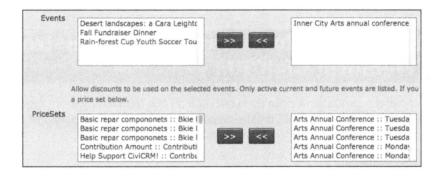

Here there is an event called **Inner City Arts annual conference** and the discount has been added to each field in the event price set.

9. Save the discount and see how it affects event registration.

Inner City Arts annual conference

If you have a discount code, enter it here   t6wan5dsx

How it works...

The event now has a box to enter the discount code.

You can now make your selections from the event price set. These discounts appear on the event registration confirmation screen.

There's more...

CiviDiscount has many other options available, and it is a good alternative to using jQuery and different price set fields for different sorts of users. It is also an example of where organizations have contributed to CiviCRM to fund a much-requested feature.

See also

▶ Find out more about supporting new CiviCRM features at `http://civicrm.org/make-it-happen`

Collecting data for a paid event registration with Webform CiviCRM

Collecting complex organizational data and user data on one form during event registration is difficult in CiviCRM. You can create profiles to gather individual contact data, but you can only collect the organization name for organizational contact data.

How to do it...

In this recipe, we will use the Drupal Webform CiviCRM module to collect the data we require and then pass the user onto the CiviCRM event registration screen, with details already filled in.

1. Download, install, and enable the following Drupal modules:
   - ❑ Webform CiviCRM (`http://drupal.org/project/webform_civicrm`)
   - ❑ Webform (`http://drupal.org/project/webform`)
   - ❑ Libraries (`http://drupal.org/project/libraries`)

2. Create a simple event in CiviCRM. The event will show a single registration fee and collect the first name and last name of the registrant and the organization they work for. Make a note of the event registration URL.

3. Create a new web form using Webform CiviCRM.

4. Enable the form for CiviCRM processing.

5. Set the form for two contacts. Contact 1 will be the individual making the registration, and Contact 2 will be the organization they work for.

6. For Contact 1, select the **Checksum** field, the **Existing Contact** field, the **Contact ID** field, and well as other fields such as **First Name** and **Last Name**.

7. You can add as many built-in or custom CiviCRM fields as you like to both contacts, and therefore, collect a lot of detailed information.

8. Enable relationship fields for Contact 2 and set Contact 2 as the employer of Contact 1.

9. Save the form.

10. Click on the **Webform** tab.

11. Change the label for Contact 1 to About you.

12. Change the label for Contact 2 to About your organization.

13. For Contact 2, the organization, click on the Edit link for the Existing Contact field.

14. In the Default Value pane, change Set the default contact from to Relationship to Contact 1.

15. Set Specify Relationships(s) to Employer of Contact 1.

16. For Contact 1, the individual, click on the Edit link for the Checksum field. You will see that Webform CiviCRM provides you with snippets of code that you can use to redirect the user once the form has been submitted. You can adapt these to redirect the user to the event registration form.

17. In a text editor, enter the following code:

```
civicrm/event/register?reset=1&id=16&cid=%value[civicrm_1_
contact_1_fieldset_fieldset][civicrm_1_contact_1_contact_contact_
id]&cs=%value[civicrm_1_contact_1_fieldset_fieldset][civicrm_1_
contact_1_contact_cs]
```

Here, the ID value is set to the ID of the CiviCRM event.

18. Click on the form settings.

19. Under **Redirection location**, select **Custom URL** and copy and paste in the code you created earlier:

20. Test the web form.

How it works...

When the user has completed filling in the individual details and organization details, they are sent to the paid event registration screen that displays minimum data prefilled through the use of the checksum.

If this were a free event, you could have added as many contacts as you like, have them mapped to the event, and then use the web form as your event registration screen instead of CiviCRM. You would not need to use the checksum at all.

Using a shopping cart and Drupal views for event registration

CiviCRM 4.2 includes a shopping cart system for event registration. This can be combined with a Drupal view of events to provide a quick and convenient event registration page.

How to do it...

We will create a list of available CiviCRM events in a Drupal view. None of the events should include any special profile or custom field requirements. We will then add shopping cart links in the view.

1. Navigate to **Administer | CiviEvent | CiviEvent component settings** and tick the **Use Shopping Cart Style Event Registrations** checkbox.
2. Create a page view of CiviCRM events in Drupal views.
3. Add a filter to show only future events.
4. Sort the list in date order.
5. Add field values for **Event Title**, **Event Date**, and **Event ID**.
6. Set **Format** to **Table**.
7. We can rewrite the **Event ID** field in the Drupal view to provide us with add/remove links to the event shopping cart:

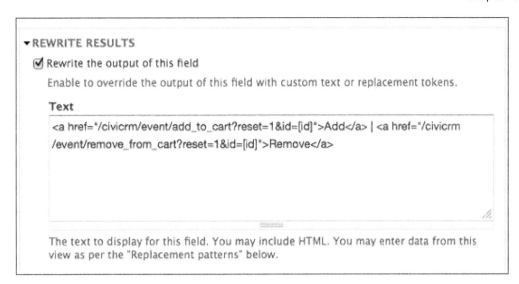

8. Save the view and test it.

How it works...

The view will now look something like this. When a user adds or removes an event from the shopping cart, a status message is displayed with a link to cart checkout:

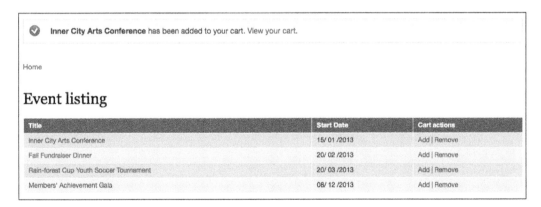

9

Using Campaigns, Surveys, and Petitions Effectively

In this chapter, we will cover:

- ▸ Using activities for campaign planning
- ▸ Designing campaign dashboards in Drupal Views
- ▸ Using surveys effectively
- ▸ Recording survey results
- ▸ Using get out the vote effectively
- ▸ Using petitions effectively

Introduction

CiviCampaign acts as a *container* for activities, events, petitions, and surveys based around a particular *organizational* goal. This chapter explores how to set up campaigns, how to display them, and how to use some of the more specialized campaigning features of CiviCRM.

Using activities for campaign planning

In any campaign, there are a million things to do and usually not enough people to do them! You can use CiviCRM to define these tasks, allocate them to people, schedule their completion, and check their progress.

How to do it...

1. Navigate to **Administer | System Settings** and enable **CiviCampaign**.
2. Navigate to **Administer | CiviCampaign | Campaign types** and add a campaign type. Name it `Community Campaign`.
3. Navigate to **Campaigns | New campaign** and add a campaign.
4. Set the title to `Stop the Supermarket`.
5. Set the **Campaign Type** field to `Community Campaign`.
6. Leave the start date as the current date.
7. Set the **Campaign status** to **In progress**.
8. Save the new campaign.
9. Navigate to **Administration | Customize Data and Screens | Activity Types** and add some activity types. For example, add an **Activity Type** called **Gather contacts**.
10. Add a custom field set for the **Gather Contacts** activity type and create a custom field to show what sort of contacts you want gathered.
11. Add an activity and assign it to a contact.
12. Set the **Campaign** field to **Stop the Supermarket**.

How it works...

Adding CiviCampaign allows you to gather related activities under one umbrella. By adding custom activity types, you can create, allocate, and schedule administrative tasks associated with your campaign.

There's more...

1. Navigate to **Communications| Schedule Reminders**.
2. Create a **two days before** reminder for each assigned contact to get scheduled activities completed.
3. Create a **two days after** reminder to contacts who have allocated tasks that activities have not been completed to schedule.
4. Navigate to **Reports | Contact Reports | Activity Reports**.
5. Create a to-do list. Change the activity report criteria. Set the assignee to you, and activity status to **Scheduled**. Save a copy of the report and add it to your CiviCRM dashboard.

See also

- The *Adding activity types* recipe in *Chapter 1, Setting Up CiviCRM*
- The *Adding custom fields* recipe in *Chapter 1, Setting Up CiviCRM*
- The *Using scheduled reminders for activities* recipe in *Chapter 1, Setting Up CiviCRM*

Find out more about setting up CiviCampaign at `http://book.civicrm.org/user/current/campaign/setup/`.

Designing campaign dashboards in Drupal Views

CiviCRM does have a campaign report, but it is based around a contact listing rather than a list of activities associated with a campaign. There is also a **Campaign Dashboard**, but this does not provide appropriate listings.

In any campaign you might want to know:

- What administrative activities are completed, scheduled, or overdue?
- What events are scheduled?
- Were events successful?
- What mailings were sent out?

- ▸ How effective were mailings?
- ▸ What petitions were organized?
- ▸ What surveys were organized?

How to do it...

We will use Drupal Views recipes to create the necessary listings. We can also use Drupal Panels or Drupal Context modules to organize our views into *dashboards*. These recipes assume that you have a working knowledge of Drupal Views.

1. Download, install, and enable the Drupal Views module: `http://drupal.org/projects/views`.

2. Add a new view of CiviCRM Activities.

3. Save the view.

4. In the **Advanced** section of the view, add a relationship.

5. Select the **CiviCRM Activity Targets: Target Contact ID** relationship. This will enable you to display the name of the target contact. Set the **Identifier** field to **Target**.

6. Add another relationship. Select the **CiviCRM Activity Assignments: Assignee Contact ID** relationship. This will enable you to display the name of the contact that was assigned the activity. Set the **Identifier** to **Assignee**.

7. Add another relationship. Select the **CiviCRM Activities: Campaign** relationship. This will enable you to display the title of the campaign for each activity. Set the **Identifier** to **Campaign**.

8. Add the **CiviCRM Activities: Subject (Subject)** field.

9. Add the **CiviCRM Activities: Scheduled Date** field.

10. Add the **CiviCRM Activities: Scheduled Activity Date (Scheduled Activity Date)** field.

11. Add the **CiviCRM Contacts: Display Name** field and set the relationship to **Target**. Set the label to **Target Contact**.

12. Add the **CiviCRM Contacts: Display Name** field and set the relationship to **Assignee**. Set the label to **Assigned Contact**.

13. Add the **CiviCRM Campaigns: Title** field and set the **relationship** to **Campaign**. Disable the **label** and exclude the field from the display.

14. In the **Format** section, set **Format** to **Table**.

15. In the **Table** settings, set **Campaign Title** as **Grouping field**.

16. Save the view.

Support safer cycling			
SUBJECT	SCHEDULED ACTIVITY DATE	TARGET CONTACT	ASSIGNED TO
Consult with city authorities	08/04/2013	Mr. Allen Ivanov	Ms. Juliann Terry
Call to check security arrangements for protest.	30/04/2013	Billy Prentice II	Troy Jameson

Stop the supermarket			
SUBJECT	SCHEDULED ACTIVITY DATE	TARGET CONTACT	ASSIGNED TO
Get sponsorship from this business	29/04/2013	Creative Technology Partnership	Nobody
Lets start gathering some data	23/05/2013	Nobody	Mr. Clint Terry
Start gathering contact data	24/05/2013	Nobody	Bernadette Cooper

How it works...

Drupal Views has powerful relationship tools that allow you to extract data from different tables and bring them into the same view.

It also allows you to summarize the data on a field—in this case, the **Campaign Title** field. The effect is a view that shows activities grouped under each campaign.

There's more...

- Remove the grouping field and add a filter for the campaign ID. This would create a display for a single campaign. Clone the display and change the campaign ID to get displays for different campaigns.

- Add filters for the Activity scheduled date. For example, you could set a filter to display activities that have passed their scheduled date and are still scheduled; in effect, overdue activities.

- Add the Contact ID for each relationship and use the Rewrite field feature in Views to make links back to the related CiviCRM contacts.

- Add the Activity ID and use the Rewrite field feature in Views to make links back to each activity.

- Add a Drupal User relationship and combine it with other relationships to get lists of activities you have assigned, or that have been assigned to you.

▸ Create another view of mailings. Add in fields for click throughs, openings, and other useful data. Link it to campaigns using the Campaign relationship. This provides a mailing report for each campaign.

▸ Create a custom field set for events. Add a field called **Event report**. Create a view of events that includes the field for the event report. Link it to campaigns using the Campaign relationship. This provides an event report for the campaign.

▸ For each view, set the campaign ID as a **Contextual filter**. Gather each view into a Panel or a page using the Contexts module. This creates a dashboard that unites events, mailing, and activities into one page for each campaign.

Using surveys effectively

In any campaign you might want to get quick answers to simple questions. For example, in an election campaign you might want to ask:

▸ Who do you intend to vote for?

▸ What issues are important to you?

CiviSurvey is used in these sorts of situations where you have a very limited set of questions to ask, and where the contacts you intend to survey are already in your database.

In **CiviCampaign**, we can use surveys and petitions to collect data to support our campaign objectives. Surveys are used to collect data from contacts that are already in CiviCRM. In this recipe we shall create a survey to ask contacts about their voting intentions. We will distribute the survey to our volunteers so that they can conduct the survey from door-to-door (a **walklist** survey).

How to do it...

We need to set up some custom fields to hold our survey questions and then link them to a survey. In this example, we will create a single question and distribute it as a door-to-door survey managed by our volunteers.

1. Navigate to **Campaigns | New Campaign**. Name the campaign `Election Campaign`.

2. Navigate to **Administer | Custom Fields** and create a custom field set. Name it `Survey Questions`.

3. Set **Used For** to **Activities**.

4. Set **Activities Options** to **WalkList**.

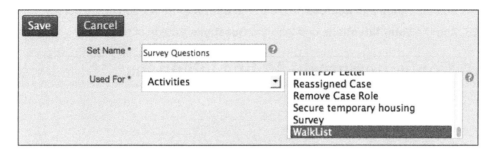

5. Add a custom alphanumeric radio button field. Name it `Which party will you vote for?`.

6. Add choices for **Labour**, **Tory**, **Green**, and **Democrat**.

7. Navigate to **Administer | Customize Data and Screens** and create a new profile. Name it `Voting Intentions`.

8. Add the **Survey Questions** custom field set to the profile.

9. Navigate to **Campaigns | New Survey** and create a new survey. Name the survey `Voter intentions door-to-door`.

10. Set the **Campaign** field to **Election campaign**.

11. Set **Activity Type** to **WalkList**.

12. Set **Maximum contacts reserved at one time** to `10`.

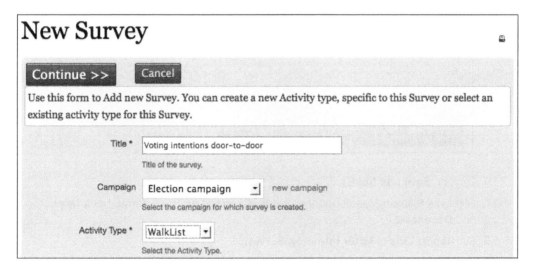

13. Click on **Save and Next**.

14. Add the **Name and Address** profile to the **Contact Info** section of the survey.

15. Add the **Voter Intentions** profile to the **Questions** section of the survey.

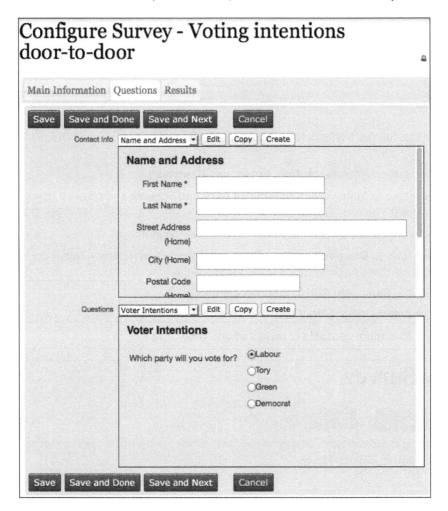

16. Click on **Save and Next**.

17. Enter the following result options: **Not in**, **Changed address**, **Come back later**, and **Deceased**.

18. Set **Report Title** to **Voter Intention Survey**.

19. Save the survey.

20. Navigate to **Contacts | New Group** and add a group. Name it Canvassers.

21. Add some contacts to the Canvassers group for testing purposes.

22. Navigate to **Contacts | New Group** and add a group. Name it `Voters`.

23. Add some contacts to the `Voters` group for testing purposes.

24. Navigate to **Campaigns | Reserve Respondents**.

25. Select the `Canvassers` group and click on **Search.**

26. Select up to 10 contacts from the list. Select **Reserve respondents** from the **Action** drop-down list and click on **Go**.

27. Navigate to **Campaigns | Campaign reports**.

28. Select the **Voter Intention Result** report.

29. Print out the report.

Voter Intention Result.

April 29th, 2013 10:06 PM

Survey   Is Voting intentions door-to-door

Respondent Status Is equal to Reserved

Respondent Name	Street Number	Street Name	Street Unit	Survey Result	Which party will you vote for?
Ivanov, Jackson				ni I mo I cbl I de	lab I tor I gre I dem
Ivanov, Andrew	829	Caulder		ni I mo I cbl I de	lab I tor I gre I dem
Ivanov, Herminia	931	Lincoln		ni I mo I cbl I de	lab I tor I gre I dem
Ivanov, Alida	54	Main		ni I mo I cbl I de	lab I tor I gre I dem
Ivanov, Allen	277	Second		ni I mo I cbl I de	lab I tor I gre I dem
González, Ivey	299	Second		ni I mo I cbl I de	lab I tor I gre I dem
Ivanov, Elizabeth	757	Van Ness		ni I mo I cbl I de	lab I tor I gre I dem
Ivanov, Delana	515	Woodbridge		ni I mo I cbl I de	lab I tor I gre I dem

Row(s) Listed 8

The report printout includes pages for canvassers to record the survey.

How it works...

We created a set of custom fields that are used for the walklist activity and added them to a profile for walklist activities. We then created a new survey and made it a walklist survey. We then added in a profile that contained the names and addresses of contacts and the profile we created for the walklist.

We then added some options for the survey result such as a change of address. We then chose a group of respondents and printed off the walklist. The names and addresses profile populates the walklist with address data and the walklist profile populates it with the question.

See also

Find out more about CiviSurvey at `http://book.civicrm.org/user/current/survey/setup/`.

Recording survey results

CiviCRM surveys are conducted offline, and so results must be entered *manually*. This recipe shows you how to manually enter results.

How to do it...

CiviSurvey has a well-developed interface for recording offline survey results. We will use this in our recipe as follows:

1. Navigate to **Campaigns | Dashboard** and click on the **Surveys** button.
2. Select a survey. In the preceding recipe, we created a survey called `Voter Intentions`.
3. In the **More** menu, select **Interview Respondents**. You are now presented with a list of possible respondents for the survey.

How it works...

At the top of the screen there is an interface to order the results. So, if a volunteer comes in with the results of a walklist survey, you can quickly navigate to the related respondents. You also have a screen where you can enter the survey results. Note that the head of the columns allows you to downfill the results.

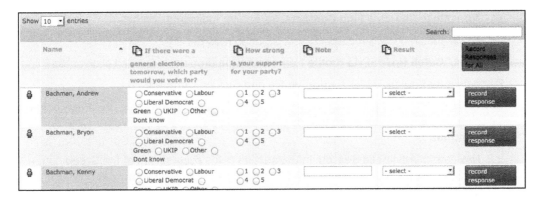

Using get out the vote effectively

Get out the vote (GOTV) is a handy tool to very quickly check off people you know have voted in an election. For example, imagine you are running a local election campaign for your party. You would want to maximize your vote, and the best way to do this is to know if your supporters have voted or not. This recipe shows you how to create reports that show how well you and your opponents are doing.

How to do it...

The CiviCRM database needs to hold party affiliation data for each individual that is going to vote for your party. The best way to hold this data is not within a survey, but in a set of custom fields organized into an individual profile. Most local political organizations have gathered this valuable data over the years, and it can be imported into CiviCRM to form the basis of your election campaign. In this recipe, we will create a set of custom fields and add them to a profile. We will then use the profile in a batch update for all the individual contacts in the sample data that is available when CiviCRM is first installed. We will then create a survey to contain our voter list and finally use a neat survey trick to record their vote.

1. Navigate to **Administer | Customize Data and Screens | Custom Fields**. Add a new custom field set. Name it `Voter allegiance`.

2. Set **User For** to **Contacts**.

3. Add a **checkbox custom field**. Name it `Party`. Add options for **Labor, Tory, Green**, and **Democrat**.

4. Navigate to **Administer | Customize Data and Screens | Profile** and add a new profile. Name it `Party allegiance`.

5. Add in the `Party` custom field and save the profile.

6. Navigate to **Search | Find Contacts**. Search for individual contacts.

7. There should be 161 records. Select 30 or so records.

8. Select **Batch Update via profile** from the **Action** drop-down list and click on **Go**.

9. Select the `Party allegiance` profile and click on **Continue**.

10. Enter a value for the first contact, for example, `Green`. At the top of the **Party** column, click on the downfill icon so that all the contacts have the `Green` value. Click on **Continue**.

11. Navigate to **Advanced Search**. In the custom fields section, select the **Green** option. Add the result set of contacts to a new smart group named **Green**. You now have a smart group that contains contacts who you know would vote Green.

12. Navigate to **Campaigns | New survey**.

13. Name the survey `Have you voted?`. You do not need to fill in any other details or add any other options.

14. Navigate to **Campaigns | Reserve Respondents**.

15. Select the `Have you voted?` survey and select the **Green** group. Click on **Search**.

16. Select all the contacts and click on **Reserve**.

17. Navigate to **Campaigns | GOTV**.

18. Select the **Have you voted?** survey and click on **Search**.

19. In the last column you can click on the checkbox for each contact you know has voted.

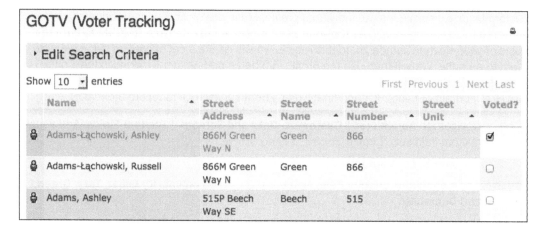

GOTV (Voter Tracking)

▸ Edit Search Criteria

Show 10 ▾ entries   First Previous 1 Next Last

Name	Street Address ▲	Street Name ▲	Street Number ▲	Street Unit ▲	Voted?
Adams-Łachowski, Ashley	866M Green Way N	Green	866		☑
Adams-Łachowski, Russell	866M Green Way N	Green	866		☐
Adams, Ashley	515P Beech Way SE	Beech	515		☐

How it works...

The `Have you voted?` survey is just a container that holds the respondents that we are interested in. GOTV provides displays for the respondents and 'interviews them' when the **Voted?** checkbox is selected. This removes them as a respondent and this is used to show they have voted.

Using petitions effectively

CiviCRM Petition allows you to gather data online. You can use the data simply as survey data, or you can use it to demonstrate support for your cause in the form of a petition. CiviCRM Petition allows you to store, enrich, and leverage the data you hold and that alone gives it a huge advantage over external petitioning applications. This recipe shows you how to set up a petition.

How to do it...

We will need to set up some custom fields to hold our petition question and put this into a profile. We will also need to create another profile to hold details of the person completing the petition. We then combine these two profiles to create the petition itself.

1. Navigate to **Campaigns | New Campaign** and set the title to `Stop the Supermarket.`

2. Navigate to **People | Permissions** and add the CiviCRM Petition permission for anonymous and authenticated users.

PERMISSION	ANONYMOUS USER	AUTHENTICATED USER	ADMINISTRATOR
CiviCampaign: sign CiviCRM Petition	☑	☑	☑

3. Navigate to **Administer Customize Data and Screens | Profiles** and create a new profile. Name it `Petition contact.`

4. Add first name, last name, and e-mail address fields.

5. In **Advanced Settings**, set **What to do upon duplicate match** to **Allow duplicate contact to be created**.

6. Navigate to **Administer Customize Data and Screens | Custom Fields** and add a new field set. Name it `Supermarket campaign petition.`

7. Set **Used For** to **Activities**.

8. Select **Petition Signature** in the **Activities** options.

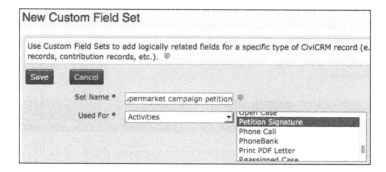

9. Add a custom checkbox field to the set. Name it Do you want a new supermarket in town? and set **checkbox options** for **Yes** and **No**.

10. Navigate to **Administer Customize Data and Screens | Profiles** and create a new profile. Name the profile Supermarket petition.

11. Add in the supermarket question.

12. In **Advanced Settings**, set **What to do upon duplicate match** to **Allow duplicate contact to be created**.

13. Navigate to **Campaigns | New Petition**.

14. Set the **Campaign** to **Stop the supermarket**.

15. Set the **Contact Profile** to **Petition contact**.

16. Set the **Activity Profile** to **Supermarket petition**.

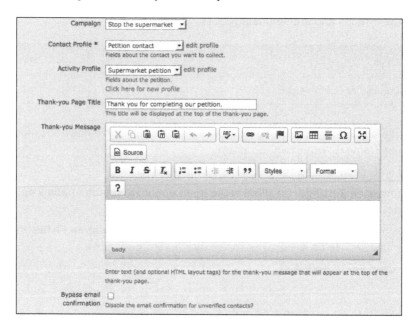

17. Navigate to **Campaign | Dashboard | Petition**.

18. Select the **Stop the supermarket** petition.

19. In the **More** menu, select **Sign**. This provides the URL for the petition.

20. In the **More** menu, select **Signatures**. This provides a report on petition signatures.

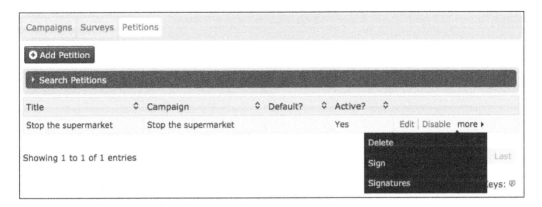

See also

Find out more about CiviCRM Petition at `http://book.civicrm.org/user/current/petition/what-is-civipetition/`.

10
Working with CiviMember

In this chapter, we will cover:

- ▶ Creating a membership directory using Drupal Views
- ▶ Updating memberships by bulk data entry
- ▶ Effective membership communications using reminders
- ▶ Using price sets for complex memberships
- ▶ Using CiviCase for membership induction

Introduction

This chapter explores CiviMember, a CiviCRM component used for membership management. We will look at a popular requirement, displaying a membership directory, and then explore linking common membership tasks with other CiviCRM components.

Creating a membership directory using Drupal Views

CiviCRM uses **profiles** to display contacts, and in most situations this is an excellent solution to displaying and sorting your membership contacts.

However, displaying membership contacts can be a problem in CiviCRM. For example, you may have a membership setup that allows both individuals and organizations to join. CiviCRM does not allow you to have a profile that combines both individual and organizational data. So, you cannot use the profile solution for your directory.

How to do it...

Using this recipe, we can use Drupal's **Views** module to create a membership directory that includes organizations and individuals.

1. Download, install, and enable Drupal's `Views` module, available at `http://drupal.org/project/views`.
2. In Drupal, navigate to **Admin | Structure | Views** and add a new view.
3. Set the view to show **CiviCRM Memberships**.
4. Name the view **Membership directory**.
5. Set the view to display a page and give the page a URL.
6. In the **FORMAT** section, set the **Display format** field to **Table**.

7. In the **FIELDS** section, add the following fields:

   CiviCRM Contacts: Display Name (Display Name)

   CiviCRM Address: City / Suburb (City / Suburb)

   CiviCRM Address: State / Province (State / Province)

   CiviCRM Email: Email address (Email Address)

   CiviCRM Phone details: Phone Number (Phone Number)

8.   In the **Filters** section, add a global filter.

9.   In **Global filter configuration**, set the filter to **Exposed**.

10. Set **Operator** to **Combined**.

11. Set **Choose fields to combine for filtering** to all the fields added earlier.

12. Save the filter.

13. In the **Advanced** section, set **Query options** to **Distinct**.

14. **Preview** the view.

Membership directory

Combine fields filter

[   ] (Apply)

Display Name	City / Suburb	State / Province	Email Address	Phone Number
Mr Sandy J Reynolds Sr	North Waterford	Maine		
Mrs Amar M Smith Jr	Arlington	Tennessee		94927088
Mr Peter J Smith Jr	West Hyannisport	Massachusetts		65041724
Ms Sheila P Roberts Jr	Trenton	Michigan	robertssheila@redimall.net.in	
Mrs Milan A Smith Sr	Saint Stephens Church	Virginia		14531182
Mr John K Yadav Jr	Allgood	Alabama	yadavjohn@npo.edu.in	

How it works...

The **CiviCRM Contact Display Name** field is available for individuals and organizations. So, all membership names will be displayed.

The global filter combines all the fields together so that you can search across them.

Setting **Query options** to **Distinct** reduces the duplication of entries.

See also

▶   Find out more about reducing duplicates at `http://dropbucket.org/node/153`

Updating memberships by bulk data entry

You may run a membership organization that takes membership payments offline.

For example, in the UK, many organizations process membership payments using the **Direct Debit** payment system. Entering these payments is time-consuming, and hitherto has required custom import scripts for large sets of payments.

How to do it...

In this recipe, we will use a new batch entry system that enables you to automate membership payments.

1. First, you will need to prepare your data for entry. You will need the contact name and the amount paid. You also need to know how many entries you are going to make and the total payment amount.

2. Navigate to **Memberships | Bulk Data Entry** and create a new bulk data entry batch.

3. Name the batch.

4. Set the **Number of items** field to the number of entries you are going to make.

5. Set the **Total Amount** field to the total amount of money being paid.

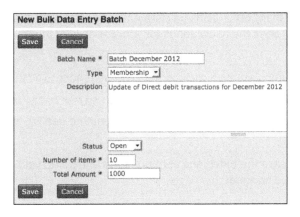

6. Save the batch.

How it works...

As you enter the data into each row, CiviCRM checks the membership details for each contact and makes the second column **Add Membership** or **Renew Membership**, depending on what membership data is held.

It also auto-enters the **Amount** column with the membership fee (not shown).

It also alters the figure entered in **Total Amount** at the top of the form entry.

The interface provides many other fields for data entry. For renewals, these do not need to be completed, as CiviCRM does the calculations for you. For new members, you will have to enter the data manually.

At the top of some columns, you can click on the column header to fill the values for each column.

Please note that caution is needed here, particularly if you are dealing with mixed membership types.

CiviCRM allows you to save the batch and continue data entry or to validate and process the batch once you have finished.

Effective membership communications using reminders

In CiviCRM 4.3, the reminder system for membership renewals has been moved from membership management to **Scheduled Reminders**. This gives us the opportunity to use these reminders in our member workflow. For example, you may have a process for membership induction. This may involve sending out information at fixed intervals.

Examples of this include a guide to the organization's website, a personalized message from the head of the organization, or a request to share some information to provide a better service for the member.

How to do it...

We will create two mail templates. We will use one to send out a guide to the website, and the other to send out a guide to local involvement. We will then schedule these mailings using **Scheduled Reminders**.

1. Navigate to **Administer | CiviMail | Message Templates**. Add a new template.
2. Set **Title** to **Guide to the website**.
3. Set the **Subject** to **Guide to the Cookbook website**. Substitute **Cookbook** with the name of your organization.
4. In the **plain text** field, enter the full details of your website guide. Insert tokens to personalize the message.
5. Copy the plain text entry into the **HTML** field and apply HTML formatting to the message.
6. Save the template.
7. Create a new template for the guide to local involvement and repeat the process.
8. Navigate to **Administer | Communications | Scheduled Reminders** and create a new reminder.
9. Set the **Title** field to **Guide to the website**.
10. Set the **Entity** field to **Membership**.
11. Set the **membership type** field to **General**.
12. Schedule the reminder for **1 day(s) after Membership Join Date**.
13. In the **Email** section, check the **Send email** checkbox.

14. Set **Use Template** to **Guide to the website**.

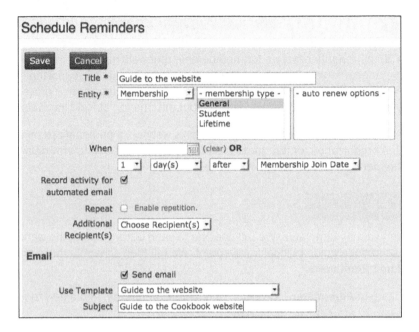

15. Set up another **Scheduled Reminder** instance for the second mailing.

16. Navigate to **Administer | System Settings | Scheduled Jobs** and enable the **Send Scheduled Reminders** job.

See also

▸ The *Using Scheduled Reminders for activities* recipe in *Chapter 1, Setting Up CiviCRM*

▸ The *Creating mail templates for CiviMail* and *Using tokens in templates* recipes in *Chapter 5, Managing Communications*

▸ Find out more about Scheduled Reminders at `http://book.civicrm.org/user/current/email/scheduled-reminders/`

Using price sets for complex memberships

Membership **price sets** are used in situations where you have a national membership plus regional sub-memberships. For example, you may run a national cycling association with chapters in each state.

How to do it...

We can create a CiviCRM price set and link it to a contributions page for online membership. The price set allows us to apply complex membership options.

1. Navigate to **Contacts | New organization**. Create a contact called **National Cycling Association**. Click on **Save and New**.

2. Add the following organizations. These will be NCA Chapters:

   NCA Delaware

   NCA California

   NCA Oregon

   NCA Florida

3. Navigate to **Administer | CiviMember | Membership Types** and add a membership.

4. Set **Name** to **NCA Full**.

5. Set **Membership Organization** to **National Cycling Association**.

6. Set **Minimum Fee** to **$100**.

7. Set **Financial Type** to **Member Dues**.

8. Set **Duration** to **1 year rolling**.

9. Click on **Save and New**.

10. Create four more membership types, one for each NCA Chapter. Set the fee for each chapter to **$20**.

11. Navigate to **Administer | CiviMember | New Price Set**.

12. Set **Name** to **NCA Membership**.

13. Set **Used For** to **Membership**.

14. Set **Default Financial Type** to **Member Dues**.

15. Save the price set and add a field.

16. Set **field label** to **NCA National Membership**.

17. Set **Input Field Type** to **Select**.

18. In **Membership Options**, set **Membership Type** to **NCA Full**.

19. Select **Required**.

20. Click on **Save and New**.

21. Set **field label** to **NCA Chapter Membership**.

22. Set **Input Field Type** to **Checkbox**.

23. In **Membership Options**, set **Membership Type** to **NCA Florida**.

24. Add in the other three chapters.

25. Save the price field.

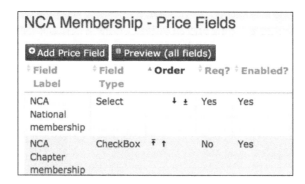

26. Navigate to **Contributions | New Contribution Page**.

27. Set **Title** to **NCA Membership**.

28. Set **Financial Type** to **Member Dues**. Click on **Save and Next**.

29. Set **Processor** to **Test Payment Processor**.

30. Uncheck **Contribution Amounts section enabled**.

31. Click on **Save and Next**.

32. Check **Membership Section enabled**.

33. Set **Title – New Membership** to **NCA Membership**.

34. Set **Title – Renewals** to **NCA Membership renewal**.

35. Set **Membership Price Set** to **NCA Membership**.

36. Click on **Save and Done**.

37. Locate the **NCA Membership** entry on the **Contribution** listing. On the **More** link, select **Test-Drive**.

How it works...

The **National Membership price** field is set to **required**. This means members have to join the national organization. NCA Chapters are not required. So, users can join none, one, or more of the chapters. CiviCRM recalculates the cost according to the users' choices.

Using CiviCase for membership induction

In this recipe, we will use CiviCase to provide a membership communication scheme for complex organizations. For example, you may have a large organization where different staff members, volunteers, and representatives have responsibility for the different stages in a membership induction program. There might be a membership officer, membership office staff, regional office staff, and specialist office staff. CiviCase allows us to allocate activities to everyone involved in this process.

How to do it...

We will create a CiviCase to handle the activities associated with a membership induction program. In our imaginary scenario, a new member induction scheme might be implemented as follows:

Relative time	Activity	Detail	Assignee
7 days	Get certificate	Get a membership certificate printed and signed by the President	Membership Officer
7 days	Identify the main contact	Contact the applicant and update our records to get the main contact details for the organization that joined	Membership Officer
7 days	Identify the local group	From the application identify the local group for the organization. Schedule a contact from the local group leader.	Local group leader
10 days	Send out the organization pack	Send out the organization pack personalized with details collected in first week	Membership Officer
14 days	Send out the certificate	Send the certificate out with a note from the President	Membership Officer
20 days	Send out the survey	Send out the online survey that collects more data about the organization	Membership Officer
27 days	Collate information and contact individuals	Collate the survey information and contact other individuals within the member organization.	Membership Officer

1. Navigate to **Administer | System Settings | CiviCRM Components** and enable CiviCase.
2. Navigate to **Administer | Customize Data and Screens | Activity Types**. Create activity types to cater to all the activities involved in your membership program.
3. Set **User For** to **CiviCase** for each activity.
4. Navigate to **Customize Data and Screens | Relationships**. Create relationships for the contacts that will be involved in the membership induction process, for example, **Membership Officer**.
5. Create the XML file that will create the activities, the activity schedules, and the necessary relationships when a new case is added to a contact.
6. Navigate to **Administer | CiviCase | Case Types** and create a new CiviCase type that uses the XML file. Name it **Member Induction**.
7. When a new member joins, add **Member Induction Case** in the contact summary screen.

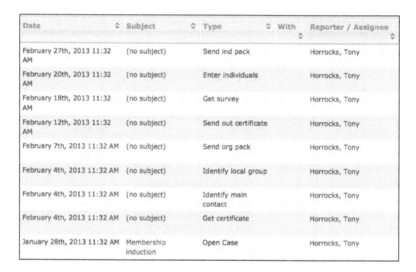

Date	Subject	Type	With	Reporter / Assignee
February 27th, 2013 11:32 AM	(no subject)	Send ind pack		Horrocks, Tony
February 20th, 2013 11:32 AM	(no subject)	Enter individuals		Horrocks, Tony
February 18th, 2013 11:32 AM	(no subject)	Get survey		Horrocks, Tony
February 12th, 2013 11:32 AM	(no subject)	Send out certificate		Horrocks, Tony
February 7th, 2013 11:32 AM	(no subject)	Send org pack		Horrocks, Tony
February 4th, 2013 11:32 AM	(no subject)	Identify local group		Horrocks, Tony
February 4th, 2013 11:32 AM	(no subject)	Identify main contact		Horrocks, Tony
February 4th, 2013 11:32 AM	(no subject)	Get certificate		Horrocks, Tony
January 28th, 2013 11:32 AM	Membership induction	Open Case		Horrocks, Tony

How it works...

CiviCase generates and schedules all the activities. All that remains is to allocate each activity to the appropriate person responsible.

See also

▸ The *Using Scheduled Reminders for activities* recipe in *Chapter 1, Setting Up CiviCRM*

▸ The *Adding custom fields* and *Creating new activities* recipes in *Chapter 1, Setting Up CiviCRM*

11

Developing for CiviCRM

In this chapter, we will cover:

- ▶ Setting up a local development environment
- ▶ Finding developer resources
- ▶ Exploring Drupal hooks
- ▶ Exploring the CiviCRM API
- ▶ Developing a CiviCRM Drupal module
- ▶ Exploring CiviCRM extension development using Civix

Introduction

This chapter looks at the software, skills, and resources you need to start developing CiviCRM in earnest. We will also cover developing a simple Drupal module and exploring the CiviCRM API.

Setting up a local development environment

A local development environment means installation of CiviCRM on your own computer so that you can do development without having to connect to a remote server on the Internet. We have seen in other recipes that having a local installation of CiviCRM makes things such as importing contacts faster and easier.

In this recipe—more of a set of guidelines—we explore how to set up such an environment.

How to do it...

We need five ingredients for our local installation to work:

- ▸ A web server: Apache will serve our CiviCRM pages
- ▸ A database: MySQL will store our CiviCRM data
- ▸ A PHP interpreter: This works with Apache and MySQL to interpret the PHP code we write and sends us back pages of HTML
- ▸ A good text editor
- ▸ A good MySQL manager

Our own computers will have an operating system such as Linux, Windows, or Mac OS, and you may have come across acronyms such as a **LAMP** environment (Linux, Apache, MySQL, PHP). So, we also have **WAMP** for Windows, and **MAMP** for Mac OS.

By far the easiest way to create these environments is to download an application called XAMPP (http://www.apachefriends.org/en/xampp.html). This can be used for Windows, Linux, and Mac OS operating systems.

This runs your local environment as an application. This means when you start XAMPP, Apache, MySQL, and PHP all start up for you. It is easy to download and install, and it is free.

For Mac OS, there is an alternative application MAMP, available at http://www.mamp.info.

Each of these applications have their own configurations, and it is not possible here to provide installation details. Once they are set up, they will do the job of serving our CiviCRM installation.

We now need to have some programs to help us develop.

There are all sorts of text editors available for Windows or Mac OS. The better ones will have syntax highlighted to show you where you are making mistakes in your code. Some will also have code-completion shortcuts, which are also useful.

Text editors for Windows include:

- ▸ UltraEdit (http://www.ultraedit.com/)
- ▸ Komodo Edit (http://www.activestate.com/komodo-edit)
- ▸ Aptana (http://www.aptana.com/)
- ▸ PSPad (http://www.pspad.com/en/)
- ▸ Notepad++ (http://notepad-plus-plus.org/)

Text editors for Mac OS include:

▶ Komodo Edit (`http://www.activestate.com/komodo-edit`)

▶ Aptana (`http://www.aptana.com/`)

▶ BBEdit (`http://www.barebones.com`)

▶ Textmate (`http://macromates.com/`)

▶ Coda (`https://panic.com/coda/`)

MySQL managers, XAMPP and MAMP, come with PHPmyAdmin, which is good enough for most purposes.

Once you have these tools installed, you are good to go for doing some development.

An **Integrated Development Environment** (**IDE**) provides a total environment for your development needs. These can be quite complex to use as they normally cater to several development environments, such as Java, C++, and so on. Popular IDE software includes:

▶ Zend Studio (`http://www.zend.com/en/products/studio/`)

▶ Netbeans (`http://netbeans.org/`)

▶ Aptana (`http://www.aptana.com/`)

▶ Komodo (`http://www.activestate.com/komodo-ide`)

Finding developer resources

CiviCRM has excellent documentation for the basic needs of most people who want to create a good CiviCRM installation.

As tasks and requirements get more and more specific, guidance becomes a little bit trickier to find. Luckily, CiviCRM has a thriving online community that can help through forums as well as an IRC channel where you can communicate with the core team. Support does not come much better than that.

How to do it...

In this recipe, we'll look at what resources are available to beginner and experienced developers.

The following table shows the CiviCRM developer continuum. Progressively more skills, time, and commitment is required as the tasks become more and more complex.

Task	Skills needed	Resources
Configuring the CiviCRM core and its components	An understanding of CiviCRM	CiviCRM books, forums, blogs, and meetups

Task	Skills needed	Resources
Basic customization of report templates and search templates	Knowledge of template structures	CiviCRM books, forums, blogs, Wiki, and meetups
Advanced customization of reports	Knowledge of Smarty templates, SQL, and PHP	CiviCRM developer resources and Wiki
CMS-specific modules	Knowledge of CMS API, OOP, and PHP	CiviCRM developer resources, CiviCRM API Explorer, CiviCRM module examples, Wiki, and IRC
Agnostic modules (extensions)	High level knowledge of CiviCRM architecture, OOP, and PHP	CiviCRM developer resources, Wiki, CiviCRM API Explorer, IRC, and code sprints

You can find basic guidance using the following resources:

- Find the latest CiviCRM announcements at `http://civicrm.org/blog-news`
- Read the authoritative guide for administrators and users of CiviCRM at `http://book.civicrm.org/user/ http://forum.civicrm.org/`
- Read the authoritative developer guide at `http://book.civicrm.org/developer/`

You can also find some advanced guidance. Here are some online resources that provide advanced guidance:

- The guide to using hooks in CMS-specific modules at `http://wiki.civicrm.org/confluence/display/CRMDOC42/Hook+Reference`
- The guide for making and customizing templates at `http://book.civicrm.org/developer/current/techniques/templates/`
- The guide to the CiviCRM API at `http://book.civicrm.org/developer/current/techniques/api/`
- The guide to advanced importing techniques at `http://book.civicrm.org/developer/current/techniques/imports/`
- Guidance for creating extensions at `http://wiki.civicrm.org/confluence/display/CRMDOC42/Create+a+Module+Extension`

Exploring Drupal hooks

You can customize the behavior of CiviCRM by developing a module that takes advantage of the **hook system**.

CiviCRM is written in a scripting language called PHP, and you use PHP to create all the functions that make CiviCRM work. Some of these functions are exposed to your CMS—in this case, Drupal. For example, there is a function called `civicrm_postProcess` that runs every time a form is submitted.

You can copy this function and customize it. Each time `civicrm_postProcess` runs, CiviCRM checks whether there is a customized version of the function, and if there is, it runs that instead. Not all CiviCRM functions are exposed in this way. If they are, they are called **hooks**.

This recipe shows you how to explore these hooks in Drupal using the `civicrm_developer` module.

How to do it...

Hooks allow the CMS to extend the functionality of CiviCRM without having to alter any core CiviCRM files. Here, we will add a module that allows us to see which hooks are available to us:

1. Install and enable the Drupal Devel module, available at `http://drupal.org/project/devel`.
2. Navigate to `https://github.com/eileenmcnaughton/civicrm_developer`.
3. Download the ZIP file for the module and expand it. It expands as a directory called `civicrm_developer-master`.
4. Rename the directory `civicrm_developer`.
5. Install and enable the module.
6. Now visit CiviCRM pages within your site.

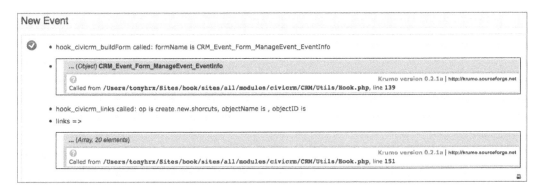

How it works...

The module shows all the Drupal hooks that can be called and allows the developer to examine objects and their values.

Exploring the CiviCRM API

Writing code is laborious. It takes a lot of skill, a lot of trial and error, and most importantly, a lot of time and cost. Rather than write the code from scratch, you can use prewritten functions that do the work. These functions, when gathered together, are called an **Application Programming Interface** (**API**).

How to do it...

CiviCRM has an API. This recipe shows you how to explore it:

1. Navigate to `http://<mycivicrm.com>/civicrm/ajax/doc/api#explorer`. Substitute `<mycivicrm.com>` with your own domain.

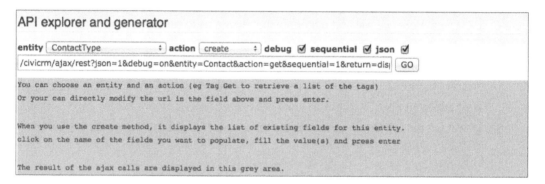

2. Select the **Activity** entity and perform a **create action** on it.
3. Click on the **Source Contact** field, the **Source Record** field, and the **Subject** field. The fields are added dynamically to the API Explorer.

4. Set **Source Contact** to **1**, **Source Record** to **1**, and **Subject** to **Test**. The values you put in each field are called **parameters**. Click on **Go**.

API explorer and generator   🔒

entity `Activity        ▾` | action `create   ▾` | ☑debug | ☑sequential | ☑json

*Available fields (click to add/remove):*Source Contact Source Record **Activity Type ID** Subject Activity
Date Duration Location Phone (called) ID Phone (called) Number Details Activity Status Id Priority Parent Activity Id Test Activity
Medium Auto Relationship Id Is this activity a current revision in versioning chain? Original Activity ID   Result Activity is in the
Trash Campaign ID Engagement Index Weight undefined undefined undefined **Activity ID**

Source Contact: `1`   X
Source Record: `1`   X
Subject: `Test`   X

`/civicrm/ajax/rest?entity=Activity&action=create&debug=1&sequential=1&json=1&source_c` [GO]

Generated codes for this api call

How it works...

CiviCRM provides us with ready-made code examples with the fields and parameters added.

URL	ajax query |REST query.
smarty	smarty uses only 'get' actions

php	```$params = array(```
	 ``` 'version' => 3,```
	 ``` 'sequential' => 1,```
	 ``` 'source_contact_id' => 1,```
	 ``` 'source_record_id' => 1,```
	 ``` 'activity_subject' => 'Test',```
	 ```);```
	 ```$result = civicrm_api('Activity', 'create', $params);```

javascript	```CRM.api('Activity', 'create', {'sequential': 1, 'source_contact_id': 1, 'source_record_id': 1, 'activity_subject':```
	 ```'Test'},```
	 ``` {success: function(data) {```
	 ``` cj.each(data, function(key, value) {// do something });```
	 ``` }```
	 ``` }```
	 ```);```

CiviCRM also provides error checking on-the-fly when you make mistakes in your API exploration.

```
{
    "fields":["one of (activity_name, activity_type_id, activity_label)"],
    "error_code":"mandatory_missing",
    "entity":"Activity",
    "action":"create",
    "is_error":1,
    "error_message":"Mandatory key(s) missing from params array: one of (activity_name, activity_type_id, activity_label
    "trace":"#0 \/home\/entity\/public_html\/sites\/all\/modules\/civicrm\/api\/v3\/utils.php(66): civicrm_api3_verify_m
}
```

 The API really does execute on your data, so any API exploration is best done locally on sample data.

There's more...

Navigate to `http://<mycivicrm.com>/civicrm/api/doc`. Substitute `<mycivicrm.com>` with your own domain.

Click on **Activity**. You will get an expanded list of the available fields and the sort of data that CiviCRM expects for the `Activity` entity.

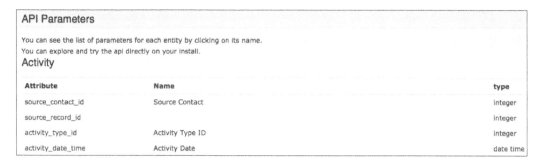

For example, **Source Contact ID** is expected to be an **integer**.

You can see that there are many CiviCRM entities that are exposed to the API, and it is not obvious what the API does for each one. For example, if you use the API call for an activity and fill in the correct parameters, what exactly does it do?

In your web server file system, navigate to `/sites/all/modules/civicrm/api/v3/`.

When a CiviCRM API runs, these are the PHP files that are called. So, for the `Activity` entity, there is a corresponding PHP file called `activity.php` that runs when the `Activity` API is called.

Open this file and look through the commented text at the start of the file; this explains what the file does. In this case, * creates or updates an activity See the example for usage. This is a good way to see what each API does.

See also

▶ Find out more about the CiviCRM API at `http://book.civicrm.org/developer/current/techniques/api/`

Developing a CiviCRM Drupal module

In this recipe, we will explore how a CiviCRM `Drupal` module works. The basic code for this module is already available online.

How to do it...

In this example, we have a contact that is in a specific group. We are going to fire off an e-mail if someone edits that contact.

1. Set up your own local development environment.

2. Download, install, and enable the Drupal Devel module, available at `http://drupal.org/project/devel`.

3. Navigate to `https://github.com/eileenmcnaughton/civicrm_developer`.

4. Download the ZIP file for the module and expand it. It expands as a directory called `civicrm_developer-master`.

5. Rename it `civicrm_developer`.

6. Install and enable the module.

7. In CiviCRM, add a contact to a group. Make a note of the contact ID; in this case, it was **51**.

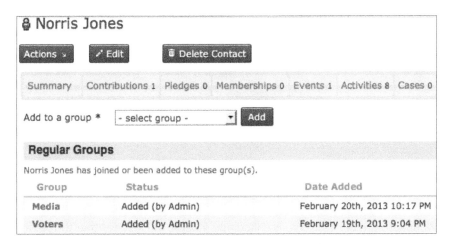

Here, a contact was added to the **Media** group.

8. Navigate to **Contacts | Manage groups**. Note the ID of the **Media** group. In this case, the ID was **7**. In your own implementation, the ID is likely to be different.

9. Click on the **Edit** button on the contact summary screen, then click on the **Save** button.

10. Click on the yellow-colored **CiviCRM Development** display at the top of the page.

    You will see that the CiviCRM Developer lists the hooks that have been called (some of them are called several times):

    ❏ hook_civicrm_buildForm

    ❏ hook_civicrm_links

    ❏ hook_civicrm_pre

    ❏ hook_civicrm_post

11. Look closely at hook_civirm_pre. In one instance, it is called when the operation is Edit and when the object name is Individual. This means it is a good candidate for the module, as you want the module to do something when a contact is edited.

12. Click on the yellow bar where hook_civicrm_pre is shown and expand it.

13. Locate the **group** array and click on it to expand it.

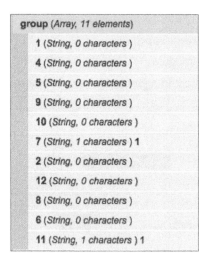

Note there is a **1** against group ID **7** and group ID **11**. This means the contact is a member of both these groups. The group set up earlier had an ID of **7** (your own ID may be different). So, you can now tell that the contact is in the **Media** group.

When hook_civicrm_pre is called, the module will test whether the contact is in group ID **7**. If it is, then it sends the e-mail. If it isn't, then it just carries on as usual.

14. Navigate to http://<mycivicrm.com>/civicrm/api/doc. Substitute <mycivicrm.com> with your own domain.

15. Click on **entity** and scroll down for group entities.

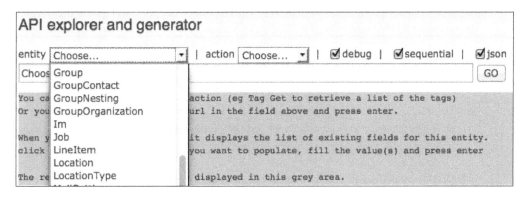

There are four entities for groups. You need to discover which one to use. The entity **GroupContact** looks like a good candidate.

16. On your web server, navigate to `/sites/all/modules/civicrm/api/v3/GroupContact.php` and open it.

```
/**
 * This API will give list of the groups for particular contact
 * Particualr status can be sent in params array
 * If no status mentioned in params, by default 'added' will be used
 * to fetch the records
 *
 * @param  array $params  name value pair of contact information
 * {@getfields GroupContact_get}
 *
 * @return  array  list of groups, given contact subsribed to
 */
function civicrm_api3_group_contact_get($params) {

  if (empty($params['contact_id'])) {
    if (empty($params['status'])) {
      //default to 'Added'
      $params['status'] = 'Added';
    }
    //ie. id passed in so we have to return something
    return _civicrm_api3_basic_get('CRM_Contact_BAO_GroupContact', $params);
  }
  $status = CRM_Utils_Array::value('status', $params, 'Added');

  $values = &CRM_Contact_BAO_GroupContact::getContactGroup($params['contact_id'], $status, NULL, FALSE, TRUE);
  return civicrm_api3_create_success($values, $params);
}
```

The code comments tell you that this API will give a list of groups for a particular contact. The code also shows what parameters the GroupContact API expects—`contact_id`.

17. Navigate to the API Explorer and select the **GroupContact** entity and the **get** action.

18. Add the contact ID parameter, `contact_id`, to the query field and give it the value of the contact ID that was edited earlier. In this case, it was **51**. Yours will be different. So, the added parameter code is **&contact_id=51**. Click on **Go**.

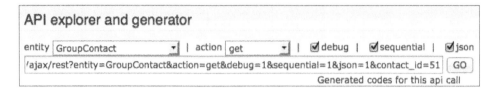

CiviCRM makes the API call and returns a result.

```
{
    "is_error":0,
    "undefined_fields":["contact_id"],
    "version":3,
    "count":2,
    "values":[{
            "id":"250",
            "group_id":"7",
            "title":"Media",
            "visibility":"User and User Admin Only",
            "is_hidden":"0",
            "in_date":"2013-02-20 22:17:13",
            "in_method":"Admin"
    },
    {

            "id":"145",
            "group_id":"11",
            "title":"Voters",
            "visibility":"User and User Admin Only",
            "is_hidden":"0",
            "in_date":"2013-02-19 21:04:40",
            "in_method":"Admin"
    }],
```

You can see that the contact **51** belongs to two groups, **7** and **11**. This is exactly what was expected. Your own results may be different as your contact ID and group ID will not be the same as in this recipe.

19. On your web server, navigate to `sites/all/modules`.

20. Create a new folder called `civicrm_custom`.

21. Using a text editor, create a file called `civicrm_custom.info` and enter the following code:

```
name = CiviCRM custom module
description = Provides custom functions
for CiviCRMcore = 7.x
package = civicrm
dependencies[] = civicrm
files[] = civicrm_custom.module
```

22. Create a file called `civicrm_custom.module` and add the following code:

```php
<?php
/**
 * Implements hook_civicrm_pre().
 */
function civicrm_custom_civicrm_pre( $op,
  $objectName, $objectId ) {
  $theGroupId = 7;
  $emailRecipient = 'johndoe@example.org';
  if ($objectName == "Individual" && $op == "edit") {
    require_once 'api/v3/utils.php';
    require_once 'api/v3/GroupContact.php';
    $params = array('contact_id' => $objectId);
    $groups = civicrm_api3_group_contact_get($params);
    $found = false;
    foreach ($groups['values'] as $group) {
      if ($group['group_id'] == $theGroupId) {
        $found = true;
      }
    }
    if (!$found) {
      return;
    }
    $emailSubject = "Contact was edited";
    $emailBody = "Someone edited contactId $objectId\n";
    mail( $emailRecipient, $emailSubject, $emailBody );
  }
}
```

23. In Drupal, navigate to **Modules** and enable the **custom civicrm** module.

24. Navigate to CiviCRM and edit a contact that is not in the Media group.

25. Check the Media group to see if the contact was edited.

How it works...

The following line stores your target `GroupID`. Your own `GroupID` may be different:

```
$theGroupId = 51;
```

This stores the e-mail address for the person we wish to e-mail:

```
$emailRecipient = 'johndoe@example.org';
```

This if statement is used to check that we are actually acting on `Individual` and that we are in `Edit` mode:

```
if ($objectName == "Individual" && $op == "edit")
```

The API is dependent on `utils.php` in order to work:

```
require_once 'api/v3/utils.php';
```

This calls the `GroupContact.php` file:

```
require_once 'api/v3/GroupContact.php';
```

This passes the contact ID into `civicrm_api3_group_contact_get`:

```
$params = array('contact_id' => $objectId);
```

The function `civicrm_api3_group_contact_get($params)` is the API call to get the contact groups:

```
$groups = civicrm_api3_group_contact_get($params);
```

The result is placed in the variable $groups. A contact can belong to many groups, so the values in $groups will be stored in an array.

```
$found = false;
    foreach ($groups['values'] as $group) {
      if ($group['group_id'] == $theGroupId) {
        $found = true;
      }
    }
    if (!$found) {
      return;
    }
```

This code cycles through the array that is stored in $groups. It checks the first group in the array and stores that in $group. It then gets group_id from $group and checks if that is equal to groupID stored in $theGroupId. This is repeated for every item in the array. If there is a match, the value of $found is set to TRUE.

If there is no match, then nothing is returned.

```
$emailSubject = "Contact was edited";
$emailBody = "Someone edited contactId $objectId\n";
mail( $emailRecipient, $emailSubject, $emailBody );
```

If there is a match, then the e-mail is sent using the function mail.

See also

- ▶ The *Exploring Drupal hooks* recipe
- ▶ The *Setting up a local development environment* recipe
- ▶ Find out more about Drupal module development at http://drupal.org/node/361112
- ▶ Find out more about CiviCRM hooks at http://wiki.civicrm.org/confluence/display/CRMDOC40/CiviCRM+hook+specification#CiviCRMhookspecification-hook_civicrm_pre

Exploring CiviCRM extension development using Civix

CiviCRM extensions are agnostic. This means that they will work regardless of what CMS you are using: Drupal, Joomla!, or WordPress. If you have ever explored the contents of your CiviCRM module directory, you'll see there are a bewildering number of directories and files. Many of these files work together. So, if you want to start developing your own CiviCRM extensions, you will need to know how the files work together.

How to do it...

Civix is a command-line tool that helps you develop CiviCRM extensions. In this recipe, we will use a MAMP local development environment available on Mac OS X and install Civix. Then, we will create our own CiviCRM extension and add a page. The recipe can be adapted to other environments.

1. Start up your local environment and set up a CiviCRM development site using your CMS of choice. In this recipe, we will use MAMP.

2. Check where PHP is running so that you can run PHP from the command line in your local development environment. Open a command-line tool, such as `Terminal`, and start typing.

which php

This will show the path to PHP. This is the PHP that runs when you type `php` on the command line.

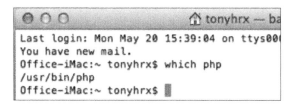

```
Last login: Mon May 20 15:39:04 on ttys00(
You have new mail.
Office-iMac:~ tonyhrx$ which php
/usr/bin/php
Office-iMac:~ tonyhrx$
```

In this example, PHP is running from the version that is installed with Mac OS X. We need to change this.

3. In your computer file system, navigate to your local development environment files to where MAMP runs PHP. In this case, it is `/Applications/MAMP/bin/php/php5.3.14`.

In your own installation, the path may be different.

4. In your computer file system, locate the file `/Users/<yoursusername>/.bash_profile` and open it in a text editor. Add the following line:

export PATH=/Applications/MAMP/bin/php/php5.3.14/bin:$PATH

Note that this recipe is for Mac OS, so details for Windows machines will be different.

5. In `Terminal`, type in the following command:

source .bash_profile

This reloads the profile you just edited.

6. In `Terminal`, type in the following command:

which php

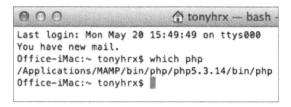

```
Last login: Mon May 20 15:49:49 on ttys000
You have new mail.
Office-iMac:~ tonyhrx$ which php
/Applications/MAMP/bin/php/php5.3.14/bin/php
Office-iMac:~ tonyhrx$
```

This shows that the correct PHP is running.

7. In your browser, navigate to `https://github.com/totten/civix/` and download the `civix .zip` archive.

8. Unzip the archive. It will unzip to a directory called `civix-master`. Rename the directory `civix` and store it in your `Applications` directory.

9. In your browser, navigate to `http://getcomposer.org/download/`. Composer is a tool that adds all the up-to-date resources that Civix needs in order to work properly.

10. In `Terminal`, enter the following commmand:

```
curl -sS https://getcomposer.org/installer | php
```

This downloads Composer.

11. In `Terminal`, change the directory to where you place Civix with this command:

```
cd /Applications/civix
```

12. Now enter this command to make Composer install all the extra resources that Civix needs:

```
php $HOME/composer.phar install
```

In the `Terminal` window, you will see Composer downloading all the files. Civix is now installed.

13. Open the `.bash_profile` again and enter the following line:

```
export PATH=/Applications/civix:$PATH
```

This ensures that Civix runs whenever you type `civix` into the command line.

14. In CiviCRM, navigate to **Administer | System Settings | Directories**. Check that you have configured the **CiviCRM Extensions Directory** setting properly.

15. In your local development environment, copy the path to the default directory that contains your `civicrm_settings.php` file.

16. In `Terminal`, type the following command, changing the path to the location of your own `civicrm_settings.php` file:

```
civix config:set civicrm_api3_conf_path /var/www/drupal/sites/
default/
```

This "connects" Civix to your development site.

17. In `Terminal`, change directories to **CiviCRM Extensions Directory**.

18. You are now ready to start your new CiviCRM extension. In `Terminal`, type in the following command:

```
civix generate:module dev.book.newextension
```

The name of the module follows CiviCRM's extension-naming conventions.

Civix generates the skeleton files for the extension.

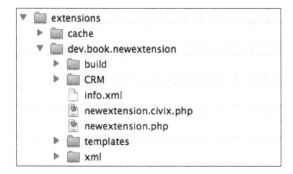

19. In `Terminal`, change directories to your new extension directory. Type in the following command:

    ```
    civix generate:page MyPage civicrm/my-page
    ```

    This generates all the files required to develop the page.

How it works...

Civix does all the basic work for you. It creates the structure and the files necessary to begin building your extension. Furthermore, each file contains template code that you can adapt to your own purpose.

This saves a huge amount of development time. Furthermore, it provides a means of exploring how CiviCRM is structured. You can generate pages, forms, searches, reports, API calls, and unit tests, and at each stage see what files Civix adds and how they work together.

See also

▶ The *Setting up a development environment* recipe
▶ Find out more about CiviCRM extension development at `http://wiki.civicrm.org/confluence/display/CRMDOC43/Create+a+Module+Extension`

Index

U

UltraEdit
 URL 196
unique ID
 creating, Google Refine used 56-58
URLs
 used, for creating newsletter subscriptions
   107
 used, for modifying profile displays 68, 69
user accounts
 creating, from contacts 135-137
 creating, with CiviCRM entities 146, 147
User Import module 135, 137
user profiles
 reCAPTCHA, setting up for 75
users
 information, updating without logging in 111,
   112

V

Views
 URL 137
Views module
 URL 148

W

walklist survey 172
WAMP 196
Webform CiviCRM
 data, collecting for paid event registration
   162-164
 URL 141
 used, for updating relationships 141-145
Webform module
 URL 141
WordPress 5
words
 replacing 12
wrapper 158

X

XAMPP 196

Z

Zend Studio
 URL 197

Thank you for buying
CiviCRM Cookbook

About Packt Publishing

Packt, pronounced 'packed', published its first book "*Mastering phpMyAdmin for Effective MySQL Management*" in April 2004 and subsequently continued to specialize in publishing highly focused books on specific technologies and solutions.

Our books and publications share the experiences of your fellow IT professionals in adapting and customizing today's systems, applications, and frameworks. Our solution based books give you the knowledge and power to customize the software and technologies you're using to get the job done. Packt books are more specific and less general than the IT books you have seen in the past. Our unique business model allows us to bring you more focused information, giving you more of what you need to know, and less of what you don't.

Packt is a modern, yet unique publishing company, which focuses on producing quality, cutting-edge books for communities of developers, administrators, and newbies alike. For more information, please visit our website: www.packtpub.com.

About Packt Open Source

In 2010, Packt launched two new brands, Packt Open Source and Packt Enterprise, in order to continue its focus on specialization. This book is part of the Packt Open Source brand, home to books published on software built around Open Source licences, and offering information to anybody from advanced developers to budding web designers. The Open Source brand also runs Packt's Open Source Royalty Scheme, by which Packt gives a royalty to each Open Source project about whose software a book is sold.

Writing for Packt

We welcome all inquiries from people who are interested in authoring. Book proposals should be sent to author@packtpub.com. If your book idea is still at an early stage and you would like to discuss it first before writing a formal book proposal, contact us; one of our commissioning editors will get in touch with you.

We're not just looking for published authors; if you have strong technical skills but no writing experience, our experienced editors can help you develop a writing career, or simply get some additional reward for your expertise.

Using CiviCRM

ISBN: 978-1-84951-226-8   Paperback: 464 pages

Develop and implement a fully-functional, systematic CRM plan for your organization using CiviCRM

1. Build a CRM that conforms to your needs from the ground up with all of the features that you want

2. Develop an integrated online system that handles contacts, donations, event registration, bulk e-mailing, case management and other functions such as activity tracking, grants, reporting, and analytics

3. Integrate CiviCRM with Drupal and Joomla!

Salesforce CRM: The Definitive Admin Handbook Second Edition

ISBN: 978-1-78217-052-5   Paperback: 420 pages

A comprehensive guide for the setup, configuration, and customization of Salesforce CRM

1. Updated for Spring '13, this book covers best practice administration principles, real-world experience, and critical design considerations for setting up and customizing Salesforce CRM

2. Analyze data within Salesforce by using reports, dashboards, custom reports, and report builder

3. A step-by-step guide offering clear guidance for the customization and administration of the Salesforce CRM application

Please check **www.PacktPub.com** for information on our titles

Implementing SugarCRM 5.x

ISBN: 978-1-84719-866-2   Paperback: 352 pages

Install, configure, and administer a robust Customer Relationship Management system using SugarCRM

1. Analyze and weigh deployment options based on your needs and resources

2. A brief overview of the benefits of SugarCRM 6.0

3. Review powerful built-in customization tools and popular third-party enhancements for your SugarCRM system

4. Learn about on-going maintenance needs such as backups and user management

Microsoft Dynamics CRM 2011 New Features

ISBN: 978-1-84968-206-0   Paperback: 288 pages

Get up to speed with the new features of Microsoft Dynamics CRM 2011

1. Master the new features of Microsoft Dynamics 2011

2. Use client-side programming to perform data validation, automation, and process enhancement

3. Learn powerful event driven server-side programming methods: Plug-Ins and Processes (Formerly Workflows)

4. Extend Microsoft Dynamics CRM 2011 in the Cloud

Please check **www.PacktPub.com** for information on our titles

Lightning Source UK Ltd.
Milton Keynes UK
UKOW05f0641260815

257515UK00005B/51/P

A BIRDWATCHING

THE PYRENEES

J. CROZIER

ARLEQUIN

TO BRIAN FOR ALL HIS HELP

ISBN 1 900159 75 9

First published 1998
Reprinted 2001

Arlequin Press, 26 Broomfield Road, Chelmsford, Essex CM1 1SW
Telephone: 01245 267771
© J. Crozier
© All illustrations James McCallum

A catalogue record for this book is available.

C O N T E N T S

LIST OF SITES

ADDITIONAL SITES

ADDITIONAL SITES

Where to watch Birds in the Pyrenees

Introduction to the Pyrenees

The Pyrenean mountains have been called "the great divide", "the barricade", a "mighty wall". More recently they have been described as the last great wilderness in Western Europe. They are all these and more.

Stretching from the Atlantic Ocean to the Mediterranean Sea, along their 435 kilometre length are beech, oak and chestnut woods, pine and fir forests; alpine pastures, semi-desert steppes, lush water meadows; hot, arid foothills; glaciers, rivers, lakes and gorges.

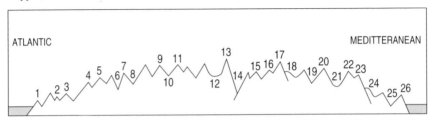

KEY: 1: La Rhune *900m* **2:**Roncesvalles*1057m* **3:**Coll d'Organbidexka *1000m* **4:**Pic Orhi *2017m* **5:**Pic d'Anie *2504m* **6:**Somport **7:**Pic du Midi d'Ossay *2884m* **8:**Portalet *1794m* **9:**Vignemale *3298m* **10:**Brêche de Roland *2807m* (Ordesa-Gavarnie) **11:**Monte Perdito *3335m* **12:**Berasque pass **13:**Aneto *3404m* **14:**Vallée de la Garonne *582m* **15:**Mont Valier *2838m* **16:**Mont Roig *2858m* **17:**Pic d'Estats *3115m* **18:**Envalira pass *2409m* (Andorra) **19:**Puymorens pass *1195m* **20:**Carlit *2921m* **21:**Eyne *1500m* **22:**Puigmal *2910m* **23:**Canigou *2784m* **24:**Ares pass *1513m* (Prats de Mollo) **25:**Perthus *277m* **26:**Pic Neulos *1246m* (Alberes).

This variety of habitat is home to a very large number of bird species – Mediterranean and northern European as well as alpine – whilst during migration periods the numbers crossing this range can be spectacular; up to thirty thousand Cranes, fifteen thousand Honey Buzzards, five thousand Red and over ten thousand Black Kites, five thousand Bee-eaters, several hundred Black Storks and over a million pigeons, to name just a few, cross at three or four main sites during their post-nuptial migration. The best observation points and times to witness this spectacle are included in the site-information.

The area covered in this Guide is based on the two language Tourist Map of the Pyrenees produced by the National Geographical Institutes of France and Spain, scale 1:400,000 or the Firestone Tourist Map T-33 of the Pyrenees, scale 1:200,000, so includes not only the higher peaks and the foothills but the plains stretching fifty kilometres or more north and south. On the northern, French side the mountains rise steeply from the plains except to the west where the hills are gentler and wetter. The northern side is generally better watered and wooded than the southern which is less cultivated, less forested and far less populated than the French side. The Spanish foothills make up almost three-quarters of the area in a series of pre-Pyrenean ranges, characterised by sheer rocky cliffs and deep ravines, divided by drier, broader valleys. For birders, these foothills are often the most productive areas, though lacking a few high-mountain species. There are over a hundred species of plants and animals that are only found in the Pyrenees.

From the dawn of history the inhabitants of this mountainous area have ignored artificial frontiers. It was not until the middle of the 17th century that the present border between France and Spain was agreed and adhered to. Even then, shepherds following their flocks to summer pastures largely ignored it, as mountain animals still do. The few remaining Brown Bears, as well as Izards, Moufflon, Marmots and Ibex wander at will across the frontiers.

The area's turbulent past is shown by the many ruined towers and castles dotted along the length of the Pyrenees; built either against the Visigoths or the Moors, or local warlords in the lawless Middle-ages; as refuges during religious wars or as evidence of the intermittent conflict between Spain and France.

Nowadays the greatest danger is likely to arise from hoards of invading tourists, especially skiers in winter. New roads leading to ski resorts make some sites more easily accessible but the development and infrastructure also erode and destroy habitat and disturb wildlife. Other threats come from forestry, modern agricultural practices, flooding valleys for reservoirs and hunting.

Introduction to the site information

The sites described run west to east from the Atlantic to the Mediterranean coasts and vary from marshes and rocky sea cliffs to 3000 metre peaks, garrigue to mountain pine forests, arid steppe to lush deciduous woods. They also range from comparatively small areas to vast National Parks. In the former, such as Organbidexka Pass, the Sierra de Boumort or Aiguamolls d'Emporda, there are large concentrations of birds at certain times. Within the very large areas a few sites that are especially rewarding for birdwatchers have been selected. They are the best places to visit if your time is limited, although many more areas are worth exploring if time allows. Finding mountain birds normally entails a reasonable amount of walking and a certain amount of luck. This guide tries to cut down on both commodities! The "Special Species" section tries to pinpoint places where certain species can usually be seen, which is not to say that they will not be seen elsewhere or will appear at all on the day you are there! The exceptions are the wintering and passage sites and the migration routes, when a large number of birds can be guaranteed at the right time of year.

Most Pyrenean valleys run north/south, so travelling east to west can be difficult, especially in Spain. However, many of the sites listed in this Guide are near each other on opposite sides of the frontier; in many cases it is possible to walk (Eyne-Nuria) or drive (Valle d'Ossau-Panticosa) from a site in France to one comparatively close in Spain. This has been noted in the text where it occurs but the sites are listed under each country for the convenience of anyone visiting one side of the range only. In a few cases, there is a cluster of sites concentrated in one, largish area (Jaca or Tremp) and these may be useful for anyone deciding to spend a holiday in one place, rather than touring. Where there is an interesting site outside the limits of this Guide but within easy driving distance, or near an airport, it has been mentioned in the text or described under "Additional Sites".

Maps

The two Tourist maps previously mentioned plus the sketchmaps in the book should be sufficient to find all the sites mentioned. Larger scale maps of the French Pyrenees (Carte Touristique 1:100,000 and Randonnées Pyrénéennes 1.50.000 – both Institut Géographique National) are fairly widely available and all National Parks have their own guides and other maps for sale. Outside these areas large scale maps of the Spanish side are few and not widely available, although there are some walking and climbing maps in the red-covered Editorial Alpina series of the most popular areas to scale 1:40,000 that also list mountain refuges, hotels and camp sites in the region.

Travelling to and around the Pyrenees

Several airlines fly twice or more daily to Toulouse, Bordeaux, Barcelona and Bilbao. There are charter flights to Girona, Lourds and Perpignan. Iberia airline has regular internal flights to Zaragoza and Pamplona and Air France to Pau. It is possible to take a car-ferry from Britain to Santander or San Sebastian. Many birders will drive their own car from Britain.

Car hire is available at all airports and most major towns and is the most convenient way of birding this area. Bus services are not available to many of the sites in this book; local buses are few and far between but anyone interested should contact local tourist offices. Four-wheel drive is not necessary for any of the sites mentioned in this book, provided the weather is reasonable. It should be pointed out that mountain weather can be unpredictable and smaller mountain roads can be blocked by snow even as late as May if there has been a freak snowstorm. Major roads are usually cleared quickly.

Since Spain joined the EU, a lot of money has been spent on roads. Almost all minor roads are now hardsurfaced and there are fast motorways running from the French frontier on the west, through Zaragoza to Barcelona. On the French side, there are good roads, mainly motorway, from Bayonne to Toulouse.

Accommodation

The Pyrenees is a tourist area, so there are plenty of guest houses (residencias), hostals or pensions and hotels in all the areas mentioned at a wide variety of prices from about 2,000 Pts. or 150 F. a night B&B upwards. Spain is nearly always cheaper than France. Many hotels are likely to be fully booked during the holiday and skiing seasons. Fortunately, the best time for birding is April to mid-June and September to November when there are likely to be vacancies. More detailed suggestions are given after each birding site.

Language

Fairly obviously, French is spoken on the north and Spanish on the south! Most people you will come into contact with probably speak both and a little English as well. National and Natural Parks have guides in English. Menus are often, in the more expensive establishments, in all three languages. However, from Pamplona westwards, notices, road signs, etc. are also in Basque (Euskara) and from Lleida eastwards in Catalan.

Food

Pyrenean food, on both sides of the frontier, is normally good but plain. There is much emphasis on meat, and green vegetables are often only served as a separate first course or the meat will come with a simple salad. Vegetarians may have problems, especially in Spain, but can usually ask for a dish of mixed vegetables (veduras) or an omelette. Each region has its own specialities; game, smoke-cured ham and various spicy sausages of the salami type are popular. There are plenty of local, quite inexpensive wines.

Almost every bar, even in the smallest village, will serve snacks of some kind for lunch or make you a sandwich (bocadillo in Spanish); half a loaf of "French" bread filled with either cheese (queso or fromage) or ham (jamón or jambon) – but don't expect butter!

Breakfast is always "Continental" – coffee and a croissant, though the more expensive establishments may offer cheese and ham as well.

It is worth noting, especially for those touring and birding until late in the evening, that the Spanish eat very late. Hotels and restaurants are not in the least fazed if you book in or ask for a meal at 10.30 p.m. Often, outside tourist areas, it may be difficult to find a restaurant that opens before 9 p.m. In France, on the other hand, most evening meals start at 7.30 p.m. and you may not be served if you arrive after 9 p.m.

Weather

It is said to snow every month of the year in the Pyrenees! However, this is only on the higher peaks and it is unlikely that it will snow below 2000 m. between May and November, though there can be freak, heavy snowfalls in these two months, sufficient to block mountain roads. At lower altitudes, April and May can often be wet and frequently windy. In addition, mountain weather is extremely changeable. You can be basking in the sun with temperatures of 30C one day and three days later shivering in biting winds with temperatures below 5C. It is also worth noting that temperatures plummet at night, especially in the spring. So bring warm and waterproof clothes as well as a sunhat and suncream at any time of the year. At high altitudes the sun burns more fiercely than lower down and it is possible to become badly sunburnt even when you feel quite cool.

Checklists

The birds referred to under each site cannot include all the species that have been recorded there but mention those that are likely to be of most interest. A checklist of Pyrenean birds is given at the end of the Guide as well as fuller information on where to find the special species likely to be of most interest to birders. As three sites are on the coast, it covers seabirds and waders as well as those species more usually associated with mountains.

Checklists of mammals as well as amphibians and reptiles and butterflies are also to be found at the end of the book; local species will be mentioned under individual sites. A plant list would be too long but a short account of some of the more widespread and common plants follows while endemics or other plants of interest are recorded under sites where they occur.

THE FLORA OF THE PYRENEES

Pyrenean plants can be loosely divided into three main types: the alpine and subalpine species to be found above 1000m in altitude; the "Mediterranean" type flora of the drier valleys and pre-Pyrenean foothills on the Spanish side and the Atlantic influence on the wetter north and west.

Most endemics are to be found in the higher areas; altitude, as well as late snow, affects the time of flowering, so while individual plants have a brief flowering period, the season extends upwards. Some of the earliest Spring flowers, appearing as the snow melts on the high passes, are the white Pyrenean Buttercups (*Ranunculus pyrenaica and R. amplexicaulis*) and the delicate Pyrenean Gentian *(Gentiana pyrenaica)*. They may be flowering at around 1800 metres as early as April but can still be found in bloom in July, a thousand metres higher in north-facing hollows where the snow has lingered. Soldanellas, Dog's-tooth Violets, Wild Daffodils, Primulas, Spring Gentians are other early flowers. In May, limestone cliffs and gorges are studded with the spectacular flower panicles of the Pyrenean Saxifrage *(Saxifraga longifolia)* and hillsides are yellow with Spanish Gorse *(Genista hispanica)* or Pyrenean Broom *(Cytisus purgans)* followed in June by the delicate white St. Bruno's Lily *(Paradisea liliastrum)*, tall Yellow and Spotted Gentians, Pyrenean Iris and Yellow Turk's Cap or Pyrenean Lily. This is the best month to look for tiny cushion alpines, saxifrages and androsaces, growing among the highest rocks. By July mountain slopes are ablaze with bright pink *Rhododendron ferrugineum* and the higher meadows are a kaleidoscope of colour and alive with butterflies. Other families well represented in the Pyrenees are the Pinks and Bellflowers. Except in the highest areas, the heat of August is starting to slow down this proliferation. Sedums and sempervivums flower on the rocks; the autumnal gentians, Field, Cross and Fringed, form patches of bright blue; the steely blue Pyrenean Eryngo *(Eryngium bourgatii)* covers swathes of the high pastures alongside clumps of tall yellow and blue Monkshood *(Aconitum sp.)*. ` The final colour of the year comes in September when sheets of lilac *Crocus nudiflorus* and rosy-pink *Merendera pyrenaica* flower under the red-berried Alpine Elders and Rowans.

Over 50 members of the Orchid family can be found in the Pyrenees, in every habitat: Marsh Orchids in wet places, Butterfly Orchids and Helleborines in light woodland, Ghost and Birdsnest Orchids favour beechwoods while the Violet Birdsnest can be found there as well as in orchards or olive groves. Pyramid Orchids can often be found in clearings in oak woods and Creeping Lady's Tresses usually on acid soil in coniferous woods. Lizard Orchids grow among warm, dry scrub in the foothills, Lady and Man Orchids (along with many other species) share a liking for dry limestone, Bug Orchids are found in damp meadows and Burnt Orchids in dry ones. Fragrant, Small White and Black Vanilla Orchids can be found growing in short grass at over 2,500 metres.

The season starts with Elder-flowered Orchid, both yellow and purple forms are out by April; another early flowerer in the lower meadows is Burnt Orchid. Many orchids are in flower by the end of May; the full flush of the Ophrys species: Bee, Late and Early Spider, Woodcock, Fly, Yellow, Dull and Sawfly, follow in June, mainly below 1000 metres. By the end of summer, Dark Red Helleborine is flowering in woodland clearings and the season finishes with Autumn Lady's Tresses.

The forests are composed of mainly Mountain Pine (Pinus uncinata) at the highest levels, mixed with Scots Pine (Pinus sylvestris) a little lower down. Swathes of Silver Fir (Abies alba) grow in damper areas, often together with Beech, forming extensive forests. The deciduous woodland on the lower slopes is predominantly Oak: Sessile, Penunculate, Downy and Pyrenean with Valencian, evergreen Holm and Kermes on the southern slopes. The dry foothills of the south are where Mediterranean maquis and garrigue are to be found.

Pyrenean Site Calendar

January   Atlantic and Mediterranean coastal sites for sea and waterbirds.

February   First week. **Gallocanta** for Cranes.
Southerly Pre-Pyrenean sites such as **Riglos, Leyre, St. Llorenç** and **Montrebei** for Wallcreeper and all resident birds (Alpine Accentor at **Riglos** during cold spells). Storks already nesting on the plains.
Alpine Accentor and Snow Finch around ski stations.
Black and White-backed Woodpeckers noisy and active at **Forest d'Issaux** and other woodland sites.

March   **Belchite and Monegros** for singing Dupont's Lark, Great Spotted Cuckoo, *Sylvia* warblers and steppe birds.
Aiguamolls d'Empordà for Gargany and other returning migrants.

April   Lower altitude sites: summer breeders arrive throughout month. Many species nesting.
Last week: best time for **Aiguamolls d'Empordà** – waders, migrants and summer breeders.
Migration through passes includes large flocks of Black Kites.

May   First week: **Aiguamolls d'Empordà.**
Migration of Honey Buzzards through passes.
Best period for summer and resident breeders at sites below 1500 m.
Last two weeks: higher sites normally accessible for Rock Thrush, Citril Finch, Water Pipit and Alpine Accentor. Wallcreepers back in breeding sites. The next two months best for Alpine flowers.

June   Ideal period for all sites over 1500 m.

July   Birds still active in highest areas: **Néouville, Gavarnie, Andorra, Nuria** for Ptarmigan, Snow Finch, Alpine Accentor. Juvenile Crossbills and Citril Finch disperse.

August   The quietest months for birds, the busiest for tourists. Good for butterflies.
Juvenile vultures flying; quite large flocks often seen feeding in non-breeding areas.
Last week: Post-breeding migration through passes commences, especially of Black Kites and Honey Buzzards at **Organbidexka** and **Eyne.** Migrating Dotterels near **Belchite.**

September Migration continues at **Organbidexka** and **Eyne.** First two weeks best for variety of species: Short-toed and Booted Eagles, kites, storks, etc.

October   Migration continues at **Organbidexka** and the Basque passes.
Waders at Atlantic and Mediterranean sites.
Steppe birds beginning to flock.

November Migration of Cranes. Last week: large numbers of Cranes at **Gallocanta.**

December First week: Cranes at **Gallocanta.**
Ordesa, Tremp, Gavarnie for displaying Lammergeiers and Golden Eagles.
Atlantic and Mediterranean sites for seabirds.

Please note that the calendar suggests ideal times to visit various sites, though extreme weather conditions may affect timing. Except for specific periods mentioned, most species will be in these sites for some time before and after the suggested month. For example, Lammergeiers may continue to display in January, woodpeckers are still active and calling in March and later, coastal sites are good throughout the winter months.

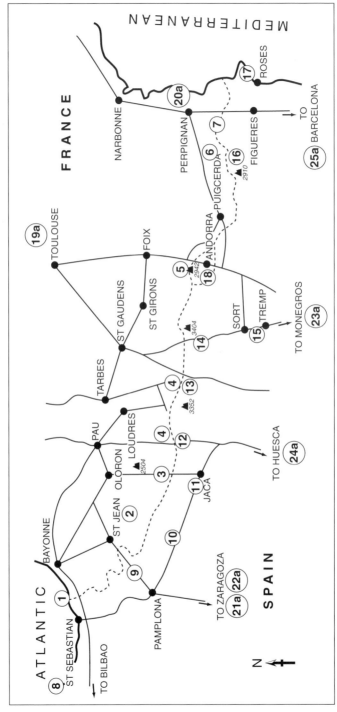

The Pyrenees. Numbers refer to sites in the main text.

10

SITES
FRANCE
1. HENDAYE AND THE ATLANTIC COAST

The seaside resort of Hendaye is situated on the north bank of the River Bidasoa, which forms the border between France and Spain. The gentle foothills of the Pyrenees rise up directly outside the town. Where the river enters the Atlantic, part of the Chingoudy Estuary has been turned into a bird reserve, La Vasiere and l'Ile des Oiseaux. There is no access to "Bird Island" but good views of the mudflats can be had from anywhere along the waterfront. There are always gulls present, mainly Yellow-legged, Lesser Black-backed and Black-headed, but also Mediterranean and a few rarities on passage. Plenty of waders and terns pass through during migration, as do Spoonbill, Black Stork and Bluethroat, which may be seen anywhere from the end of August to October. When north or north-west gales drive seabirds inshore, divers, auks, sea-ducks, shearwaters and petrels may be seen in the bay. A headland just north of the town beach, easily reached on foot, is a good spot for sea-watching.

A larger headland juts out to sea south of the river, in Spain, and this is an even better site to sea-watch. It is possible to drive over one of the bridges that separate Hendaye from its Spanish twin-town of Hondarribia where a road, not too easy to find, leads up along the bay to the headland, cape Higuer, and the lighthouse (follow the signs for "faroe"). This road gives good views down onto the bay. If it is raining, as it frequently is in the Basque country, there are two small bars beside the lighthouse from where one can look out to sea, protected from the worst of the weather.

Similar species to those at Hendayecan will be seen at other places along the Atlantic coast. Further north in France, **Hossegor Lake** is a natural lake, some 20 km north of Bayonne. It is separated from the sea by dunes but linked by a canal at its south end, and turns into mudflats at low tide. It is a good site for waders and gulls during migration and in winter, when divers, shearwaters and petrels may be seen offshore in the right weather conditions. The best place to sea-watch is from the harbour-wall where the canal enters the sea at Capbreton, south of the lake. Leave the N10 main coastal road, or the A-63 motorway at the junction signed Hossegor-Capbreton. Follow the signs to Hossegor "lac". A road runs along the east side of the Lake, with several places to park and it is possible to walk close to the west side of the lake. The lake is much used in summer, so this is really only a migration and winter site.

Accommodation

There are plenty of hotels in both Hendaye and Hondarribia and a campsite right beside the lighthouse on cape Higuer.

2. ORGANBIDEXKA

This pass, for long infamous as a shooting site for the hundreds of thousands of pigeons that cross the Pyrenees in autumn, was the first pass to have a bird observatory set up (partially to deter hunters and protect birds at the start). Soon, however, the variety and number of birds of prey using this pass led to increasingly organised and extended counts being carried out. Volunteers now man the site from mid-July to November and welcome about 8,000 visitors. Two hectares of Organbidexka are leased by agreement between a nature conservation organisation, Organbidexka Col Libre (O.C.L.) and the Ministry of the Environment. The area is classified as a reserve but this does not stop the hunters at the other sites nearby. Birdwatchers are often subjected to abuse, sometimes more than verbal, by the hunters but the growing number of birders provides an increasing deterrent. In addition, many birds other than pigeons, often protected species, are killed or injured. Recently the local mayor has tried to close footpaths during the hunting season from the beginning of October to the end of January.

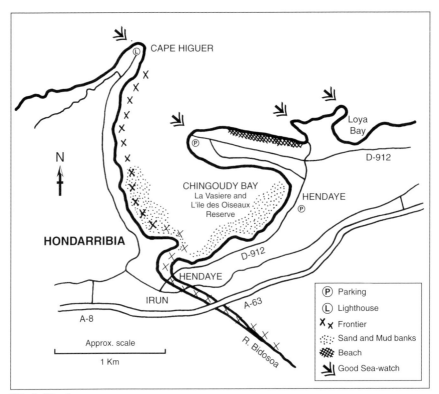

Site 1. Hendaye.

Some 10,000 Black Kites and almost 8000 Honey Buzzards cross here, the majority during the last few days of August and the first week in September. Early September is probably the best month for variety of species; in addition to smaller numbers of the above species, Black Stork, Hobby, all three harriers, Osprey and spectacular numbers of Swallows fly over. Most Red Kites, almost 3,000, pass through in October and a similar number of Cranes in November. (Figures based on 1996 count.)

Organbidexka (1355 m.) is on the Haute-Soule, some 10 km west of Larrau, along the minor road leading to Iraty and Saint-Jean-Pied-de-Port. Larrau is some 40 km south-west of Oloron-Sainte-Marie. A small path to the observation site leads off on the north side of the pass and when it is manned there are signs leading to it but birds can be seen from any vantage point on the grassy slopes of the pass.

O.C.L. also organises counts at two other sites on the Atlantic side from the end of September until the middle of November: **Lindux**, near Roncevalles, is some 30 km south of Saint-Jean-Pied-de-Port and the other Basque pass is **Lizarrieta**. This is the most accessible as there is good all-round visibility from the open area at the top of the pass. It is also a pigeon-shooting site and you can drive or walk up along the line of gun butts to other open areas. The narrow roads leading up to the pass twist through deciduous and mixed woodland. Take the D-306 to the Spanish frontier from Sare (which is 15 km from the coast at St. Jean-de-Luz, north of Hendaye) or the N-121 which runs along the Spanish side of the frontier from Hendaye towards Pamplona, turning off to Echalar and France. Much the same species cross at both these passes but in considerably smaller numbers. O.C.L. can be contacted at 11, Rue Bourgneuf F-64100 Bayonne. Tel: 05 59 25 62 03

The nearest village with a hotel is Larrau. Otherwise there are several in all the surrounding larger towns.

3. FOREST D'ISSAUX AND SOMPORT PASS

The forest lies to the west of the N-134 which runs from Oloron Ste. Marie to the Somport pass on the Spanish frontier through one of the loveliest Pyrenean valleys. Most woodland birds can be found in the forest but it is included here as one of the best sites for White-backed Woodpecker. About 4 k. north of the village of Bedous, 26 km from the Somport, there is a turning west signed to Lourdios-Ichère (this is much easier than trying to find your way through Bedous). Drive along this narrow road, passing through Lourdios village until there is a junction signed to Forest d'Issaux on the left. Drive south down this road, which passes through a rocky gorge that is a wintering site for Wallcreeper, until you come to another junction. Park here. The birds can be heard anywhere around here. Listen for their weak drumming, which has been likened to a creaking branch. They have been seen most frequently, however, from the small forestry track some 400 metres west of the junction. Take this track deeper into the wood. Stop at any areas with dead and fallen trees. The birds are easier to see in early spring before the trees are in full leaf and when they are calling. Early morning is the best time for these and all woodpecker species. If you do not succeed here, and do not wish to continue to the Somport, it is possible to drive to the Roncal valley in Spain (10), where there are other sites for this species. Follow the very minor road in the opposite direction from Bedous and turn left (south) towards the frontier. High altitude species can be found around the Somport pass but the main road carries a lot of traffic. Walking above the ski station of Astun can be more rewarding. The road to Astun is clearly signed on the Spanish side of the frontier. Snow Finch and Alpine Accentor have been seen around the buildings in winter and early spring, Water Pipit and Black Redstart in summer. Alpine Chough are common and it is a good area for raptors.

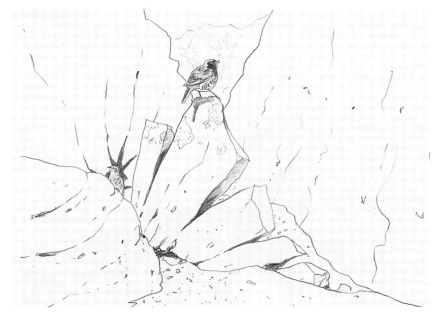

Black Redstart

13

There are small hotels and camp sites in all the larger villages on the French side. The hotels in the ski resorts may be closed off-season. There are plenty of hotels in Jaca.

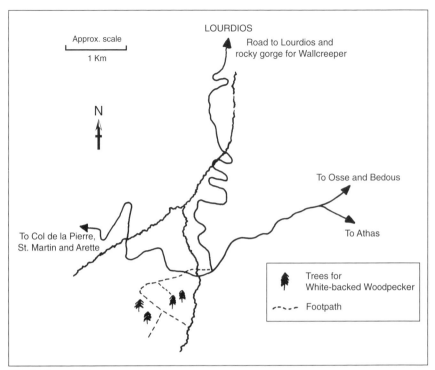

Site 3. Forest d'Issaux

4. PYRENEES NATIONAL PARK

The Parc National des Pyrenees was created in 1967. It comprises over 45,000 hectares (113,000 acres) of mountainous terrain lying between 1000 and 3000 metres and joins the Spanish Parque National de Ordesa. It is easily reached by good roads. There are many footpaths running through it and over the frontier but some parts are inaccessible.

Vallée d'Ossau

The Ossau Valley runs from the frontier at Portalet (12) towards Pau along the D-934. It was created a "Réserve Naturelle" by the National Park in 1974. At the highest point, near the frontier, the same species occur as can be seen at Portalet. Alpine Accentor may feed around the cafés on the pass in winter. Lower down the valley, between Laruns and Louvie, a quieter, minor road – the D-240 – runs parallel to the D-934. Off this road, near the villages of Aste-Béon, the cliffs are the site of one of France's Griffon Vulture colonies. There has been a winter "vulture restaurant" nearby since 1969, leading to a spectacular increase in the number of nests and young birds surviving into adulthood in the past two decades, and the expansion of the species' range east and west. Consequently, Griffon Vultures are one of the commoner birds to be seen in the skies over the Park. Lammergeiers are often seen over the Benou plateau, on the D-294 which runs west off the D-934, above Bielle and Bilhères villages 4 km north of Béon. Buzzards and both Kites are frequently seen.

Gavarnie

The Cirque de Gavarnie is the best-known and most-visited site in the whole of the Park. The scenery is certainly spectacular; waterfalls plummet thousands of metres from the top of the mountain amphitheatre which is streaked with snowfields, even at the height of summer. Birds and butterflies migrate through Gavarnie, as they do through most Pyrenean passes, but even outside the migration periods, Gavarnie is a good site.

The village of Gavarnie lies at the end of a no-through road, the D-923, from Gèdre. Park in one of the many car parks in the village and take the well-marked track towards the Cirque. The path follows the river, where Dipper can be seen, through light woodland. There are Citril Finch here, as well as Crested Tit and Crossbill among the pines. Alpine Swift fly overhead. Keep checking the mountain ridges all round; Griffon Vulture are common in summer when there are animals on the high pastures, Golden Eagle and Lammergeier can be seen year round. As you near the Cirque, search the cliffs and the small gorge for Wallcreeper, especially in spring and autumn. There is a hotel with a terrace at the end of the track; a good place to sit and watch for raptors. Footpaths lead on to the scree and snowfields below the rock walls; look for Alpine Accentor and Snow Finch. One footpath climbs westwards towards the Port de Boucharo, but this pass can very easily be reached by car.

Return to Gavarnie village and take the road signed to the ski-station. This leads upwards, through mountain moorland; Black Redstart, Wheatear and Water Pipit are the characteristic species of this habitat. Rock Buntings flit among the rocks and Marmots are very common; their alarm whistles can be disconcerting until familiar. There are plenty of places to stop on the way up and a car park at the top of the pass. This is a good viewpoint, especially for migrating raptors. You can often look down on Griffon Vultures and Alpine Chough hang around the cars, hoping for scraps. Beyond the parking the road is blocked for vehicles but walkers can continue into Spain or to the footpath that runs up through the scree and snowfields. It may be worth walking a short way along this, before it climbs too steeply, searching among the rocks for Alpine Accentor and Snow Finch.

The third road leading from Gavarnie village is a very minor one along the Ossoue river. It eventually turns into an unsurfaced track leading up to a lake. Bird species are likely to be the ones mentioned above but the alpine meadows are a botanist's dream, studded with Pyrenean Iris in early summer.

If you wish to continue eastwards from Gavarnie-Gèdre, towards Néouvielle, it will be necessary to drive over the Col du Tourmalet, where the birds and flowers are typical of bare mountain moorland, and then over the wooded Col d'Aspin to Arreau. The pinewoods on the latter pass are worth a short search.

Néouvielle

The Réserve Naturelle de Néouvielle (the name means "Old Snow") was created in 1935. It covers 2,313 hectares ranging in height from 1,800 to over 3,000 metres. It is easy to drive to above 2000 metres and the scenery is wild and majestic but although all the high Pyrenean species are to be found in the Reserve, actually seeing them is quite difficult, and involves a considerable amount of walking; even then, no sightings can be guaranteed.

A road up to the lake area of Néouvielle branches off the D-929 Arreau-St. Lary road in the village of Fabian, signposted to the Reserve. After 9.30 a.m. there is no entry to the final 6.4 km which is closed by a barrier, though you can leave at any time. It is worth going up to this top car park between Lakes Aubert and Aumar as Citril Finch are very common in the scattered pines here. If you arrive too late, there is a car park near the barrier served, in the summer season, by a shuttle-bus to the top car park.

From the top car park, footpaths lead in several directions. Several climb up to scree-covered slopes where Alpine Accentor and Snow Finch breed and can sometimes be found. One of the nearest is the Col d'Aumar. Walk back along the road to the south-eastern tip of lake Aumar and climb up to the low pass on the left. Besides Citril Finch,

Ring Ouzel

there are Siskin, Firecrest, Coal and Crested Tit in the pines here and Ring Ouzel nearer the top of the pass. Capercaillie breed in the pinewoods but they are always difficult to see. They prefer the highest strands of pines. If there is still snow, you can sometimes see their tracks. In summer, when the steep slopes are most accessible, there are many walkers and the birds are well away from the footpaths. Black Woodpecker is another forest species; look for them lower down in the taller forest, near the first two parking areas.

Other wildlife and flora

Most mountain species – Izard, Marmot, Pine Martin, Red Squirrel and Pyrenean Desman among them – can be found within the Park. Look for the desman in fast-flowing, unpolluted mountain streams with rocky banks. The rare Seoanei's viper occurs in Néouvielle. The whole area is rich botanically; the Park publishes its own guides – "Fleurs du Parc National", showing 573 of the plants to be found here. There is a Botanical Garden on the Col du Tourmalet. Such an abundant flora hosts abundant invertebrates; butterflies include species such as the rare and local Gavarnie Blue and Glandon Blue. Many of the butterflies which occur on mountains can be found at Néouvielle (which has over 1,200 plant species), including the Apollo and many species of ringlet.

<u>Accommodation</u>

There are plenty of hotels and campsites in all the villages and small towns near the Park but in high season (July/August) it is almost impossible to find a room unless you have previously booked.

16

Plate 1. *Rocky headlands, plantations and moorland – typical habitats on Atlantic coast near Urdaibai Reserve.*   *J. Crozier*

Plate 2. *Rocky Islands just off the Atlantic coast near Lekeitio – breeding grounds for Shag, Blue Rock Thrush and petrels.*   *J. Crozier*

Plate 3. *Typical woodland habitat in the Basque region. This is near the Spanish frontier south of St. Jean-Pied-de-Port.* *J. Crozier*

Plate 4. *Organbidexka. The main trans-Pyrenean migration pass.*

J. Crozier

Plate 5. Griffon Vultures circling above wooded ridge in the Sierra de Leyre. Feeding station in the foreground   *J. Crozier*

Plate 6. Pre-Pyrenean range at Riglos. Griffon and Egyptian Vultures, Blue Rock Thrush, Black Wheatear and Red-billed Chough nest on the cliffs; Spectacled and Dartford Warblers in the Scrub below.   *J. Crozier*

Plate 7. *Foz de Ayuban. Central Pyrenean gorge. Breeding site for Griffon Vulture, Lammergeier, Eagle Owl, Red-billed Chough. Wintering site for Wallcreeper.*　　　　　*J. Crozier*

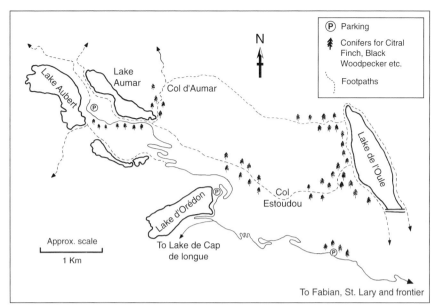

Site 4. Néouvielle

5. VICDESSOS

The head of the Vicdessos-Auzat valley is an easily accessible site for high-mountain species such as Water Pipit, Alpine Accentor, Rock Thrush, Alpine Chough and Ptarmigan. Lammergeier can sometimes be seen and, during migration periods, Black Kite, Honey Buzzard and other birds of prey.

Leave the N-10 at Tarascon-sur-Ariège (16 km south of Foix) and take the D-8 towards Vicdessos and Auzat. About 1.5 km after Auzat the road forks; take the road signed Monicou. A few kilometres after this village the hard surface runs out but the track is still driveable in summer, except in very bad weather. You can drive right up to Soulcem reservoir where Alpine Chough are often to be seen and scan the ridges from here. But for the other species you need to drive on for a further 2.5 km and then walk. Park by a stream which runs into the Vicdessos river near a small building. From here there is a marked trail (spots of red paint) along the right-hand bank of the stream which runs down from Soucarrane Lake (2292 m). Walk along the left-hand side of the lake and climb for 2 km to the Port de Bouet (2509 m). Ptarmigan can be seen on the scree between the lake and this point. Continue northwards with Soucarrane now on your right to the foot of Pic de la Rouge (2902 m). Alpine Accentor and Rock Thrush can be seen on the slopes of Pic de la Rouge. The climb up is likely to take at least two hours. Return the same way.

The driveable track peters out soon after where you have parked but it is possible to continue on foot over the Port de Rat into Arcalis in Andorra (see sketch map site 18). Snow Finch are sometimes seen here.

Wildlife and flora

Most of the mammals and invertebrates listed under Andorra can be found here. The flora is also similar.

Accommodation

There are small hotels and campsites in all the villages in the Vicdessos-Auzat valley, and more in the nearest, larger town of Tarascon-sur-Ariège.

6. EYNE

The plateau near the village of Eyne is one of the more important migration routes across the Pyrenees. In autumn up to 20,000 birds fly over the site, the majority Honey Buzzard and Short-toed Eagle. Other species include Black Kite, Black and White Storks, Sparrowhawk, Hen, Montagu's and Marsh Harriers as well as large numbers of Bee-eaters and quite a few Dotterel. The Bee-eaters often follow flocks of migrating dragonflies! The Honey Buzzards and Black Kites cross early, during the last few days of August and the first week of September. Black Stork numbers peak during the last two weeks of September. Like all post-nuptial migration sites, weather conditions play a large part in determining whether the migration is high or low, spectacular or very disappointing.

Eyne used to be manned from August until early November by a team from O.C.L (see Organbidexka (2)) counting the migrating birds. Recently they seem to have abandoned Eyne and concentrated their efforts on the east. However, Eyne is still a good site if you are in the area in early autumn. There are a variety of habitats on the plateau: hay meadows, pine woods, wooded streams, and several footpaths. It is a good area for Red-backed Shrike.

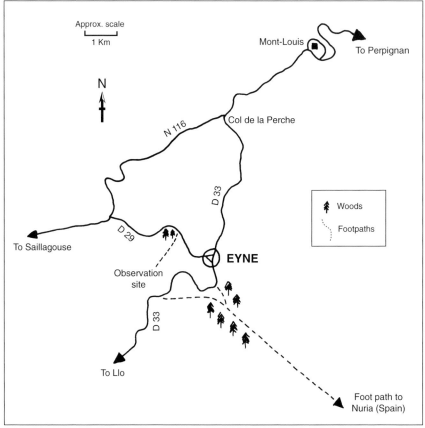

Site 6. Eyne

The best observation point is 2 km from the village where the plateau looks across the valley to Font-Romeu and the northern foothills. If coming from Perpignan take the N-116 through Prades up to Mont-Louis and continue towards Saillagouse. Turn left after 2.5 km onto the D-33 signposted Eyne. In the village (do not at this point continue on the road to Llo) turn right onto the D-29 and after half a kilometre the path to the site is on the left just before a conifer plantation. If coming the opposite way from Saillagouse, the D-29 leading to Eyne is on the right after some 4 km and the site is then on the right before you reach the village.

If you want to walk across the frontier to the site at Nuria (16), return to the village and turn towards Llo where marked footpaths on the left lead up the Eyne Valley following the river towards the Nuria Pass, 8 km away. The path at first goes through pine woods that gradually thin out near the Refuge de Orry de Baix, about half way to the pass. Citril Finch are likely here. After this point all the high mountain bird species are likely to be seen: Rock Thrush, Alpine Accentor, Alpine Chough and Golden Eagle. When you reach the pass with the Pic de Nuria (2794 m) on your right and the Pic d'Eyne (2786 m) on your left and start the descent, Ptarmigan and even Snow Finch are possible. The walk, with birding, is likely to take all day. The Eyne Valley is a famous botanical site with most of the eastern Pyrenean specialities growing there. The Yellow Turk's-cap Lily (*Lilium pyrenaicum*) is especially fine in June.

Accommodation
There are a couple of small hotels in Eyne itself and others in Saillagouse and Mont-Louis as well as campsites nearby.

7. PRATS-DE-MOLLO – LA PRESTE

This high mountain Reserve is located at the extreme east of the Pyrenean chain, about 60 km south-west of Perpignan. It is also the most southerly reserve in France; right on the Spanish frontier with its north-eastern limits extending to the lower slopes of Mount Canigou, at 2784 m. the most easterly high peak in the Pyrenees. Adjoining its north-western slope is the Reserve of Py-Mantet. The site is included because it is the best place to see mountain species if you are on the Mediterranean coast. It is possible to drive up to over 2000 m. Take the D-115 westwards from Boulou, which is 21km south of Perpignan, to Prats-de-Mollo, a further 39 km. In the village the very minor N-115A leads to La Preste and continues up to the southern end of the reserve. Another road leading north branches off 2.5 km before La Preste at St. Saveur. They may be blocked by snow as late as May.

The woodlands hold Black Woodpecker, Crested Tit and Bonelli's Warbler; Citril Finch can be found where the trees start to thin out. Rock Bunting, Rock Thrush and Alpine Accentor can all be found around the highest slopes and Ptarmigan on the topmost screes. It is also an excellent site for both species of Chough and birds of prey: Golden, Short-toed and Bonelli's Eagle can all be seen here and occasionally Lammergeier. Eagle Owl also breed here.

Other wildlife and flora
There are Izard on the highest slopes; Wild Boar, Wild Cat and Pine Martin in the woods, all difficult to see. The rare blind scorpion *Belisarius xambeui* is found on some limestone outcrops. It is excellent for mountain butterflies (see under Andorra which has similar species) and the rare and beautiful Spanish Moon Moth *(Graellsia isabellae)* is found in the pinewoods. The higher areas are excellent for alpine flowers.

Accommodation
There are hotels and campsites in both Prat de Mollo and la Preste, which are spa towns.

SPAIN

8. GUERNICA ESTUARY AND URDAIBAI RESERVE

North of Guernica (or Gernika in Basque) lies the estuary of the River Oka, an area of marsh, salt-flats, sand and mud banks that comprises the Urbaidai Reserve. Around the estuary there are conifer plantations, Holm oak woodlands, moorland and farmland set in a landscape of rolling, emerald green hills and rocky sea-cliffs. Although geographically the area is Cantabrian rather than Pyrenean, many birders will fly to Bilbao or arrive at the ferry-ports of Santander or San Sebastian and may wish to visit this area before driving east.

Access to the estuary is limited, but there are roads running from Guernica along both the right (east) and left (west) banks with many opportunities to stop and scan the river. You will need a telescope. A small railway also runs close to the river along the left bank and roads leading down to the railway stations ("estacion") give access to or views of the estuary. Like all river estuaries, low tide is best. On the mud flats you should see the normal gulls and water birds. Numbers increase during migration periods when you may find Bluethroat, Spoonbill from August to October and Crane later in the autumn.

Where the estuary enters the sea, on the west shore, you reach the fishing port of Bermeo, which is a good spot for sea-watching, especially from the jetty or the viewpoint above the village. Shags breed nearby and can be seen on the rocks, as well as auks, divers and Purple Sandpiper in winter.

From Bermeo you can drive westwards along the coast road where there are several good sea-watch points. These are always best when north or north-west gales drive birds inshore. The first is the lighthouse at Cape Matxitxako. Peregrine and Blue Rock Thrush breed on the cliffs. Look out for the signs to "faroe" on the right in Bermeo. Retrace your path to the coast road and turn right where you will soon reach another but more beautiful sea-watch point at San Juan de Gastelugatxe. This small island is linked by a causeway to the mainland. You can drive down 1.8 km to a parking area, walk over the causeway and up hundreds of steps to the old hermitage. On the inland side of the coast road there are several open areas with gorse scrub and Holm oak where you may see Hen Harrier, Cirl Bunting, Sardinian and Dartford Warblers and, in summer, Wryneck and Red-backed Shrike.

Peregrine

24

Site 8. Guernica and Urdaibai Reserve.

Return to Guernica, either by the same route or by the minor roads inland. The road along the east bank of the estuary is signed to Laida-Laga and Lekeitio. Just over 5 km from Guernica, you should fork left towards Playa de Laida. At Kanala there is an excellent view over the marshes below, opposite a parking area on the right hand side of the road. Continuing along the estuary, it is worth stopping at Playa de Laida to check the gulls and terns on the sandbanks. Shortly after this village, the road turns east along the coast. The Cape of Ogoño juts out into the sea, with rocky bays each side of it. Shag, Storm Petrel, Blue Rock Thrush and Peregrine breed here. On its west side you can drive down to Laga beach for a view of the cliff and on the east more views can be obtained from the port of Elantxobe, which is also a good sea-watch point in winter. There are Firecrest and Crested Tit in the strands of conifers on the hillsides, Great Reed Warbler is a summer visitor to the reed beds, Cetti's and Fan-tailed Warbler can be heard year round.

Flora

The heavy rainfall and mild climate of this coastal region produce a very western Atlantic type flora; Gorse *(Ulex europaeus),* for example, has replaced the Pyrenean and Spanish Brooms found further east.

Accommodation

Foreign tourism is not highly developed in this area. There are hotels in Mundaka and Lekeitio. In the latter, the Hotel Zubieta, on the road to Markina and Muntibar, is a traditional building tastefully restored in a quiet parkland area on the edge of town. It does not serve evening meals but there are several good restaurants nearby.

9. QUINTO REAL FOREST AND URKIAGA PASS

The beech woodland north of Pamplona, known as Quinto Real, is the western fringe of the vast beech and silver fir forest of Irati that stretches from Roncevalles over the frontier and becomes the Foret d'Iraty in France. A minor road leading from Zubiri (20 km north of Pamplona) towards the French frontier and Aldudes crosses the Collado (low pass) of Urkiaga after 16 km. The pass is used for pigeon shooting in autumn and paths to the gun butts as well as forestry tracks give easy access to a part of these woods.

There is space to park at the Urkiaga pass. On the west side a path leads up to the gun "towers" along the ridge and a wider forestry road runs in the same direction but lower. The latter is closed to vehicles by a chain but there is no problem in walking along it. As it climbs through the woods there are many places where the trees thin out and give views over the woods below and the high pastures above where migrants may be seen. White-backed and Black Woodpeckers are found here and can sometimes be heard and seen quite close to the road. Listen for their calls. Honey Buzzard are another woodland breeder and can be seen soaring over the woods below. Tree Pipit, Pied Flycatcher and the local Marsh Tit are other woodland species. If you climb through the woods towards the open ground Citril Finch can be found where the trees thin out and Water Pipit on the moorland.

You can return by the same forestry road but it is possible to return along the ridge past the shooting butts. Watch for a small track that leads off to the left. This track follows the ridge and the butts and ends at the car park on the pass. The same woodland birds will be seen here.

This pass also has a good passage of migratory raptors in autumn; in addition, Black Storks and Cranes pass in smaller numbers as well as thousands of pigeons and doves which unfortunately are the targets of the local hunters (see Organbidexka 2).

Other fauna and flora

Painted Lady and Long-tailed Blue butterflies use the passes to migrate northwards in August and September. Chequered Skipper, Swallowtail, Scarce Swallowtail, Cleopatra, Silver-studded Blue, Silver-washed and Dark Green Fritillaries are among the hundred or so species recorded here. St. Dabeoc's Heath *(Daboecia cantabrica)* grows together with Heather in clearings in the higher woods. Martagan Lily and the strange parasitic Toothwort *(Lathraaea squamaria)* grow in the beech woods and Lady's Slipper is among the orchids that can be found here and in the meadows. In spring, *Narcissus bulbocodium* is only found in the west of the Pyrenees.

Accommodation

There is accommodation and restaurants in the attractive village of Eugui, beside the reservoir of the same name which is some 7 km north of Zubiri. Pamplona is a large city with many hotels in all price ranges.

10. SIERRAS DE LEYRE, RONCAL AND SALAZAR VALLEYS

The Roncal valley, with the pre-Pyrenean range of Leyre to its south, runs north parallel to the valleys of Hecho and Anso (see Jaca 11). As a bird flies, these three valleys are quite close together, (18 km between Hecho and Roncal) but driving to the head of the Roncal Valley entails a considerable journey – some 125 km from Jaca.

The next north/south valley, continuing westwards, is the Salazar, carved out by the river of the same name. There are two impressive gorges at the entry to the Salazar Valley, the Foz de Lumbier and the Foz de Arbayún and another, the Foz de Burgui, in the south of the Roncal Valley. All four valleys are linked by minor west/east roads but the Roncal and Salazar Valleys can most conveniently be reached from the main Jaca-Pamplona road, the N-240, by taking the turning to Lumbier. By following the route below, each can be visited in turn; birds seen will be much the same in all three gorges.

The most common species around these gorges is Griffon Vulture; some of the largest colonies in Spain are to be found here. If any birder thinks that they will never tire of

Griffon Vulture

watching soaring vultures, then a few days in Navarra and Aragon may change their minds! Perhaps because of the high population density, it has recently been discovered that some Griffon Vultures in Navarra have changed from being purely carrion feeders and have started to attack sheep and other live stock. They are currently being studied to see if this is just a temporary aberration. Other cliff-nesting species include Eagle Owl, Peregrine Falcon, Egyptian Vulture and Alpine Swift (both summer visitors), Crag Martin, Red-billed Chough, Rock Dove and Blue Rock Thrush. In winter, Wallcreeper may be seen on the walls of any of these gorges and hundreds of Yellow-billed (or Alpine) Chough are likely to have joined the flocks of Red-billed Chough. Alpine Accentor is another winter visitor. Lammergeier are likely to be spotted overhead in either summer or winter; other raptors include Golden Eagle year round, Booted and Short-toed Eagles from April to September.

Some 500 metres after the Lumbier turning off the N-240, there is a feeding station on the right, looking towards the Foz de Lumbier. A parking area and a hide have been constructed overlooking this "vulture restaurant". When carrion has been put out, two hundred or more vultures can often be seen feeding and circling overhead. An unforgettable spectacle!

To walk through the most southerly gorge, the Foz de Lumbier, turn right at the signed road just before reaching the village of Lumbier. The road finishes after 2 km at a car park at the edge of the gorge. A footpath continues into the gorge, passing through two disused railway tunnels. It is possible to take a circular, marked footpath from the end of the gorge back to the car park.

The Foz de Arbayún can be reached by taking the main road out of Lumbier that leads towards Navascués. There is no access into this gorge but 11.6 km after Lumbier, on the right-hand side of the road, an excellent viewpoint (or "mirador") has been built overlooking it. Scan the rock ledges where you may be lucky enough to find a Lammergeier or Eagle Owl as well as numerous Griffons. Another viewpoint is the television mast on the peak of Arangüite (1356 m). Not only is the view stunning but you should see

27

Griffon Vultures, and other raptors, above, below and at eye level – as close as you are ever likely to see them! 2.4 km beyond the "mirador", just after the road crosses the Salazar River, turn right onto a minor road leading to Bigüezal and Salvatierra. Just past the village of Bigüezal, where a road sign states "Bigüezal 0.9", the road to the mast turns sharply back right. It is narrow but hard-surfaced all the way to the top and passes through woodland, where there are Citril Finch and Crossbill, before reaching an open area of box and broom scrub on the summit. This area, like the Foz de Arbayún, is a Zone of Special Protection for Birds (ZEPA). Dartford Warbler, Red-backed Shrike, Whinchat, Rock and Ortolan Bunting are some of the species to be found here.

To continue to the Burgui gorge, return to the Bigüezal road but turn right (not back left into the village) towards Salvatierra de Esca. This quiet road runs through a variety of habitats and it is worth making several stops for buntings, chats and finches. In Salvatierra, turn left onto the C-137 towards Burgui. The gorge lies between this junction and the village of Burgui. Drive through it, stopping where possible to scan the rock walls, or park and walk along the road. The rock walls are closer at both ends of the gorge. Just before the beginning of the gorge, an unsurfaced track turns right leading up to the hermitage of "La Virgen de la Peña" which can be seen perched on top of the cliff 8 km away. The road is rough, though a 4-wheel drive vehicle should manage it. Alternatively, it is an hour and a half walk. It passes through box/juniper scrub, where Sardinian, Dartford and Sub-alpine Warblers, Stonechat, Rock Bunting can be found. Like the television mast at Arangüite, you can look down on soaring raptors from the top of the cliff.

The head of this valley contains several sites for White-backed Woodpecker, mostly

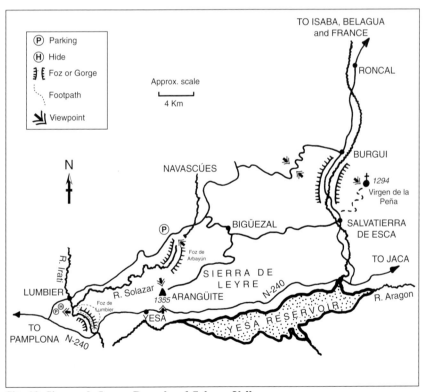

Site 10. Sierras de Leyre, Roncal and Salazar Valleys

28

difficult to work. After Burgui the road continues towards Roncal and Isaba. In Isaba follow the main road for Belagua and France. White-backed Woodpecker are found in the beechwoods here. The first possible site is the beechwood behind the carpark, which you will find on the right, 12 km after Isaba. There are several tracks here; try all of them.

After a further 6 km, you will see the refuge of Belagua just off the road on the right. If you park at the refuge, you can walk across open moorland with Water Pipit, Black Redstart, Red and Yellow-billed Chough, towards a mixed beech/fir wood. This is a cross-country skiing area and there are plenty of marked trails. White-backed Woodpecker are among the woodland species that occur here.

If you continue on this road over the frontier into France, then you will come to the Forest d'Issaux (3), a much easier site for White-backed Woodpecker.

Other fauna and flora

This area contains both the beechwoods of the previous site, a high Alpine zone and the more Mediterranean climate of the southern gorges. So floristically there is a mix of the species listed above for the west and those given below for the Jaca area. This also applies to the butterflies and other fauna. Butterflies are numerous including The Hermit and Cleopatra which is very common in late summer. Pyrenean Desman can be found in fast flowing rivers and the Pyrenean Brook Salamander in smaller streams and damp places.

Accommodation

There are hotels in Isaba, Roncal, Burgui and Lumbier as well as campsites near all these villages.

11. JACA AREA

The small Aragonese town of Jaca is located just west and south of some of the highest peaks in the Pyrenean range and is in the centre of what is probably the best birdwatching area in the Pyrenees. Most of the Pyrenean specialities can be seen from here, as there are a wide variety of habitats within easy driving distance.

Jaca is situated at the junction of the N-330 which runs from Huesca to the French frontier at the Somport pass (when it becomes the N-134) and the N-240 from Pamplona. It lies at an altitude of 818m.

The town itself offers some good birding. In the town park (or "Paseo") situated on the west of the town just off the main road, Scops Owls are always to be found in the summer. Track them down by their calls just after dark. They frequently perch in the light from street lamps. This park, and the avenue running from it overlooking the countryside below, is also good for Firecrest, Crested Tit, Nightingale, Short-toed Treecreeper and warblers.

The old Citadel, just north of the park, is probably the best place in the Pyrenees to see Rock Sparrow; listen out for their distinctive "wheeze". Dozens of pairs breed here, together with Little Owl, Kestrel and hundreds of House Sparrows and Swifts. A few pairs of Pallid Swifts are usually among them and can be picked out when they fly low enough.

The River Aragon runs just below the town and a road from near the end of the park leads down to it. Dipper and Common Sandpiper breed near the road bridge and Golden Oriole in the riverside trees. There are always a few Bee-eaters around the small village of Asieso, which can be seen from the bridge, as well as Spotless and Common Starling, Corn Bunting, Red-backed Shrike, Blue Rock Thrush, Black-eared and Northern Wheatear and often a pair of Hoopoes. Quail call in the fields nearby and Red and Black Kite and Griffon Vulture frequently soar overhead.

The old packhorse bridge further down river is another good spot for Golden Oriole as well as Tree Sparrow, Cirl Bunting, Woodchat Shrike and Melodious Warbler. Hobby has been seen from here, chasing the many swifts and martins overhead. From this bridge there is a footpath which leads back to the park in Jaca.

The wooded slopes and flat top of Oroel (1769m) are a landmark from everywhere in or around the town. The cliffs hold a colony of Griffon Vultures, frequently to be seen

Pallid Swift

flying over the town. It is also a good place to watch for Lammergeier, Egyptian Vulture and Short-toed Eagle. The woods contain, among other species, Firecrest, Crested Tit, Crossbill, Bonelli's Warbler and in the clearings, Woodlark and Tree Pipit but Oroel is best known for being one of the easiest places to see Black Woodpecker. Take the road that leads from Jaca towards Bernues and turn off left at the sign Mirador or Parador d'Oroel. Park at the Mirador (the word means viewpoint) where there is a small carpark, picnic area and restaurant and listen for the drumming or calls of Black Woodpecker, then follow the sounds. A pair can often be seen in the picnic area. Otherwise there is a footpath to the top of the peak and the birds sometimes call from about 200 metres along this. Early morning is the best time. Other previously mentioned species can be seen from this footpath or by walking along the hard-surfaced road beyond the Mirador which is also another possibility for Black Woodpecker.

San Juan de la Peña

The Sierra (a pre-Pyrenean range) and two monasteries of San Juan de la Peña can be reached from Oroel by returning to the Bernues road and turning right at the village. From here it is 12 km to the higher, 18th century monastery. You can park beside the Monastery, where Black Redstart breed, and walk through the woods on the right of it towards the Mirador de los Pirineos. The path ends at a sheer cliff with a spectacular view of some of the highest mountains stretching east and west as far as you can see. There is an orientation slab naming them. This is another good spot for Black Woodpecker. One can often be heard calling or flying over the trees below. Griffon Vultures also fly past towards their colony and anywhere along this cliff edge is a good raptor watch-point. Bonelli's Eagle and Lammergeier have been seen from here. The path runs right to the highest point (1552m) or left towards another viewpoint before circling back through the woods to the Monastery. Look out and listen for Crossbill, Crested Tit and Firecrest.

The road continues down from this Monastery towards the much older, 10th century one and then twists and turns down to the typically Aragonese village of Santa Cruz. There are several lay-byes along this road; all are worth stopping at to look at the Griffon Vultures on their breeding ledges. Egyptian Vulture and Common Chough are also here and Hobby, Peregrine and Golden Eagle have been spotted. The woods around Santa Cruz hold Bonelli's and other warblers.

4 km after Santa Cruz the road meets the N-240, turn right and it is 11 km back to Jaca.

Binies and the Hecho Valley

The Hecho Valley lies 20 km to the west of Jaca, off the N-240 Pamplona road just after it has crossed the bridge over the Aragon river at Puente de la Reina. These 20 km are the best place in the area to observe both Red and Black Kite, which are numerous here. In addition Booted and Short-toed Eagle can often be seen from the bridge as well as Cetti's and Melodious Warblers, Little Ringed Plover and Common Sandpiper.

The upper reaches of the Hecho Valley are the best for birding. Once past Hecho village look out for Red-backed Shrike, frequently perched on the top of bramble bushes. Raptors likely to be seen include Goshawk, Sparrowhawk, Griffon and Egyptian Vultures and Booted Eagle. Wallcreepers nest in the rocky gorges beside the river, especially near the tunnel known as the Boca del Infierno (Hell's Mouth). This is one of the lowest (980m) and easiest places in the Pyrenees to observe Wallcreeper. Patience is needed; keep scanning the rock walls. This is also a good place for spotting Lammergeier. Higher up, near the forest called Selva de Oza, Citril Finch can often be seen as well as many woodland birds. Golden Eagle fly above the ridges. If you are unlucky with Citril Finch here, drive back past the Boca del Infierno and turn left up to the mountain refuge and cross-country ski resort of Gabardito (1,300m). There are nearly always Citril Finch here as well as Crossbills while Black Woodpecker have been seen in the conifer woods through which the road winds up. The ridges here are worth scanning for Golden Eagle and Lammergeier as well as for flocks of Alpine and Common Chough. If you want to walk from here, Rock Thrush and higher up Alpine Accentor, Ring Ouzel and Snow Finch can be found. From the refuge there are marked footpaths which lead upwards towards the peak of Visuarín. This is another area to search for Wallcreeper.

At Hecho, a road runs west to the parallel north/south valley of Anso. Take this road and stop at the coll on the top to search for raptors, especially Goshawk, over the wooded slopes below. At the junction with the Anso road you can turn right, northwards towards the village of Anso and beyond, where the species are similar to those at the head of the Hecho valley, or left towards Binies. Southwards the road runs through the gorge or Foz de Binies before the village of that name can be seen perched on a small hill beside a ruined watchtower. In the gorge look out for breeding Crag Martins, Griffon Vultures, Peregrine and Blue Rock Thrush (at the end nearest Binies village). On the rocky slopes below the village, search for Thekla Lark and Tawny Pipit. The scrub alongside the road continuing south towards Berdun is good for Dartford and Subalpine Warblers; Dartford prefers the low-growing, prickly broom while Sub-alpine is found in the slightly taller brambles and box. Orphean Warbler can be found in the trees and orchards. Other species along this stretch include Cirl, Corn and Ortolan Buntings and Stonechat. Just before the hilltop village of Berdun, take one of the tracks that lead off to the left through the cornfields towards the hamlet of Santa Engracia. This is the best place to find Montagu's Harrier, although there are very few breeding pairs and they can be elusive. From Santa Engracia and Berdun the roads leads back to Puente de la Reina.

Riglos and Agüero

50 km by road south-west of Jaca lie the extraordinary puddingstone peaks known as the Mallos (or fingers), with the tiny, white villages of Riglos and Agüero at their feet. Once again, leave Jaca on the N-240 westwards to the Puenta de la Reina, but instead of crossing the bridge, continue southwards towards Ayerbe and Huesca. Stop where the river widens into the reservoir de Peña. There are Great Reed Warblers in the reed beds, easily located by their song, Marsh Harriers fly over the reeds and Sub-alpine Warblers can be found in the bushes.

31

Thekla Lark

Turn right towards Huesca on the bridge across the reservoir. Soon the Mallos will loom up on your left beyond the Gallego river but it is necessary to continue on for several kilometres more before the road to Riglos turns off on the left. First stop in the village of Morillo de Gallego. There are usually a few pairs of Pallid Swifts among the common ones that scream around the church. Soon after Morillo there is a turning to the right towards Agüero and a little further on the road to Riglos turns off to the left. Very much the same species can be seen in both villages. Black Wheatear is especially easy to see in Riglos. Park outside the village and walk through it towards the church. Just below the church is a footpath that scrambles up the rocky, *maquis* covered slopes towards the cliffs. Take this path for about 100 metres and stand just below the cliffs for long enough and Black Wheatear should easily be seen, flicking among the rocks. Other species here are Spectacled, Sardinian and Dartford Warblers, Black Redstart, Ortolan Bunting. In spite of disturbance from climbers, Chough, Blue Rock Thrush, Griffon and Egyptian Vultures, Kestrel, Peregrine and a few genuine Rock Dove still breed on the cliffs. In winter, Wallcreeper and Alpine Accentor can be found here. There are no climbers at Agüero and in addition to the above species, Black-eared Wheatear, Rock Bunting, Sub-alpine and Orphean Warblers, Rock Thrush and Woodchat Shrike can be found.

From Ayerbe there is a road to the Castle of Loarre which gives good views over the Sierra beyond. It is possible to walk from here to a raptor observation point but doubtful if any different species will be seen.

To return to Jaca, you must retrace your path to the reservoir where you can turn right after the bridge and take the minor road along the eastern part of the reservoir which eventually leads to Bernues and then Jaca or you can turn left and go back the way you came.

Other wildlife and flora

Red Squirrel can be seen in the park in Jaca. Chamois (or Izard, as the two species have been separated) as well as Marmot are often to be found on the slopes above the top of the Hecho valley – though a scope is necessary. Both species can be seen much closer at Panticosa and Marmots are especially easy to observe at close range at Portalet – see site 12.

There are several orchid species on the grassy slopes between Jaca and the River Aragon and around Agüero. They include several *Ophrys* species as well as Pyramidal, Fragrant, Lady and Greater Butterfly Orchids. The roadside verges near Sant Juan de la Peña are good for Pyrenean species, including the Pyrenean Bluebell *(Hyacinthus amethystinus)*, Rush-leaved Narcissus *(Narcissus requienii)*, Pyrenean Bellflower *(Campanula speciosa)*, Tuberous-rooted Meadow Rue *(Thalictrum tuberosum)*, Pyrenean Flax *(Linum suffrutaicosum)*, Pink or Pyrenean Rockrose *(Helianthemum pyrenaicum)* and *Dianthus hispanicus*. The Pyrenean Saxifrage (S. *longifolia)* and other saxifrage species can be found growing on the cliffs below San Juan, in the Boca de Infierno gorge and the Foz de Binies. Pyrenean Honeysuckle *(Lonicera pyrenaica)* also grows at the last site. The Yellow Turk's-cap Lily *(Lilium pyrenaicum)* grows in clearings around the Mirador of Oroel and in the higher valleys.

Accommodation
Jaca is a ski resort and there are plenty of hotels at all price ranges. There are also campsites nearby. All the villages mentioned (except Riglos) also have small hotels and bars.

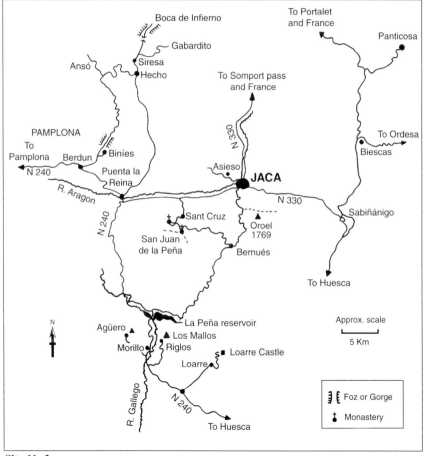

Site 11. Jaca

12. PANTICOSA AND PORTALET

The 19th century spa or Balneario de Panticosa (1659 m.) lies at the head of a side valley branching off the N-260 that runs from Huesca to the French frontier at the Portalet pass. The modern ski resort of Panticosa is lower down and far less rewarding. Footpaths lead from the old spa high into the mountains and walking along any of them could result in sightings of Rock Bunting, Crested Tit, Firecrest, Crossbill, Alpine and Common Chough, as well as Izard and Marmots. One of the best paths starts from a flight of steps on the right of the square, opposite the Casino. You will reach a junction where there are red/white paint marks. Take the left-hand track. Follow this track which leads up to an avalanche wall. Do not cross the wall but follow the track which bends upwards and to the right. It is easy walking to above the treeline at 2000 m. The surrounding ridges are worth searching for Golden Eagle and Lammergeier.

The Spanish side of the Portalet pass (1792 m.) is even better for sightings of Marmots and is one of the easiest places to see Rock Thrush without too much walking. Park near the "duty free" tourist shops. Face south towards Spain and walk along the track that runs from behind the right-hand shops towards the disused mine. Rock Thrush can be seen and heard on the rocks around the mines. Typical birds of high alpine meadows such as Water Pipit, Skylark, Black Redstart are also to be found here. Alpine Chough is frequent, so is Lammergeier. There is also a track leading off the main road on the left. This is almost as good as the wetter right-hand side and easier walking. There is a wealth of alpine flowers on both sides. To reach the Vall d'Ossau (4) continue over the pass into France.

Other wildlife and flora

Marmots can be seen very easily at Portalet, even from the road. Listen for their far-carrying whistle and look out for the males on "guard duty" on top of prominent rocks. At Panticosa, Izard and Marmots can be seen on the slopes above the spa and even near the road leading up to it.

Both Portalet and Panticosa are good for mountain species of butterfly. The Apollo flies at Portalet from the beginning of June to September.

The alpine meadows just below Portalet are one of the easiest places to find the endemic Pyrenean Snakeshead *(Fritillaria pyrenaica)* at the end of May when the Black Vanilla Orchid (Nigritella nigra) and the Horned Pansy *(Viola cornuta)* are just coming into flower. There are in addition gentians, saxifrages and hosts of narcissi. It is a wonderful spot for botanists, as is Panticosa.

Red-billed Chough

There are hotels in all the nearby ski resorts, although these may not necessarily be open in early summer. Balneario de Panticosa has its own hotels but they are likely to be full of tourists taking the spa waters. Jaca, where there are plenty of hotels, is within easy driving distance.

13. ORDESA NATIONAL PARK

This 15,608 hectare Park runs along the frontier adjoining the French National Park of the Pyrenees. Its full name is the National Park of Ordesa and Monte Perdito (the "Lost Mountain"), whose 3355 metre high peak dominates the park. The area was made a National Park in 1918, not only because it is an area of outstanding natural beauty but, in part, to protect one of the last remaining strongholds of the Spanish Ibex. Sadly, the numbers of this species have continued to decline.

The huge cliffs towering above the Ordesa Valley leading to the Soaso Pass have been described as "Spain's answer to the Grand Canyon". Certainly they are unique in the Spanish Pyrenees. The site is included in this book as it is a very good place to see Lammergeier, as well as worth visiting for its own sake.

From Jaca, turn onto the N-260 at Sabiñánigo and continue to Biescas. From France, cross the frontier from the Vallée d'Ossau (4) at Portalet (12). At Biescas, turn in the direction of Torla and Broto. From here there are signposts to the National Park.

3 km from Torla, a minor road leads off to the left towards Bujaruelo. There are several campsite and restaurant notices. Stop here and scan the high peaks around for Lammergeier. It is also a good spot for Goshawk, which often flies over the woods, Alpine Chough and Golden Eagle. Continue another 3 km to the car-park, restaurant and information centre. Maps are available here but all paths within the Park are very well marked. The main footpath to Soaso follows the river on its left-hand side. Just after the car-park, you can cross to the right-hand side of the river. This is a quieter path. After about 2 km you have to cross the river again and rejoin the main track. Both tracks lead through beech and silver-fir woodland. Listen out for Black Woodpecker and other woodland birds. Take a good look at the Long-tailed Tits; they belong to the darker, Spanish race. Wherever there is a clearing, scan the skies for raptors and Alpine Swifts and the rock faces for Izard and Ibex. The path continues past several spectacular waterfalls, where Wallcreeper have been seen occasionally. Once you are above the treeline there will be the usual high-mountain birds: Black Redstart, Dunnock, Water Pipit and Wheatear. There is a refuge at the foot of Monte Perdito if you wish to stay overnight or continue climbing into Gavarnie. Otherwise, the walk to the waterfalls and back takes about four hours.

It is also possible to visit the eastern end of the Park, though it needs some quite steep climbing to penetrate far into it. However, there are three roads that enable you to drive to the eastern edge and all pass through incomparable scenery.

To reach the eastern side, the twisting but very scenic C-138 road runs from Broto to Ainsa where you turn north for Bielsa. If coming from France, a road from St. Lary and Néouvielle (4) runs due south over the frontier to Bielsa which is 18 km from the frontier and 34 km from Ainsa.

At Bielsa a minor road runs west, through the Pineta valley, alongside the River Cinca towards Monte Perdito and the National Parador (an expensive state-run hotel in a dramatic setting). It is worth driving along this road, stopping at intervals. It passes through woodland; massive cliffs with tumbling waterfalls tower up on the left. You will see the same birds as on the west side. If you would like closer views of woodland birds, about a third of the way along the road, a tarmac road leads up to the village of Espierba. From here a driveable track runs through the woods, gradually emerging onto higher ground. From the little old Chapel of Nuestra Señora de Pineta, just before the Parador, a footpath signed "Llanas de la Larri" leads up through the beechwoods towards alpine meadows. Other footpaths run along the river and to the foot of the cliffs and are worth walking if you have time. Siskin and Marsh Tit are two very local breeding species that can be found in the woods here.

The minor roads between Bielsa and Ainsa leading westwards into the Park, though often blocked by snow in early spring, are definitely worth driving along, stopping at intervals and strolling around any likely habitat. This is a good area to spot Lammergeier and Golden Eagle. The eastern side of the Park, at these lower altitudes, is drier than the west and so has a more Mediterranean type vegetation preferred by species such as Sub-alpine, Dartford and Sardinian Warblers, Blue Rock Thrush, Wryneck. Bee-eaters can be seen around Ainsa.

The first road, 18 km south of Bielsa that runs to the edge of the park is signed Tella and a large plan just after the junction shows two minor roads leading to Revilla and Estaroniello. Take the hard-surfaced one that climbs through Cortalavina towards Revilla, stopping by suitable habitat and scanning the cliffs and ridges. This is an excellent area for raptors and Lammergeier.

The second road, 6 km further south, runs into the Park through the spectacularly scenic Añisclo gorge, one of the longest and most dramatic in the Pyrenees. The road is one-way only through the gorge and entails a circular drive starting and finishing at the village of Escalona. There are several lay-byes along the very narrow road which runs though pine, beech and fir woods, where it is possible to stop and scan the sky and rock walls for raptors and vultures, choughs and Alpine Swift. There are Goshawk and Black Woodpecker, among other species, in the woods.

Where the gorge branches north towards the Añisclo pass, there is a car park and a cliff footpath leads up the gorge (only for those with a head for heights). Even if you do not want to walk, this is an excellent viewpoint towards the Tres Sorores and Monte Perdito mountains.

The road branches just beyond the car-park. Take the left-hand road back to Escalona. The first village you come to, Vio, is another good viewpoint and there is some excellent scrubby habitat (Box, Holm Oak) along the road towards the next village, Buerba. Look out for Red-backed Shrike on the Box bushes.

Other wildlife and flora

All the alpine flowers, including Edelweiss, of the central Pyrenees can be found around Soaso. There is an interesting woodland flora that includes Helleborines and, on wet rock faces, Long-leaved Butterwort *(Pinguicula longifolia)* can be found. Other rock-loving species include saxifrages, *Ramonda myconi* and the endemic Pyrenean Yam *(Borderea pyrenaica)*.

There are Marmots, Izard, Spanish Ibex and Wild Boar in the Park. Red Squirrels can be seen in the woodland. It is an excellent area for butterflies; both woodland and mountain species including Gavarnie, Spanish Chalkhill, Glandon and Black-eyed Blues, The Dryad, High Brown, Silver-washed and Dark Green Fritillaries.

Accommodation

There are good hotels in Torla, the nearest village to the western Park entrance. All nearby villages have hotels and campsites. On the east side, in addition to the Parador, there are hotels in Bielsa and Ainsa and a large number of campsites, sophisticated and more primitive, including one at the park entrance, right in front of the Parador.

14. AIGÜESTORTES NATIONAL PARK

The eastern part of this high mountain Park is conveniently situated for anyone birding the Tremp area. In addition, the Park runs a four-wheel drive "taxi" service, enabling visitors to explore the higher areas without hours of climbing. As most ordinary cars are not suitable for the terrain and are not, anyway, allowed into the park, it is an ideal site for

Plate 8. *Boca de Infierno. Hecho valley, Wallcreeper and Crag Martin breed in this gorge.*

J. Crozier

Plate 9. *Some of the heighest peaks in the central Pyrenees near Garvanie where Snow Finch, Alpine Accentor and Yellow-billed Chough can be found.* J. Crozier

Plate 10. *Neovielle for Snow Finch and Alpine Accentor on the higher peaks and Citril Finch, Black Woodpecker and Capercaille in the pine woods.* J. Crozier

Plate 11. *Mont-rebei, an eastern Pyrenean gorge. Site for Griffon Vulture, Lammergeier, Golden Eagle and Red-billed Chough. Wintering site for Wallcreeper.*   J. Crozier

Plate 12. *Aiguamolls d'Emporda. View towards Cap de Creus.*   J. Crozier

Plate 13. *El Planeron reserve showing typical steppe habitat favoured by Dupont's, Lesser Short-toed and Short-toed Larks, Sandgrouse and Little Bustards.*   J. Crozier

Rock Bunting

those unable or unwilling to undertake a long climb. Aigüestortes (the name means "Tumbling waters") is also one of the most beautiful Parks in the Pyrenees, if not outstanding birding.

From La Pobla de Segur take the C-147 through the Collegats gorge and Sort until you reach the turning for Espot, a distance of 52 km. There is a Park Information Office for maps and advice in the centre of Espot and beside it, the "taxi service" office. The "taxis" – white jeeps – leave very regularly for Sant Maurici lake at a cost of 500 pts. for a single trip. They also run, provided there are six people wishing to go, to the further lakes of Ratera, d'Amitges and Negre. They will drop those wishing to walk at any of these lakes and arrange to collect them later at Sant Maurici. Return fares for this service vary between 1500 to 2700 pts. If you wish, it is quite easy to walk to Sant Maurici lake. It will take about two hours at birding speed.

At Espot, a narrow tarmac road continues on to the lake of Sant-Maurici 8 km away. It is possible to drive for 3 km from the end of the village (by the electricity sub-station) to a parking area. From here you have to walk, by well-marked footpaths, to the lake. This route is called the "Ruta d'Isards" and Izards can frequently be seen on the grassy slopes high above.

The path runs through pine forest with the usual birds: Coal Tit, Crested Tit, both Treecreepers, Firecrest, as well as areas of sub-alpine meadow. These are a feast for botanists and butterflies throughout the summer! Rock Bunting breed in them. As you walk higher, the pines become older and larger. Black Woodpecker may be seen flying above the trees; listen out for its calls, especially early in the morning and at dusk as well as noting any dead trees where they have been feeding. In this area, also listen out for the "chip, chip" calls of Crossbill flocks. The peaks to your right as you walk towards the lake should be continually checked for Lammergeier, Griffon Vulture and Golden Eagle; this is one of the most likely places to see them as they soar above the ridges. They usually fly over the open, grassy slopes rather than the rocky ones. Nearing the lake, watch out and listen for Citril Finch near the woodland edges and Dipper in the river.

Most visitors venture no further than Sant Maurici lake, where another small Information Office is open in summer and jeeps wait for return passengers. But the footpath to the Ratera lake is well signed. The birds are much the same as lower down and there is an interesting alpine flora. The yellow *Lilium pyrenaicum* is splendid in June, so are the views. There are Capercaillie in the forest near the Ratera lake and waterfall; they have been seen flying across the lake at dawn and in the evening. Tengmalm's Owl also breed in the Park. You will probably need to reach the Amitges lakes (where there is a mountain refuge) to see Alpine Accentor.

It is possible to walk across the Park to the west side but most visitors drive around as roads run outside the northern and southern boundaries. The southern route runs from Espot back to Sort and La Pobla de Segur. Here take the C-144 over the Port de Perves pass (a good place for Rock Thrush and Red-backed Shrike as well as watch raptors) to Pont de Suert. Continue northwards towards Viella and the Vall d'Aran but turn off after 3 km onto the L-500 road towards Caldes de Boí. The drive will take almost a whole morning, with stops for birding.

There are car parks beyond Boí and Caldes de Boí and taxis are available from both, as they are from Espot on the east side. It is possible to drive up to the Cavallers lake and walk along the footpath on its right side or take the right hand track towards the Llebreta lake and the Aigüestortes plateau. The latter is probably the most interesting. There is a damp, mixed woodland beyond the lake; Marsh Tit and Goshawk are two new species that can be seen here, in addition to the usual woodland birds. Among the pines and firs, the forest species mentioned for the Sant Maurici area can be found, including both Serin and Citril Finch. Rock Bunting breed among the rocks, Dunnock in the *rhododendron* bushes. Griffon Vulture, Golden Eagle and Lammergeier fly above the sheer cliff faces. If you walk as far as the Llong lake, flocks of Yellow and Red-billed Chough are often seen flying and Capercaillie and Black Woodpecker are to be found in the pines on the right.

Other wildlife and flora

Izard are quite plentiful on the upper slopes. Two endemics, the Pyrenean Desman and the Pyrenean Brook Salamander are to be found in the Park; the first in the fast-flowing rivers and the second in the smaller streams, especially the Sant Nicolau stream below the Llebreta lake. A few brown bears were reintroduced by the French just over the frontier from Aigüestortes and have been reported in and near the Park. They wander at will across the border. There is a new Spanish breeding and reintroduction programme where bears can be seen in captivity in the village of Arties, north of the Park. Otters have also been the subject of reintroduction and conservation and their numbers are increasing. They can be seen in the deeper rivers nearby, especially the Noguera north of the Park. There is a breeding centre, which can be visited, at Pont de Suert, to the west of the Park and a "Ruta de la Lludriga" (Otter Route) runs through the park. Details are available from the centre or any Park Information Office.

The rich flora is typical of the central high Pyrenees, especially the *Dactylohiza* and *Gymnadenia* orchids. Late May, June and July are the best months for quantity and variety. They are also a good time for butterflies, although there are still plenty on the wing in September. The mountain species listed under Andorra (18) can all be found here and many others: at least 19 blues, 12 skippers and 17 fritillaries.

Accommodation

There are hotels, restaurants and campsites in Espot and its ski station, Super Espot, as well as all nearby villages. In the Park itself, there are four mountain refuge huts: at Sant Maurici (open all year) and d'Amitges, near the Negre and Llong lakes. They are wardened and have a radiotelephone for emergencies. On the west, there are hotels in the villages in the Boí valley.

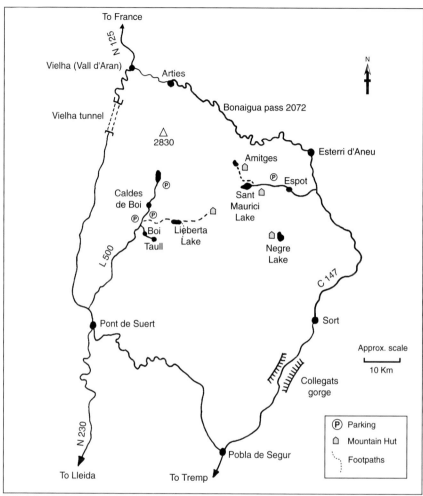

Site 14. Aigüestortes.

15. TREMP AREA

This area includes three sites, to the north, west and south of the town. Each site probably needs a full day. From France they can be reached by taking the N117 westwards from St. Gaudens to Montrejeau. Here you turn south onto the N125 which becomes the N-230 when it crosses the border to Vielha in Spain. From here continue on the N-230 through the Vielha tunnel, turning off onto the N-260 at El Port de Suert to Pobla de Segur. The National Park of Aigüestortes (14), north of Pobla de Segur, is conveniently situated to be visited before or after this site.

From Spain take the C-1313 from Lleida (or Lerida) to Balaguer and then turn onto the C-147 towards Tremp.

43

Sierra de Boumort

The Sierra (or Serra) de Boumort, a huge limestone ridge, is part of the pre-Pyrenees. The west end is the site of the largest Griffon Vulture colony in Catalunya and this area, fortunately, is easily accessible. Other parts of the Sierra are used for hunting and access is difficult or prohibited. The nearby Gorge de Collegats on the N-260 at the western end of the ridge is also interesting and is partly protected. The artificial lake (Embalse or Panta) of Talarn in the valley below the sierra is worth visiting, especially during migration periods. The reservoir near Cellers, about 25 km south on the road from Tremp to Balaguer is even better for waterbirds, being reed fringed.

Boumort is situated off the N-260 at La Pobla de Segur. Turn east onto the minor road immediately north of the bridge crossing the river. It is signposted to El Pont de Claverol, Hortoneda, St. Marti and Aramunt. At El Pont de Claverol, there is a sharp right turn over another bridge. At the far end of the bridge, turn right again. Continue for approximately 2.5 km to a junction; turn left here following the signs for St. Marti and Pessonada. When you reach St. Marti, turn left. This unsigned road leads up to the small hamlet of Pessonada, lying directly below the sierra. Just before the hamlet the road forks and here you should take the left-hand lane to a pig farm. Here either park and walk or drive slowly along the rough track that leads left past the farm. The cliff with the colony is immediately above you on the left. The best viewing spot is about 500 metres past the farm.

About fifty pairs of Griffon Vulture nest here and can be seen all year round, although they are best observed from April to July when they still have young on the nest ledges. This is also the best time for other summer breeding species, although the lakes are more interesting during migration periods. Half a day is probably sufficient for the cliff itself but the scrub, olive groves, orchards and farmland around are also worth exploring.

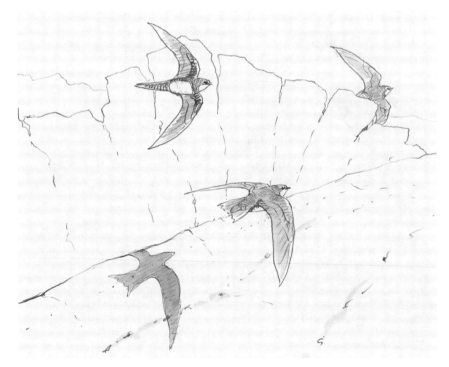

Alpine Swift

44

Besides the Griffons, a pair of Lammergeier nest nearby and can often be seen flying over Boumort. Egyptian Vulture also breed alongside the Griffons and can be seen in summer flying over the lake or near their nest sites. Golden Eagle breed near here though these are best seen early in the year before nesting or in late summer when the young are flying. The cliffs are also the home of hundreds of pairs of Common Chough, Alpine Swift and a few pairs of Peregrine. Hobby can usually be seen hunting near the lake throughout the summer. Booted and Short-toed Eagle are more usually seen over the open fields and wooded hills to the north and south of the site.

There is a colony of Bee-eaters beside the road which runs along the east shore of the lake after the village of El Pont de Claverol. The birds can be seen anywhere along here. There are several places to scan the lake from this road that runs to a small bar (only open in summer) and beach. Besides the resident Great Crested Grebe and Mallard, Red-crested Pochard, Black-headed and Yellow-legged Gull, Black Stork and Black and Whiskered Tern occur on passage. Red and Black Kite frequently fly over the far side of the lake. The

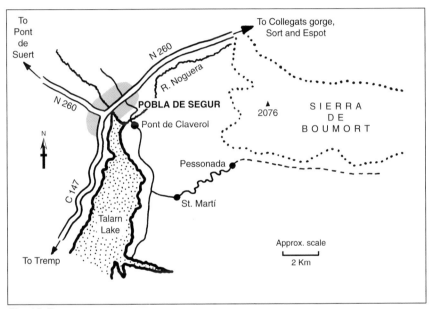

Site 15. Boumort area.

orchards and scrub at the foot of the cliff attract various passerines including Cirl and Ortolan Bunting, Stonechat, Woodchat Shrike and Sub-alpine Warbler. Firecrest can be found in the woods, Golden Oriole in the taller trees near the lake and Hoopoe around the villages.

There are picnic/parking areas just north and south of the tunnels that by-pass the Gorge at Collegats. Just scanning the ridges and the river from these parking areas can be rewarding (the one to the south is one of the best places for Lammergeier) but it is possible to walk through the gorge on the old road alongside the river as the main road now runs through two tunnels. Lammergeier frequently fly over the Collegats gorge, where Blue Rock Thrush and Crag Martins nest and Wallcreeper can sometimes be seen, especially in winter. There are Dipper in the river. It is another area where Alpine Swifts are often seen.

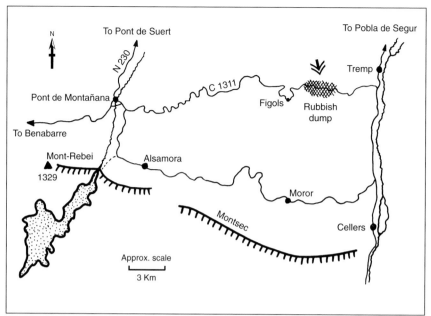

Site 15. Mont-rebei area.

Mont-rebei Gorge

This is one of the few gorges in the eastern Pyrenees that does not have a road cut through it and so has remained relatively wild and unspoiled; it was in fact, created a Partial Nature Reserve to protect an otter colony. There is a narrow footpath cut high into the cliff above the river which makes for a spectacular walk but is not for those who suffer from vertigo. Most birds can be seen from the path along the lakeside leading to the gorge but for views of Wallcreeper it is necessary to walk almost to the end of the cliff path, searching the rock walls above and below you. Mont-rebei is primarily a wintering site for this species but a pair sometimes breeds here. Certainly they can be seen as early as mid-September.

To reach the gorge, take the C-1311 which runs west just south of Tremp, signposted Figols de Tremp and Benabarre. Set your trip meter at the junction. 5.4 km from the junction there is a large rubbish dump on the right hand side. This is a good spot to see Black Kite and Egyptian Vulture in summer and Red Kite and Raven all year round. At 25 km from the junction, just before the C-1311 meets the more major N230 at Puente de Montañana, turn left (signposted Castissent) and continue along this narrow, hard-surfaced road for 2.5 km At this point you will see a house and a gravel track (signed La Clua low down) on the right-hand side. Follow this gravel track for 3.1 km, and then take the right fork which has a footpath notice GR1 – Congost de Mont-Rebei. After 1.2 km there is a track leading down on your right towards the lake. Although you can drive down a short way and park, the track become rough and after rain very muddy, so it is probably better to park at the junction and walk.

Blue Rock Thrush, Rock and Cirl Buntings, Dartford and Sardinian Warblers can all found, in suitable habitat, along the C-1311 or the track leading to the gorge. At Mont-rebei, look out for the local Golden Eagles, which are frequently seen here. Check the ruined watchtower on the right-hand side before the entrance to the gorge; an eagle often perches here. It is also an excellent spot for Lammergeier, Griffon and Egyptian Vultures. Other raptors which can be seen include Goshawk, Sparrowhawk, Kestrel and Peregrine. Alpine and Common Chough fly above the gorge. As mentioned above, this is a good site for Wallcreeper. In addition, Eagle Owl breed in the area and can be heard early in the year, although your chances of seeing them are remote. Along the river, which at times widens to a small lake before the gorge, you may find grebes, cormorants, duck, Kingfisher, Grey Heron, Grey and White Wagtails and the occasional wader.

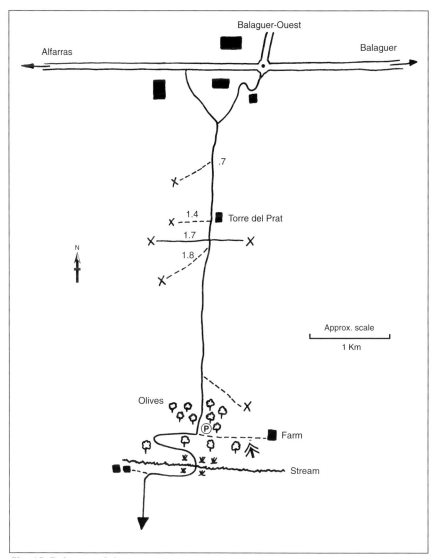

Site 15. Balaguer plains.

Balaguer plains and St. Llorenç Lake
The plains lie to the west and the lake to the north-east of Balaguer, 58 km south of Tremp. Both the plains and the lake can be visited in a day if you start early enough. To reach the plains area, take the C-148 towards Algerri and Alfarras which can now be reached from the new by-pass round Balaguer. On the outskirts of the town, there are some warehouses,

one on the right and three on the left. Two tracks lead off between the left-hand buildings. Take the unsigned track which leads off from the small roundabout at the end of the new by-pass. (The road opposite is signed "Balaguer-Oest"). Zero your trip meter here. (If you miss this turn, take the next left-hand track but deduct .2 km from all distances quoted – both tracks join after the buildings.) Continue along this track until you reach a fork at .7 km. Take the left-hand fork. At 1.4 km you will pass a building on the left-hand side marked "Torre del Prat" on the entrance gate. Continue for another .3 km and you will come to a crossroads. Carry straight on towards a fork about 100 metres past this junction. Take the left-hand fork (1.8 km) and continue straight on ignoring any turnings until you reach a T-junction at 5.2 km. You will see a farmhouse at a short distance on your left and olive groves on both sides of the road. Park here, look out over the valley and explore the olive groves. Roller are frequently seen here, together with Hobby, Bee-eater, Little Owl and Golden Oriole. Stone Curlew are often among the olives. They can be hard to find as they frequently crouch in the long grass under the trees. Orphean and Melodious Warblers breed here.

You can continue down into the valley and cross the river, though it may sometimes be quite deep. Check the reeds. The track climbs up the far side. Look out for Little Owl, Black-eared Wheatear and Thekla lark. Avoid the private road leading off to the farm buildings on the right. At the top of the valley, there is a T-junction, turn right and after about one hundred metres, turn left. Continue along the track, ignoring turnings to left or right and check all the fields on both sides for 3/4 km for Little Bustard. Should you deviate from the main track, keep careful note to avoid getting lost!

Return to Balaguer by the same route, stopping, if you have time, to walk around the small hillocks you can see from the track, which are also good vantagepoints for raptors hunting over the plains.

This is one of the nearest areas to the Pyrenees to find typical steppe birds such as Sandgrouse, Little Bustard, Roller and Stone Curlew (though the Fraga and Belchite areas listed under "Additional Sites" are better for these species). Much of the area is now sown with winter barley and these fields are good for Calandra Lark, Corn Bunting and Little Bustard in spring. Little Bustard calls at dusk and frequently performs display flights at the same time. Stone Curlew are also most likely to be seen and heard in the evening or very early in the morning. Red-legged Partridge and Bee-eaters can be seen around the fields and in the drier areas and Little Owl on old walls and buildings as well as both Spotless and Common Starling. White Storks nest in Algerri and several nearby villages. Crested Lark are often observed at the roadsides, Short-toed Lark and Tawny Pipit in the drier, scrubby areas while Thekla Lark are only to be found on the dry, rocky slopes of the hills. Immature Bonelli's Eagle sometimes fly over the plains, especially in autumn and spring

St. Llorenç lake can be reached by leaving Balaguer on the L904 and branching right towards Gerb (or Gerp) 3 km from the end of the town. In Gerb, keep right in the direction of Sant Llorenç de Mongai and after 5 km the lake comes into view on the right. It is possible to scan the lake from the entrance to the dam; the small spinney to the right of the dam path is worth checking, as are the reedbeds. The cliffs on the opposite shore of the lake are a breeding site for Bonelli's Eagle and Eagle Owl, which can be heard at dusk early in the year. Drive on another kilometre towards the village where it is possible to park right on the lakeside; this is the best place to scan the cliffs opposite for Bonelli's Eagle which often seems to fly mid-morning. It is also possible to sit on the terrace of the lakeside bar to watch in comfort. Continuing through the village and along the lakeside, rocky cliffs rise up on the left. In winter this is a good spot for Wallcreeper. Before the lake ends just after a bridge, there are several lay-byes from which to scan the lake, the cliffs and the reedbeds. The road continues to a junction with the C147 near the village of Camarasa where Rock Sparrow can be found.

Black Wheatear

Purple Heron breed in the reeds, as do Cetti's, Great Reed and Fan-tailed Warblers. Golden Orioles and Penduline Tits can be found in the riverside woodland on the far bank. In winter, hundreds of duck, mainly Tufted, Teal, Mallard and Common Pochard can be found on the lake, together with the resident Great Crested and Little Grebes. Blue Rock Thrush and Crag Martin are present on the cliffs all year round, together with a few genuine Rock Doves. Chough can be seen overhead and Alpine Swift in spring and summer. The scrub below the cliffs holds Sardinian Warbler, which can also be found behind the railway station in the village, together with Black Wheatear, Rock Sparrow and Cirl Bunting.

Other wildlife and flora

The flora of this area is exceptional, especially from April to June, being a combination of Alpine and Mediterranean plants. Collegats gorge is a convenient place to see some Pyrenean endemics, especially the spectacular Pyrenean Saxifrage (*S. longifolia*), *Ramonda myconi* and Creeping Snapdragon *(Asarina procumbens)*.

Over one hundred and fifty butterflies have been recorded in the area, including Scarce Swallowtail, Spanish Festoon, Moroccan Orange Tip, Cleopatra, Nettle-tree Butterfly, Two-tailed Pasha, Indian Red Admiral, Forster's Furry Blue and Camberwell Beauty.

Otters can sometimes be seen in the Noguera River and below Mont-rebei gorge.

Accommodation

Pobla de Segur and Tremp have a couple of small hotels each. Balaguer has a more expensive Parador. Probably the most congenial centre from which to explore the whole area is the Casa Guilla, somewhat off the beaten track, in the small village of Santa Engracia near Tremp. (Tel: 973 67 61 06) It is run by an English couple who are knowledgeable about the local wildlife and there is excellent birding in the immediate vicinity.

There is a convenient campsite "Collegats" situated about midway between the gorge of the same name and Pobla de Segur. There is another campsite opposite the dam at St. Llorenç lake. They are only open in summer.

There are several small bars serving food in all the towns and villages mentioned. The lakeside bars serve meals but are open only in the summer and early autumn. (This area is shown on sketch map for 'Additional Sites' 21a-23a).

49

16. NURIA

Reached by the only rack-railway in Spain, Nuria is a neat, Swiss-looking little resort. It has been a Sanctuary for a thousand years; nowadays it is also a small ski-resort. It lies at 2000 m. within the Freser National Game Reserve, whose highest point is Puigmal (2913 m)

The rack railway starts at Ribes de Fresner (905 m), with a halfway stop at Queralbs. You can drive to Queralbs but no further. It is approximately 7 km from Ribes to Queralbs and the road passes through deciduous woodland and other habitats where you may see Wryneck, Goshawk, Honey Buzzard, Tree Pipit, Bonelli's and Cetti's Warblers among other species, so it is worth making several stops wherever possible. From Queralbs it is possible to walk up to Nuria along a well-marked G-11 footpath but it is easier to take the train up to the Sanctuary and walk back down to Queralbs. The first trains leave Queralbs at 7.52 and 9.39 and then every two hours in spring and autumn, every hour in summer until 17.39. They return from Nuria at ten minutes past the hour from midday until 18.10 or later in summer. There is a large carpark next to the station at Queralbs.

When you arrive at the Sanctuary, a large turn-of-the-century building, look in the pine trees around it for Citril Finch and in winter for Snow Finch and Alpine Accentor, which feed near the restaurants. There are several marked walks from Nuria but to reach the nearest scree area take the one towards Puigmal. Walk past all the buildings to the stream that runs to the left of the Sanctuary. Follow the path on the right-hand bank for about 500 metres, then cross by a bridge and take the smaller track signed Puigmal. It is also marked with blue paint that runs out after a while but by then the track is obvious. This track runs uphill to another, smaller stream where it turns left again following the stream towards its source. It is quite a steep climb from here to the scree areas below Puigmal and Pic de Segre. It will take about three hours if you are also looking at birds. The commonest birds from here on are Water Pipit, Northern Wheatear, Dunnock and Black Redstart. There are Citril Finch and a few Ring Ouzel around the scattered pine trees, as well as Crested Tit and the much commoner Coal Tit. Look out for Rock Thrush on the rocks near the stream. Short-toed Eagle breed in the woods lower down and you should get good views of this species as they fly over the slopes looking for snakes and lizards. Keep looking above the ridges for Golden Eagle, Buzzard and Lammergeier. As you climb higher you should see quite large numbers of Izard. Start checking the scree slopes for Ptarmigan as you climb nearer.

The most productive scree area is marked by a couple of rain gauges on a ridge to the right of the path that leads to Puigmal. Ptarmigan can be anywhere in the scree below the

Grey Wagtail and Dipper

50

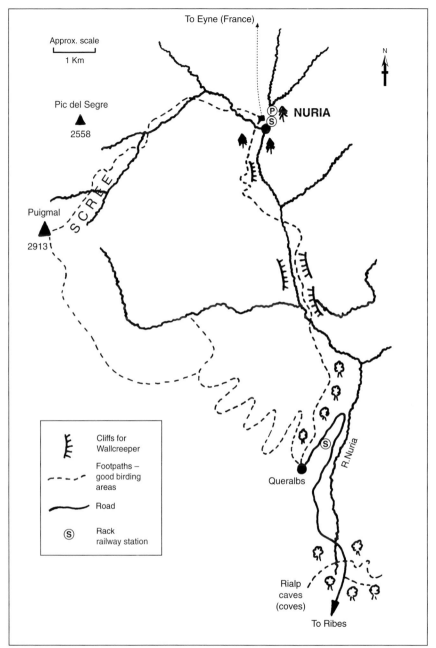

Site 16. Nuria.

ridge which runs from Pic de Segre to Puigmal and on the lower slopes of the latter. They are very difficult to see unless they are flushed. Then they usually only fly a short distance and drop down into a dip just out of sight. But look around the hollows where snow still lies. Snowfinch search for seeds around the snow, too, and have been seen near the top of the ridge in summer. Wallcreeper have also been seen in summer around the ridgetops and the higher crags. Early spring and autumn are probably the best time to see all these birds but there can be a lot of snow about then. To see Ptarmigan in winter plumage, you would need to be here at the end of November or early December but snow can make walking on scree very dangerous and it should never be attempted.

It is possible to climb to the top of Puigmal and descend by the ridge on the opposite side but for birds it is probably better to return to the Sanctuary and then walk down to Queralbs station. The walk will take you through alpine meadows, good for Ring Ouzel, woodland for Citril Finch, Crossbill and tits and, about halfway down, through a narrow gorge where Wallcreeper breed. Scan the cliff faces above you and listen out for their high-pitched double whistle. Crag Martins breed here too. Alpine Swift can be seen over the high cliffs anywhere in the area, as well as both Choughs, Lammergeier and Golden Eagle. The path follows the river where Dipper can be seen. Rock Bunting, Citril Finch, Red-backed Shrike, Short-toed Treecreeper and Firecrest are all species that can be seen nearer Queralbs village.

Other wildlife and flora

Izard are very easy to spot above Nuria. There are also Moufflon and Marmots. Most of the mountain butterflies listed for Andorra can also be seen here. In addition Common Brassy Ringlet and Alpine Grizzled Skipper are common near the Sanctuary in summer and Dewy Ringlet can be found higher up.

This is also a good area for botanists as it, like Eyne in France, has species only found in the eastern Pyrenees. Grey Alpine Grounsel *(Senecio leucophyllus)* grows all over the lower scree slopes and higher up the strange endemic umbellifer, *Xatradia scrabra*, that Izard like browsing on.

<u>Accommodation</u>

There are hotels in Ribes de Freser. There is a hotel and campsite in Nuria as well as several restaurants, a children's playground, boating lake, shops and exhibitions; all of which make it a good place for families to spend some time while the birding member(s) of the family is slogging up the slopes. There are restaurants and a small pension in Queralbs.

17. CAP DE CREUS AND AIGUAMOLLS D'EMPORDÀ

The Cap de Creus peninsular is the most easterly point of Spain where the foothills of the Pyrenees plunge into the Mediterranean. The Aiguamolls (the word means marshes in Catalan) of Empordà are the saline and freshwater lagoons lying just south of the cape around the mouths of the rivers Muga and Fluvia. They are now a Natural Park, and a Ramsar Site, 867 hectares of which are Integral Nature Reserves (access only on designated tracks). The Cap de Creus area is protected by a preliminary conservation plan and may become a Natural Park.

Both areas contain a variety of habitats. Cap de Creus has scrub covered hills which hold many warblers; Holm and Cork Oak woodland; cliffs and coves which make excellent areas for spotting birds migrating along the coast as well as for watching seabirds and raptors. The marshes, beaches and rice-paddies of Aiguamolls are an important resting-place for waders on passage as well as holding sizeable numbers of wintering wildfowl and breeding terns and herons in summer. The water meadows, riverside woods and drier agricultural land are interesting for summer visitors.

The migration periods, mid April to the end of May and September to November are the best times to visit but the winter months can also be rewarding. July and August are the least interesting months; water levels are often low and there are too many tourists about. Morning and dusk are the best times to visit Aiguamolls Reserve and for sea-watching, be at Cap de Creus in the afternoon, when the fishing boats are returning.

Alpine Accentor

There are marked walks and well-placed hides in Aiguamolls. Outside these drive slowly along the minor roads, stopping frequently by olive and almond groves and look at wires, bushes and posts. The Information Centre at El Cortalet, within the Natural Park, will always give information on what birds are present and the currently best areas.

You will need two full days at least to cover both areas, and could spend up to a week here in spring. A car is necessary for Cap de Creus. Always lock your cars and leave nothing valuable inside. Car thieves are a real problem here, even out of season.

Cap de Creus lies just south of the French border. The A-9 motorway from Perpignan crosses the border at Le Perthus and becomes the Spanish A-7 to Gerona and Barcelona. If you wish to avoid the motorways, the N-9 in France and the N-11 in Spain run parallel to them. The only delays at the frontier may be on Bank Holidays and during the summer months. Both sites can be reached by taking the C-252 or the C-260 from Figueres. The very minor roads leading from these last two are worth exploring.

Cap de Creus

The rocks at the tip of Cap de Creus are a good place to look for Black Wheatear, Blue Rock Thrush all year round and Rock Thrush in spring. Park near the lighthouse; there are numerous tracks leading over the rocks towards the sea. Thekla Lark is found among the rocks just before the cape. In winter Wallcreeper and Alpine Accentor can sometimes be seen as small numbers regularly winter here, but they take a lot of searching for. The terrace of the café gives good views over the sea. Large numbers of Balearic Shearwaters, which winter along the coast, can often be seen quite close inshore, as well as Gannets, Sandwich Terns and Cory's Shearwaters. Yellow-legged Gulls are common.

One way to reach Cap de Creus is to take the road from Vilajuiga, signposted to San Pere de Rodes monastery, which leads up through olive groves, haunt of Hoopoe,

Sardinian and Orphean Warblers, through scrub where Spectacled Warbler breed in the more sparsely vegetated areas and Subalpine and Dartford in thicker scrubland. Birds that prefer open ground, such as Rock and Ortolan Bunting, Tawny Pipit, Thekla Lark and Black-eared Wheatear choose the rocky or stony areas. The cistus scrub both along the cliff tops and further inland are good for migrating passerines. Alpine, Pallid and Common Swifts, as well as Crag Martins, can all be here and at Cap Norfeu.

It is worth stopping at the monastery and climbing up from it to San Salvador, at 670 m. the highest peak of the peninsular. Many of the species mentioned above will be seen in the scrub and the top is a good spot to watch out for raptors, especially during migration. Black Wheatear can usually be seen here too, as well as Alpine Accentor in winter. Wryneck, Melodious and Olivaceous Warblers have been found right beside the monastery in spring.

From the monastery car park a road leads down to Port de la Selva before turning inland towards Cadaques 11 km away. Just on the outskirts of Cadaques you turn left, following the signs for Cap de Creus; they are not always very easy to see. The cistus scrub as you near the headland is especially good for *Sylvia* warblers. Stop where any tracks lead off and take a short walk.

Cap de Creus can also be reached from Roses; follow the signs for Cadaques. Cap Norfeu can only be reached from Roses and is more difficult to find. The main road into Roses takes you to the sea-front. Turn inland and look for a sign to Cala Jóncols and Cala Montjoi on a road leading uphill west from the town. Cap Norfeu is 10 km from this junction and the road passes through very similar habitats to those previously described. Look out for Blue Rock Thrush in the quarries near Roses and stop at the old tower house you pass after 3 km. There are often good birds around here. When you reach Cap Norfeu, recognisable by its tower, you will have to park and walk along the tracks leading around the headland. The complete circuit could take several hours but if you are pushed for time, a short stroll towards some ruined buildings and careful observation of the scrub could produce almost as many birds. Rufous Bush Robin has been seen here during migration. The track that leads inland is not so rewarding.

Aiguamolls d'Empordá

The Reserve can be reached by returning to Roses and taking the C-260 towards Castello d'Empuries and Figueres. This busy road bypasses the village of Castello but you must take the turning to the left, signed San Pere Pescador, just before the bridge leading right to the village. The Reserve is signed at this junction. If you pass a large Danone factory on your left you have missed it. If you are coming from Figueres, look out for the turning just after the Danone factory. The Reserve lies on the left of the San Pere Pescador road and the main, El Cortalet, entrance is clearly marked shortly after a petrol filling station on the opposite side of the road.

In the olive groves and fields inland – between the Cape and Aiguamolls – Bee-eater, Hoopoe, Golden Oriole, Great Spotted Cuckoo and Woodchat Shrike can be seen in spring and summer. It is also the best area in northern Spain to see breeding Lesser Grey Shrike. There are not very many but they perch conveniently on olive trees or telegraph wires. Look especially along the minor roads around Castello and Perelada and when walking along the path to the Estany de Vilahut (or Vilaüt), where there is a hide. During migration Red-backed Shrike are also present and Great Grey in winter. Sometimes all four species can be seen in early May.

The best strategy to adopt at the Reserve is to go first to the Information Centre at El Cortalet. Check the notice board for interesting species, note where they have been seen and ask at the counter for a plan of the Reserve. Many of the staff and wardens speak English. All hides and trails are clearly marked, on the plan and in the field. You have to walk around the main part of the Reserve but you can drive to the old rice silos, now converted into an observation tower. Return to the Sant Pere Pescador road, continue in the

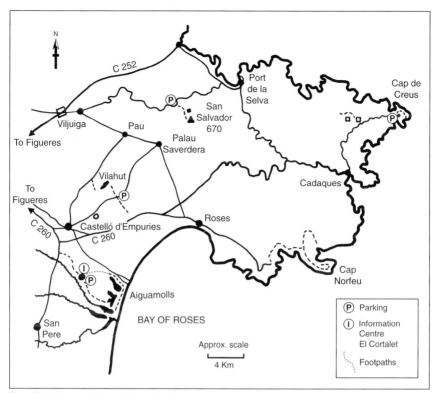

Site 17. Aiguamolls and Cap de Creus.

direction of San Pere and turn left at the clearly signed turning to Camping Nautic Almata. A track to the tower and hides on this side of the Reserve branches off the campsite road.

It is also necessary to drive to Vilahut, situated on the other side of Castello from El Cortalet. Cross the bridge into Castello village and then turn left after the traffic lights towards the centre of the village. Do not go into the old part with its narrow streets but look for the signs to Palau-Saverdera on the right. This is a very minor road and the signs in the village are not easy to see. Drive slowly along this road which runs alongside the River Mugeta through cultivated fields. There are several places to stop. The road crosses three bridges over canals running through reedbeds. The footpath to Vilahut hide is just after the third bridge. Drive past the entrance and park your car at the nearby restaurant. Walk back and take the marked path to the hide.

During migration most of the commoner European waders can be seen in the marshes and flooded rice fields. Other migratory species include Greater Flamingo, Great White Egret, Squacco Heron, Glossy Ibis, Spoonbill, Pratincoles, Avocet, Whiskered, Black and Gull-billed Terns. Black-winged Stilt, White Stork, Gargany, Purple Heron, Bittern, Little Bittern and Night Heron all breed here in greater or lesser numbers. White and Cattle Egrets can be seen all year round. Purple Gallinule were reintroduced some years ago, are breeding well and can now be seen easily from El Cortalet and Vilahut hides, especially in the early morning. Great Reed, Fan-tailed, Cetti's, Moustached and Savi's Warblers, as well as Penduline Tit, breed in or near the reed beds. Moustached Warbler and Penduline Tit can also be found in winter, especially in the reed beds near the three bridges on the road to Vilahut. Marsh Harriers can be seen flying over the reeds all year round. Kentish

Plover and Little Tern breed on the beaches; as a result, long stretches adjacent to the Reserve are out of bounds in spring and early summer. Red-breasted Pipit is seen most springs in the fields behind the Information Centre; small numbers of Stone Curlew breed in the same area and larger flocks overwinter most years. A few Bluethroat can also be seen from September to March. Rarities keep turning up at this Reserve and you never know what you may discover; a few years ago a Black-shouldered Kite wintered here. Red-footed Falcon are seen regularly during the spring migration and Pectoral Sandpiper in autumn.

Other wildlife and flora

Otters, fairly common until fifty years ago, have recently been reintroduced to the Reserve, although you will be lucky even to see their prints on the beach or beside the rivers. Fallow Deer are common. There are Stripe-necked Terrapin in the freshwater pools and streams where Painted Frogs can also be found and Stripeless Tree Frogs are noisy and abundant. The dunes hold Psamodromus *sp.* and skink *(Chalcides chalcides)*.

Among the characteristic saline and marshland vegetation, the blue *Iris spuria* which flowers in May and June is noteworthy, as is the Sea Daffodil *(Pancratium maritimum)* in late summer. Brackish Water Crowsfoot *(Ranunculus baudotii)* covers Vilahut Lake in summer.

Hermann's Tortoise can be found on the lower, eastern slopes of the Albera hills and on Cap de Creus, which has a typically Mediterranean flora. The butterfly species on the check-list which prefer Mediterranean coastal regions will be found here.

Accommodation

The Hotel Allioli on the San Pere Pescador/Castello d'Empuries junction (by the Danone factory) serves good food and is within walking distance of the Reserve. However this is a tourist area and there are other small hotels, bars and restaurants in both villages as well as a large number of hotels and hostals, ranging from one to four star, in Roses. There are also campsites near the beaches within the park area, though some are only open in summer. The nearest is Nautic Almata, adjoining the Reserve along the San Pere road, which also has bungalows, a supermarket, etc. It is probably not necessary to book in advance except in the summer months when a call to the Tourist Information Bureau in Roses (tel: 972-2573 31) is advisable.

18. ANDORRA

Andorra is a small, independent state covering some 486 square kilometres mainly on the southern slope of the Pyrenees. Within the country, which is approximately the size of the Isle of Wight, there are a wide variety of habitats from Mediterranean-type garrigue to mountain pine forest, so most Pyrenean species can be found there. Unfortunately the country has been over-developed in the last twenty years and a lot of habitat lost. There are seven ski stations, which makes access to the higher areas relatively easy. As well as the three sites described, many of the high altitude species can be seen on the approaches to and around the ski-stations, in summer as well as winter. Alpine Accentors can be commonly found picking up crumbs around the restaurants in the ski season. Of the three sites described below, only one involves much walking. At any of them, even using a car, you should be able to see the more interesting species without an all-day trek.

Coll d'Ordino

A recently constructed, hard-surfaced road leads from Canillo to Ordino, driveable thoughout the year except in exceptionally bad conditions. Turn off the main road running south from the French frontier at Canillo, just after the huge ice-rink (Palau de Gel). Drive to where a footpath is marked Vall de Riu. Park here and walk a few hundred metres along a newly-made track towards some ruined barns. Rock Bunting, Citril Finch, Black Redstart, Red-backed Shrike and Rock Thrush can be seen along this stretch in spring and early summer. Golden Eagle and Lammergeier often fly over this valley. Drive on, looking out for raptors, until you reach a parking area marked by a modern sculpture resembling totem poles. This is the Roc de Quer and is a good spot to spend an hour or two on a raptor watch, especially at mid-day, as there is 360 degrees visibility and a superb view down into the main valley. Lammergeier can appear from any direction, Griffon Vultures fly over the peak of Casamanya to the north, especially in summer when livestock are grazing there. Black Woodpecker, Crested Tit, Woodlark, Short-toed Treecreeper, Bonelli's Warbler, Firecrest, Crossbill and Citril Finch can be heard, and sometimes seen, in the surrounding trees. Both Short-toed Treecreeper and Eurasian Treecreeper occur in Andorra, as elsewhere in the Pyrenees. Usually Short-toed is to be found in mixed woodland and gardens below 1500 m. and Eurasian in coniferous forests above this altitude. But there is some overlap. Unless the bird sings, it can be very difficult to be sure which species it is. If you have time, walk over the meadows towards the stream, below and to the northeast. After some time here, continue on to the Coll d'Ordino, where you can park beside the road and explore this open, grassy pass. Much the same birds can be expected as at Roc de Quer, but if you failed to see any species there, you may well find them here. On the left-hand side, as the road starts to descend, a footpath leads up through the pinewoods to a radio mast at a peak known as Bony de les Neres. Capercaillie can be found here, but when they are perching in trees during the day, it takes a lot of thrashing around on steep slopes to spot one. The road then continues down to the village of Ordino.

Arcalis and Sorteny
From Ordino a road leads north, through several villages, to El Serrat and the ski resort of Ordino-Arcalis. The road does not stop at the main ski buildings but continues up to two further sub-stations with chairlifts and a restaurant. Alpine Accentor can be seen around any of the three, even as late as May when the skiing has finished but the best birding is between the second and top sub-station. On the lightly wooded, rocky slopes Citril Finch and Rock Thrush can be found. Around the top restaurant you may be lucky enough to find a few Snow Finch soon after the snow has thawed, although they breed higher up. Both Choughs, Raven and sometimes Golden Eagle, can be seen over the ridges. Water Pipit, Northern Wheatear, Black Redstart and Dunnock are common.

   When you have birded this area, drive down through the tunnel. Before the village of El Serrat, there is a road off to the left, marked Sorteny. The tarmac finishes, after about a kilometre, near a picnic site but a driveable track continues up for a further kilometre until it is blocked by a wall and gate. Park here and walk up the valley towards a refuge. Crossbill, Crested Tit, Rock Bunting, Goldcrest and Firecrest can be found among the trees; there are Citril Finch near the refuge and often Rock Thrush a little further on. If you are lucky you may see Goshawk, Golden Eagle or Lammergeier flying overhead. There is an ill-defined narrow track leading upwards from the refuge to the ridge to the north. (Do not take the main footpath which runs along the valley and is marked by paint on the wall and rocks.) When you reach a fairly level, open area, turn right (east) and continue climbing up towards the pinewoods. Capercaillie can be found here with diligent searching. Look for droppings under their roosting trees. Sorteny is an excellent area for flowers and butterflies (see below).

La Rabassa
The third Andorran site is in the south of the country, on the Spanish border. From Sant Julia de Loria, the southernmost town, take the road that leads off from the centre of town towards Aubinya and Juberri. The road is now hard-surfaced for 18 km to the cross-country ski resort of la Rabassa. For Sub-alpine Warbler, stop at suitable habitat (bramble bushes, tall scrub) during the first few km. Look up for Short-toed and Golden Eagle. Park where the road ends, near the restaurant, and walk around the large, open picnic area to the south of the restaurant. Crossbill, Citril Finch, Crested Tit, Firecrest, Woodlark and Ring Ouzel can all be found here. This area is right on the Spanish frontier which is not marked and there are various tracks (much used by smugglers) that lead into Spain.

If you wish to see Alpine Accentor and Ptarmigan, as well as Marmots, then you must take the track through the pinewoods, which starts on the left-hand side, just before you reach the restaurant. This is driveable if you have a four-wheel drive vehicle with high clearance. Otherwise it is a long walk towards Pic Negre (2665 m). When you emerge from the trees, the track, which is very rough in places, leads over alpine meadows above the tree line. The same species as above can be seen here. At the top of Pic Negre, recognisable as it is composed of dark grey shale, there is a footpath marked with paint spots on the rocks, which leads along a ridge running south east, following the frontier, towards the next peak, Torre dels Soldats (2761 m.). The driveable track continues in the opposite direction from the footpath, towards a radio mast but if you are driving you should park at the top of Pic Negre. Between the two peaks, you should search the scree for Ptarmigan and Alpine Accentor, which are always here though difficult to see. Dotterel has bred here and can sometimes be found during migration periods. Return the way you have come. Take care as mountain weather is very changeable; you are very exposed if there is a thunderstorm and clouds can descend with little warning, reducing visibility to almost nil.

Other wildlife and flora
Marmots can be seen between la Rabassa and Pic Negre. Look for their holes among the rocks that dot the grassy slopes. Other mammals include Izard, Wild Boar, Moufflon (introduced), Fallow and Roe Deer. There are Genets in the woods around Sorteny but they are nocturnal and very difficult to see as during the day they sleep in the top of thick foliaged trees. Red Squirrels (a very dark, almost black form) are common.

Over 100 species of butterfly have been recorded in Andorra; they include Swallowtail and Scarce Swallowtail, Apollo, Clouded Apollo, Mountain Dappled White, Moroccan Orange Tip, Camberwell Beauty, Mountain Clouded Yellow, High Brown Fritillary, Mountain Fritillary, Great Banded Grayling, Spanish Brassy, Mountain, Gavarnie, Piedmont, Lefèbvre's, False Dewy, de Prunner's Ringlets, Large Blue, Eros Blue, Silvery Argus, Tufted Marbled and Dusky Grizzled Skipper. The Sorteny valley and the slopes above are good for butterflies, especially late in the summer. Many of the mountain species that occur above 1700 m. can be found on the grassy uplands above la Rabassa.

Both Sorteny and la Rabassa are exceptional sites for the botanist. In early spring, Sorteny is covered with sheets of white Pyrenean Buttercup *(Ranunculus pyrenaeus)* and Dog's Tooth Violet *(Erythronium dens-canis)*, a little later the yellow form of the Alpine Pasque Flower *(Pulsatilla alpina ss apiifolia)* appears, followed in June by the violet-blue Pyrenean Iris *(Iris latifolia)* and the Yellow Turk's-cap Lily *(Lilium pyrenaicum).* By July the slopes are bright pink when Rhododendron ferrugineum is in flower. The Pyrenean Gentian *(Gentiana pyrenaica)* grows among the Spring and Trumpet Gentians. Later in the summer there are Great Yellow and Spotted Gentians *(Gentiana lutea and G. punctata).* One of the commonest orchids is the early Elder-flowered Orchid *(Dactylorhiza sambucina)*, both yellow and purple forms.

La Rabassa is less immediately colourful but hidden among the scree slopes are the Parnassus-leaved Buttercup *(Ranunculus parnassifolius)*, the Spring Pasque Flower *(Pulsatilla vernalis),* Purple Saxifrage *(Saxifraga oppositifolia ss paradoxa)*, Moss Campion *(Silene acaulis)*, *Viola diversifolia* and many other eastern Pyrenean specialities. The Pyrenean Gentian grows in the high pastures as well as the Southern Gentian *(G. alpina).* The endemic Soft Snapdragon *(Antirrhinum molle)* grows on the old bridge in Santa Coloma.

<u>Accommodation and transport</u>
Andorra's main industry is tourism, so there are hotels at every price range in all the towns and villages and several campsites. They are only likely to be full at peak holiday periods. The coach company, Nadal, in Andorra la Vella, runs trips in amazing four-wheel drive buses right up to Pic Negre but they only stop here for a few minutes, not long enough to walk to Torre del Soldats. It will, however, give you a chance to see this high-mountain

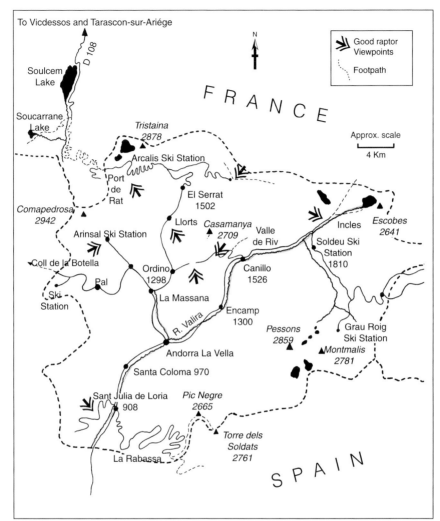

Site 18. Andorra and Vicdessos

area if you have no other way of getting there. Jeeps can sometimes be rented from Hertz and Avis in the capital.

Additional sites

These sites, although just outside the geographical limits of this guide, are within easy driving distances and worth visiting, or are ones that are less important but have at least one good species.

FRANCE

19a. Toulouse

Anyone arriving at the airport, or driving through Toulouse, might like to visit a small reserve that the local authority has made out of some disused gravel pits alongside the junction of the Rivers Ariège and Garonne. Its main attraction is the number of Night Heron that breed along the river and roost in the dead trees around the flooded pits but Hobby, Golden Oriole, Woodchat Shrike, Nightingale and Cetti's Warbler are among other species noted here. There is a colony of Pallid Swift in Toulouse and some can often be seen flying over the river with the many Common Swift.

To reach the reserve, take the A-64 motorway south out of the city. Branch onto the N-20 towards Auterive (signed Foix and Andorra) and in a very short distance, at the next roundabout, turn left towards Lacroix. This minor road runs back towards Toulouse. The reserve is on the left after approximately four km.

20a. Perpignan

Anyone flying into the airport here or spending time on the Mediterranean side of the Pyrenees might like to visit some of the sites in this area. A good wetland site is the Étang (or lagoon) of Canet or Saint-Nazaire, a large shallow lake of variable salinity on the coast just south of Perpignan. Take the D617 to Canet-en-Roussillon, then turn south towards Saint-Cyprien Plage. The D81 runs along the eastern shore of the lake. Stop wherever you have a good view of the lake and walk along any track that runs towards it. It is also possible to view the west side by going to St. Nazaire and taking the track that runs from the petrol station beyond the village towards the lake.

Flamingos can be seen on the lake most of the year. It is good for waders in spring and ducks in winter. The reedbeds hold much the same species as Aiguamolls. A pair of Purple Gallinules bred here in 1996.

North of Perpignan, the limestone plateau near the lighthouse at **Leucate** is a site for spring migration. Many raptors, especially Honey Buzzard and Short-toed Eagle, cross the coast here as well as storks, Bee-eater, Hoopoe, Black-eared Wheatear and many passerines. Other species that have been seen on the plateau include Great Spotted Cuckoo, Blue Rock Thrush, Crested Lark, Tawny Pipit, Ortolan Bunting and Orphean, Spectacled, Subalpine, Dartford and Sardinian Warblers. Be warned that like all migration sites you can hit lucky or spend an almost birdless day. It all depends on the weather.

South of Perpignan, right on the frontier, runs a range of wooded hills known as the **Albères**. From the coast road, le Perthus or Céret, several minor roads lead into them, often just winding up to viewpoints. These are worth exploring. Many of the species mentioned above will also be found here as well as woodland birds.

SPAIN

21a. Gallocanta

The shallow, reed-fringed lake of Gallocanta lies some 100 km south of Zaragoza at an altitude of 1000m. surrounded by farmland and low hills. It is considered to be the largest natural lake in Spain but, since it is fed by rainwater, its size and depth vary dramatically. It is largely saline though some fresh water springs feed it.

It is a vital stopping place for the majority of Europe's cranes after they have crossed the Pyrenees on their autumn migration to Extremadura and North Africa. In some years up to 50,000 can be seen around the lake in early December. Although a few thousand may winter there, very cold weather will drive the majority further south, to return at the beginning of February.

Gallocanta, however, has more to offer the visiting birdwatcher than just cranes, however spectacular their numbers. Thousands of waterfowl winter there, including important numbers of Red-crested Pochard. Steppe birds such as Little Bustard, Stone Curlew and Black-bellied Sandgrouse can be found in the scrub-covered hills and neglected fields to the south-east. The latter can be seen when they come to drink from the lake at dusk – just when the cranes are returning. Dupont's Lark also breed nearby but an easier site to see them is at Belchite, described below. The best time to visit is between November and March but be warned – it can be bitterly cold.

To reach Gallocanta take the N-330 from Zaragoza to Daroca (84 km), then the C-211 for 18.7 km to the Gallocanta junction and finally the Z-4241 leads to the small village of Gallocanta situated on the northeast shore of the lake (3.6 km).

Gallocanta is part of a Hunting Reserve (Refugio Nacional de Caza) and in theory it is necessary to obtain permission and contact a warden if you want to walk right down to the lakeshore and take photographs. In practice, however, the Conservation Office in Zaragoza seldom replies to requests and perfectly good views of the lake can be had from the lakeside square in the village of Gallocanta or by taking the often muddy tracks that run from the village to a restored hermitage and two "observatories" on low hills that give good views over the lake and surrounding countryside and are the best place to watch the evening flight of cranes returning to roost beside the lake. If there is a warden here, a useful map of the reserve can be obtained from him and he will also show you the best observation points.

A minor road runs from Gallocanta village around the lake, passing through four other tiny hamlets. Footpaths from all these villages lead to the lakeside and other marked "observatories" on the reserve map. Some of these are towers and others are rather dilapidated hides; whether they are for hunters or birdwatchers is not clear but several of them afford good views of the lake and the reedbeds. The cranes can often be seen well from the south-eastern shores of the lake and this is also the most interesting area for other birds in spring.

Accommodation

There is a small Albergue Rural (Country Inn) in Gallocanta village, catering especially for birdwatchers. Phone (976) 803137 or fax (976) 803090. Daroca, 25 km away is the nearest town and has a 2-star hotel and a hostel, both simple but adequate. The hotel only offers bed-and-breakfast in the winter but there are several small bars serving food in the town. Slightly further away, the beautiful old Monastery of Piedra, now converted into a fairly expensive hotel, lies 49 km to the west of Gallocanta and is surrounded by a spectacular park and waterfalls. The road to it leads through several good birding areas and anyone wishing to treat themselves to a luxurious short winter break could not do better. Dipper, Crossbill, Blue Rock Thrush, Crag Martin and Chough are some of the birds to be found in the grounds.

If you wish to write for a permit, the address is: Servicio Provincial de Agricultura, Ganaderia y Monts, Sección de Conservación del Medio Natural, c/ Vazquez de Mella, 10; 50009 Zaragoza. The Service also runs the Lomazas Steppe Reserve, near Belchite but the same birds can probably be seen as well, if not better, from El Planeron Reserve (see below) without the need to obtain visiting permission in advance.

22a. Belchite

The Spanish Ornithological Society (SEO) owns and runs the steppe reserve of El Planeron, close to the village of Belchite. It is probably the best place in Spain to see Dupont's lark, with a high breeding density of around 400 pairs in a comparatively small area.

The reserve lies on the road between Belchite and Quinto and is clearly marked on the left-hand side of the road if coming from Belchite. If coming from Quinto, the sign is more difficult to see but there is now an observation area overlooking the reserve some way before the turning. If, coming from this direction, you reach the village of Codos, you have gone too far! If you are travelling on the Zaragoza-Barcelona motorway, turn off at exit 3 (Bujaraloz). Here you should turn south towards the old road (N-2). When you reach the village of Bujaraloz, which is 4 km from the motorway, turn west onto the N-2. The turning to Gelsa and Quinto is 18 km towards Zaragoza. It is another 18 km through the village of Gelsa, crossing the River Ebro, to Quinto where you join the N-232. The turning to Belchite is rather badly signed at the end the village. Turn left and follow this minor road to the reserve which from this direction will be on your right.

Dupont's Lark is resident but can be seen most easily in early spring when it is singing. After this you have to work harder! Drive down the track into the reserve and stop by the first stretch of natural vegetation – clumps of esparto grass. This is its favoured habitat. Listen out for its distinctive song and try and find it in the sky. This can be difficult as it is often very high and plummets to earth very quickly. Stand on the road and keep looking for it running through the grass. Lesser Short-toed Lark, also resident, are very common in this habitat too as well as in the areas with low scrub; in summer, they are joined by Short-toed Lark. Black-eared Wheatear and Spectacled Warbler are other summer visitors. There is another area of esparto grass at the very end of the reserve, where the track peters out; try here too. While you are searching for the larks, keep a lookout for Sandgrouse; both Black-bellied and Pin-tailed fly over to drink at the nearby reservoir in the morning. Hen Harriers hunt over the plains in winter and Montagu's in summer.

There is a farm track on the opposite side of the road to the reserve which can be worth driving along. Sandgrouse can sometimes be seen if you stop on a small rise and search the steppe area below.

El Planeron has no information centre on the reserve but SEO have a small office in Belchite, signed from the centre of the village, though it may only be open at weekends. The ruins of old Belchite, destroyed in the Civil War and left as a memorial, deserve a short visit. Black Wheatear and Blue Rock Thrush can be seen around the ruined churches.

23a. Los Monegros

The Monegros is an area of steppe, cultivated fields and low, scrubby hillsides in the driest part of the Ebro basin. Shallow saline lagoons, called "saladas" dot the plain. Steppe birds can be seen in almost any part but the area is vast; one can drive around all day and see very little. However, the following two small sections are usually very productive.

Purburell area

From Belchite take the C-221 east to Azaila. The road runs through a steppe area good for Calandra Lark and where in September and October Dotterel can be found. After Azaila turn left but continue on the C-221 to Escatron. From here cross the River Ebro and follow the signs to the village of Sastago. Take the road leading to Alborge but before crossing the Ebro again, check the rocky cliffs for Black Wheatear.

In Alborge take the road to Bujaraloz. It climbs out of the river valley onto flat plains. Where the road bends right, turn left onto a wide, unsurfaced track. It is not signed but obviously much used. It leads through an area of steppe and agricultural land with several lagoons. Drive slowly along the track looking out for Little Bustard, both Sandgrouse, Stone Curlew, Tawny Pipit and Black-eared Wheatear. Early morning and dusk are the best times. During migration and in winter, there may be waders and ducks on the lagoons. There is a tiny relict population of Great Bustard in Aragon. This is one area where they have been seen but they are notoriously difficult to find. The track eventually rejoins the Bujaraloz road.

Cadnasnos – Ballobar – Alcolea triangle

About 18 km to the east of Bujaraloz lies the village of Candasnos, which is the starting point for this itinerary to the north-eastern part of the Monegros. Take the minor road north to Ontinena and Alcolea de Cinca. Approximately 5 km from the village (just before the 47 km marker sign) there is a small hill on the left. Black Wheatear and Spectacled and Dartford Warblers breed here. Search the rocky cliffs for the Wheatear and look among the lowest, scattered bushes for the warblers. 600m further on a track on the right leads to a sheep watering hole. Spend some time near the drinking pool and scan the nearby fields. Pin-tailed Sandgrouse sometimes come to drink here early in the morning. Great Spotted Cuckoo, Stone Curlew, Hoopoe, Lesser Short-toed Lark, Tawny Pipit are among other birds that have been seen here regularly. Dupont's Lark can be found on the higher ground beyond the watering hole.

Black Wheatear

About 9 km from Candasnos a very minor road leads to Ballobar. Spectacled Warbler and Great Spotted Cuckoo have been seen along it. Turn right onto it and 6 km from the junction there is a crossroads. Take the unpaved track to the left that runs parallel to a high tension cable over saline steppes that are full of larks, including Dupont's. In some years, when there has been heavy winter rain, a large, shallow lake forms below the pylons. When this happens it attracts large flocks of migrating ducks and waders, including good numbers of Garganey. Near the end of the saltings there is a crossroads; on the left, near a small stone building, is another watering hole where Black-bellied Sandgrouse come to drink, slightly later in the morning than Pin-tailed. The left-hand track past the watering hole leads up to a flat-topped plateau where Sandgrouse can also be found as well as Thekla Lark which prefer stony hillsides, helping to distinguish them from Crested Lark, which are nearly always on the flat plain.

Having explored the higher areas, return to the waterhole and follow the original track which now curves towards the north-west, away from the power lines, until you regain the Candasnos-Ontinena road, or return the way you came to the Ballobar junction and turn right for Ontinena. Go through the village, cross the river, where you can stop to look for warblers and Penduline Tits, and continue to a road junction. Turn left and then 600m further on, right towards Alcolea de Cinca, 8 km away. This is the end of the steppe area and you can either retrace your route or continue on the west bank of the River Cinca to Fraga. Drive through the village, taking care not to miss the church which has about twelve pairs of White Storks nesting on it. Keep on in the direction of Chalamera and you will pass some tall cliffs on the right. Search them for Black Wheatear, Blue Rock Thrush, Rock Sparrow. It is also a good area for raptors; besides the cliffs, check the rubbish dump between Alcolea and Chalamera. Immediately after this village you will meet the Sarinena-Fraga road, C-1310; turn left towards Fraga. Several of the villages along this road also have storks' nests on the churches, while Night Heron, Penduline Tit and Golden Oriole breed beside the river (check the areas where it runs nearest to the road). At Ballobar, you can take the road that leads through the town up onto the high plains behind the church for another chance to find Dupont's Lark or continue into Fraga and turn right onto the NII back to the starting point at Candasnos. A few Lesser Kestrel have recently begun to recolonise northern Spain and can sometimes be seen along this stretch of road.

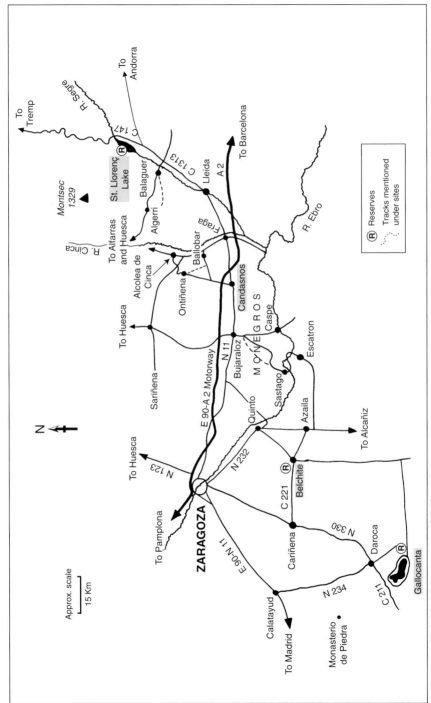

Gallocanta, Belchite, Monegros and Balaguer areas.

There is quite a large hotel in Fraga and a very basic hostal in Belchite (though the food is fine) but the most central place to stay for both Monegros itineraries and Belchite and one that can be recommended is La Cruzanzana, on the N 11 just east of Candasnos.

24a. Huesca

Just south of Huesca, to the west of the road leading to Sariñena, lies an interesting range of rocky hills known as the Serreta de Tramaced. This is a good area for Black Wheatear, Rock Dove, Thekla Lark, Dartford and Sardinian Warblers and in summer, Black-eared Wheatear and Bee-eater. Scan the skies for raptors which in summer include Short-toed Eagle and Egyptian Vulture.

At Sesa, 26 km from Huesca, turn right towards the small village of Tramaced. Just before the village you will see an area of much eroded, rocky hills on the left. Scan and where possible walk towards these. When you reach a crossroads, turn left (south) where there are further, similar hills. When you reach the village of Fraella, turn back towards Tramaced but this time carry straight on. After a couple of kilometres you will see the village of Piracés on your right, at the foot of more low hills. Take the road towards the village that skirts it and then climbs up to overlook a valley with a radio mast on the hills in the background. The rocks beside the road are an excellent site for Black Wheatear. You should also search the valley below. This road eventually takes you back to the main Huesca-Sariñena road.

If you are continuing south to Sariñena, the large reed-fringed lake here can be worth birding. It is clearly signed from the village and a driveable track runs down to the edge. However views over the water are difficult because of the high reeds. Summer visitors include Little Bittern and Purple Heron; there are waders during migration periods and duck in winter.

25a. Barcelona

Many birders who start their holidays here are unaware that there is an excellent birding site right beside the airport which was built on part of the delta of the River Llobregat. Much of the remainder is now built over but just south of the airport a stretch of river and marsh has been saved and turned into a small reserve, which is currently being extended and improved. The Llobregat area seems to turn up more rarities, especially during migration periods, than many better-known sites in Spain but this may be because it is more watched.

To reach the Remolar-Filipines Reserve, continue on the airport road – the dual

Mixed group of Waders

carriageway C-246 – in the direction of Castelldefels for approximately 3 km. Turn left by the 11km post, signed "Camping Toro Bravo". This entails turning across the on-coming traffic but is permitted. If there is a lot of traffic or you miss the turning, go on for about 3 km to where there is another place to make a U-turn. It is not far, so it would be feasible to take an airport taxi if you do not have a hire car.

Start birding as soon as you turn off the main road. The small San Climent river is reed fringed and has plenty of duck, especially during migration periods and in winter, when they can include Red-crested Pochard and sometimes Ferruginous, as well as egrets and water-birds. Marsh Harriers and other raptors fly above the marsh on the far bank. Stop the car wherever there is a lay-by. A little further on you will see an observation tower on the right hand side of the road. This is a good place from which to scan the marsh. On the left-hand side there is a hide but it is just as easy to search the river, which widens at this point, from the bank. Access to the marsh on the far bank is proposed. Little Bittern breed in the reeds and a few Penduline Tits in trees nearby, though there are more in winter and on migration. Serins are common, as are Cetti's and Fan-tailed Warblers, which can be seen and heard all year. Reed and Great Reed Warblers are common in summer.

The road stops here, outside the campsite but it is possible to walk to the beach, where there is another observation tower. The beach is good for a sea-watch and for waders during migration

It is also possible to get down to the beach (platja) from north of the airport, opposite the Pryca supermarket but it means trying to find your way through industrial estates towards the El Prat golf course.

In the centre of Barcelona, any of the numerous city parks can provide quite interesting bird watching, especially the Parc de la Ciutadella where the Zoo is. Both Monk and Rose-ringed Parakeets have quite large feral breeding populations. The nests of the former can be found in palm trees all over the city.

Special Species (numbers in brackets refer to sites in the main text)

Balearic Shearwater *Puffinus maurentanicus* Now split from both Yelkouan and Manx Shearwaters. Breeds around the Balearic Islands, so a few can sometimes be seen out at sea in summer from Cap de Creus. In winter, quite large flocks are often close inshore around the Bay of Roses. (17).

Lammergeier *Gypaetus barbatus* Numbers have been increasing slowly but steadily over the past decade, largely due to conservation programmes in both France and Spain that combine protection of nesting sites with "vulture restaurants"; the latter in particular helping young birds survive their first few winters. On the Spanish side of the Pyrenees, where numbers have always been greater, there are now 66 occupied territories, an increase of 24 in 10 years; a total of some 150 individuals spread the length of the range, except for the extreme west and east. There are 11 occupied territories in France.

The easiest place to see this species is probably around Ordesa National Park. They frequently fly over the car park at the main, west entrance (11). They can also be seen in the east of the Park, where there is a feeding station. Other good areas are all the sites around Jaca (13), the Sierras de Leyre (10), Boumort and Collegats Gorge in the Tremp area (15) and on the French side, Vallee d'Ossau, Gavarnie (4) and Vicdessos (5).

Bonelli's Eagle *Hieraetus fasciatus* Pairs breed around Jaca (11), St. Llorenç lake (15) and near Prats-de-Mollo (7). This species breeds on cliffs in the warmer, pre-Pyrenean ranges, often above woods and with water in the vicinity. The best months to see them are from mid-June (when the young are on the wing) to the end of the year, when they start displaying. When they are breeding (mid-February to end of May) they are more difficult. For some reason, they often seem to fly at mid-day.

Ptarmigan *Lagopus mutus* The remnant Pyrenean population keeps to the highest mountain tops and a considerable amount of walking is always necessary to see this species. Best places are the scree slopes above Nuria (16), the flat top leading to Torre del Soldat in Andorra (18) and the Vicdessos scree slopes (5). By the time they are in their winter plumage, end-November and early December, these areas can be dangerous.

Capercaillie *Tetrao urogallus* Another remnant population, stranded in the Pyrenees since the ending of the last ice-age. This species has suffered much disturbance recently through forestry and the spread of off-piste skiing and snowmobiles and is consequently in decline. Nowadays birds can only be found in the central 350 km of the Pyrenees, between 400 and 2000 m. They seem to prefer the higher mountain pine *(Pinus uncinata)* forests. They can be seen in the woods around Néouvielle (4), Andorra (18) and many of the forests on the French side as well as on the north slopes of the Cadi chain, between Andorra and Eyne. However, they are very difficult to see except by luck or if you should happen to disturb a roosting bird while walking through the forests. In spring, when they lek, sightings are easier but most leks are protected by wardens who will certainly turn you away.

Purple Gallinule *Porphyrio porphyrio* This species was reintroduced from the Coto Donaña into the Natural Park of Aiguamolls d'Empordà (17) in 1989 and 1991. The programme has been extremely successful and now it is now almost easier to see them here than in Andalucia, including plenty of un-ringed birds. The hides around the Cortalet scrape, right outside the Information Centre and the hide at Vilahut are two places that practically guarantee good views, especially at dawn. In 1996, two pairs bred in the Etang de Canet-St. Nazaire, near Perpignan; a "first" for France.

Stone-curlew *Burhinus oedicnemus* This bird of dry steppe-land can be found on the meadows around Cortalet at Aiguamolls (17), on the Balaguer plains (15) and near the additional sites of Belchite and Gallocanta. Listen for its curlew-like call at dawn and dusk.

Little Bustard *Tetrax tetrax* Can be found on the dry plains around Balaguer (15) or on the additional sites of Belchite and the Monegros. A tiny remnant population of Great Bustards are also in the latter area but extreme luck will be needed to see them.

Audouin's Gull *(Larus audouinii)* This species has been one of Spain's breeding successes. Only 36 pairs bred in the Ebro Delta in 1981; now there are over 7000 pairs. Birds can be seen flying past the beach at Aiguamolls (17) in spring and summer.

Pin-tailed and Black-bellied Sandgrouse *Pterocles alchata and P. orientalis* These are only found in the same areas as Little Bustard.

Great Spotted Cuckoo *Clamator glandarius* This summer visitor arrives at the end of February and is often gone by June. Most likely to be seen March-April when its harsh calls give away its presence. Young birds are flying by early May. It parasitises magpies, so look out when you see a pair getting very excited. It favours the same habitats as Stone Curlew – Aiguamolls (17), Balaguer (15) and the Monegros.

Scops Owl *Otus scops* An urban little owl, most likely to be seen in town parks and around villages with tall trees. Its "sonar blip" call, given as soon as it is dark, is the best way of find it and Jaca town park probably the easiest place (11).

Tengmalm's Owl *Aegolius funereus* A small remnant population was discovered in the Pyrenees as recently as the 1960's when a pair was found in a nest-box. They prefer north-facing slopes above 2000 m. with large, old conifers and normally take over a Black Woodpecker's hole as a nest site. They call early in the year when these areas are inaccessible to walkers, breed irregularly and move around frequently. Consequently they are very difficult to find. Any tree with a hole high up in the right habitat is worth tapping with a stick, to see if a head peers out!

Eagle Owl *Bubo bubo* This can be a very difficult bird to see. They call mainly very early in the year, at dusk, and are relatively quiet when breeding and feeding young. They prefer inaccessible and remote cliff faces, not necessarily very high, for breeding and though a pair stays in the same territory for many years, they move the nest site frequently. The best hope of seeing one is to be at one of the smaller sites, Foz de Binies (11), Mont-rebei and especially St. Llorenç (15) just before it is dark, scanning the cliffs and listening.

Red-necked Nightjar *Caprimulgus ruficollis* This species can only be found in Spain, on dry sunny slopes, sparse dry woodland and cultivated areas below the altitude of 600 m. Listen for its repeated "kutook" call at dusk in the right habitat around Balaguer (15) and the Monegros (additional sites). It arrives in early May and leaves in September. The **European Nightjar** prefers shady areas and hillsides, especially bracken covered ones, at altitudes up to at least 1200 m.

Alpine Swift *Apus melba* This species arrives in the Pyrenees in the latter part of March and leaves in September-October. It breeds on high cliff faces and can be seen over Boumort (15), Riglos (11), Ordesa (13) and Gavarnie (4).

Pallid Swift *Apus pallidus* Arrives earlier and leaves later than Common Swift. It can still be seen until October-November. Usually found near the Mediterranean - see Cap de Creus (17) but a few pairs can sometimes be seen around Jaca and Riglos (11) and in Toulouse. (19a).

Bee-eater *Merops apiaster* This typically Mediterranean species is more likely to be seen on the south and east sides of the chain, though it may be found anywhere during migration. It is present from end-April to September when it breeds colonially in holes in soft banks. Jaca (11), the Tremp area (15) and Aiguamolls (17) are breeding areas and Eyne (6) is a good spot for migrating birds.

Roller *Coracias garrulus* A scarce bird in this region and possibly in decline. It can be found in the dry, open areas favoured by Little Bustard and Stone Curlew. The best sites are Aiguamolls (17) where it is rare and the Balaguer plains (15), as well as the appropriate additional sites. Their habit of perching on electricity wires makes them easy to spot.

Black Woodpecker *Dryocopus martius* This large woodpecker is relatively common in mixed and coniferous woodland the length of the chain. Pairs are resident but young birds can fly considerable distances to find their own territories during their first autumn. It only nests in large trees and its nesting hole, often 5 metres or more from the ground, is large and distinctively pear-shaped. Listen out for its very loud drumming and take note of dead trees where they have been feeding; look for large areas of stripped-off bark and deep holes.

White-backed Woodpecker *Dendrocopus leucotos* Although it is worth searching any suitable habitat (old beech-fir woods with plenty of decaying trees) in the centre-west of the chain for the rarest of the Pyrenean woodpeckers, the site in the Forest of Issaux (3) is the best place where there is a good change of seeing them.

Thekla Lark *Galerida theklae* A bird of stony Mediterranean hillsides and plateaux, only found on the south-east side of the Pyrenean chain, from Jaca (11) to the Mediterranean coast at Cap de Creus (17). **Crested Lark** is widespread and essentially a lowland bird.

Dupont's Lark *Chersophilus duponti* This lark needs vast, dry plains, preferring those parts covered with esparto grass. It cannot be seen nearer to the Pyrenees than Belchite Reserve (see additional sites), though there are a few in the Monegros area. Early spring is the easiest time to locate it, when it is in song-flight at dawn. Otherwise listen for its nasal "wolf whistle" uttered as it briefly perches on top of a low plant or stone. **Short-toed and Lesser Short-toed Larks** will be found in the same areas.

Calandra Lark *Melanocorypha calandra* This large, chunky lark is usually seen flying over lowland meadows and arable land when the white trailing edge of its wings is distinctive. It is not found on the Atlantic side of the Pyrenees nor in higher, rocky areas.

Crag Martin *Ptyonoprogne rupestris* is a very common resident, although it is a partial, altitudinal migrant and some birds move down from the higher breeding grounds in late October-November to return in February, if the weather is mild. It can be seen around gorges, cliff faces and the higher villages, often with House Martins.

Alpine Accentor *Prunella collaris* This resident species is an altitudinal migrant; breeding in rocky scree slopes above 2000 m but comes down to ski stations and lower mountain areas in winter. Andorra (18) and Nuria (16) are two places where they can be seen all year round. There are usually easy to see in the villages of Riglos and Agüero (15) in winter, as well as round the frontier passes.

Black Wheatear *Oenanthe leucura* This resident species is always found on the south side of the Pyrenees, around warm, dry rocky areas with little vegetation below 1000m. It is a typically Mediterranean species and numbers in the Pyrenees have been decreasing. It is quite easy to see throughout the year at Riglos (11), Cap de Creus (17) and on the cliffs outside Cinca (23a). The only site in France is on the rocky slopes around the Tour Medeloc near Banyuls-sur-Mer, just north of the Spanish frontier.

Rock Thrush *Monticola saxatilis* A summer visitor to the Pyrenees. It can be found in both high mountain areas and the lower foothills between April and September. It often sings from a prominent rock or telephone wires. The Portalet pass (12) is one of the most regular sites; others include Arcalis in Andorra (18), Vicdessos (5), the Perves pass (14) or at several spots along the N-260 between Adrall and Sort. The first is at the turning to Guils del Canto, 19.2 km from the Adrall junction. Turn off the main road just past the car park and check the rocky cliff face below. The second site is around the Bar del Canto, just after the pass, opposite the little hamlet of El Rubio.

Blue Rock Thrush *Monticola solitarius* Inland, this resident species likes much the same dry and rocky habitat as Black Wheatear. The two can be seen together at Riglos (11). It can also be found near St. Llorenc Lake (15), in the Foz de Binies (11), near Collegats gorge (15) and in France near the village of Prats-de Mollo (7). It also breeds on sea cliffs near Urdaibai (8) and Cap de Creus (17). Search the top of a cliff face or the highest rocks where the male often perches. It has a distinctive long-billed silhouette even when the blue coloration is not obvious (much longer beak than a Blackbird's, for example, whose song is somewhat similar).

Spectacled Warbler *Sylvia conspicillata* This rare and local warbler breeds in dry places with low and sparse vegetation, sometimes alongside Dartford Warbler. In the area covered by this guide, it is most likely to be found in Spain on the Cap de Creus (17), Riglos (11) and near Candasnos in the Monegros (23a) where they can be seen from the end of March until mid-October. Its rufous wings and white throat immediately distinguish it (it looks very much like a small Whitethroat).

Subalpine Warbler *Sylvia cantillans* This migrant breeder reaches the Pyrenees at the end of March and stays until October. It breeds in taller scrub and undergrowth, seeming to have a preference for brambles and drier areas, at low as well as higher altitudes up to about 1200 m. In the right habitat it can be seen at almost all the sites described, except high mountain and wetland ones. It is, however, very skulking and difficult to see except when the males are singing from the tops of bushes early in the season.

Bonelli's Warbler *Phylloscopus bonelli* One of the commonest warblers in woodland, found in deciduous and mixed woods in the foothills and in pinewoods up to almost 2000 m. It seems to prefer sunny slopes and the edges or clearings of woods but can also be found in plantations. It is most easily located by its two-syllable "hoo-eet" call and short single-note trill. In lower areas its range overlaps with that of Chiffchaff but replaces it at higher altitudes. It arrives in the Pyrenees at the end of March and leaves during August.

Short-toed Treecreeper *(Certhia brachydactyla)* Both species of Treecreepers can be found in the Pyrenees. Generally, Short-toed Treecreeper is found in deciduous and mixed woodland, as well as around parks and gardens, up to an altitude of about 1,600 metres, while Eurasian Treecreeper *(Certhia familiaris)* prefers the higher, coniferous forests. But there is an overlap where both occur as the latter species can be found between 900 and 2000 metres. Song is the easiest way to distinguish between them as their calls can sound similar.

Wallcreeper *Tichodroma muraria* One of the "most wanted" Pyrenean birds. It tends to breed at very high altitudes but also favours narrow, shady gorges close to fast flowing water or a waterfall much lower down. Two such sites are given for Hecho valley (11) and

Mont-rebei gorge (15). In winter birds move to lower altitudes and at this season it is often easier to see them when they can be found in the foothills on almost any rocky cliff face or even sea cliffs or tall stone buildings. Cap de Creus (17), Mont-rebei, Collegats, St. Llorenc (15) and on the French side, the Lourdios gorge and the main road between Urdos and the Somport (3) are some of the areas where they have been seen in this season. Additional sites are around the gorge and town of Alquezar, between Barbastro and Ainsa or on the rocks walls of the tunnelled gorge on the HU 904, between Barbastro and Graus, south of Ainsa (13). Listen for their high, thin whistle and watch rock faces for a flash of crimson when they flick their wings.

Spotless Starling *Sturnus unicolor* Considered a southern Spanish bird until quite recently, this species continues to extend its range northwards and a few birds now breed on the north side of the Pyrenees in France. Around Jaca (11) and Tremp (15) they can be found side by side with Common Starlings in many of the villages. Outside the breeding season they can be difficult to tell apart.

Snow Finch *Montifringilla nivalis* This large finch only breeds on the highest rocky slopes above 2,200 m. and is very difficult to find at this season. It descends lower in winter when small flocks can often be seen around ski resorts, especially those near the Somport pass (3) or at Nuria (16), often in the company of Alpine Accentors.

Rock Sparrow *Petronia petronia* Undoubtedly the best place to see this species is on the Citadel in Jaca (1) where there are many breeding pairs. Otherwise single pairs may be found on rocky cliffs, or around small villages in the warmer areas. Its distribution is very local.

Citril Finch *Serinus citrinella* This small mountain finch breeds on the edge of the tree line in subalpine areas above 1500 m. In autumn young birds may be found higher and in winter it flocks with other finches, especially Serins and Siskins, at lower altitudes. They are quite easy to see at the top of the Hecho valley (15), in Andorra (18), Aiguestortes (14) and in many parts of the French National Park (4)

Bibliography and recommended books

Site Guides
Where to Watch Birds in Catalonia. J. de Hoyo et al. Lynx.
Where to Watch Birds in Spain. SEO. Lynx.
Where to Watch Birds in France. LFPO. Christopher Helm.
(All three books include more sites in the Pyrenees as well as outside the area covered by this guide. The first is the most detailed and highly recommended for anyone visiting this area.)

General
Pyrenees. The rough guide series.
Pyrenees. Landscapes countryside guides.
Walking the Pyrenees. Footpaths of Europe series. Robertson McCarta (Good maps but only covers French side).
Walks and Climbs in the Pyrenees. Reynolds Cicerone (Useful if wanting to walk in higher areas than this book covers).

Birds
The Birds of Britain and Europe. New Edition. Heinzel, Fitter and Parslow. Harper Collins
Birds of Europe. Jonsson. Helm.
The Birds of Prey of Britain and Europe. Gensbol. Collins
Flowers
Mediterranean Wild Flowers. Blamey/Grey-Wilson. Harper Collins.

Alpine Flowers of Britain and Europe. New Edition. Blamey/Grey-Wilson. Harper Collins
Wild Flowers of Britain and Northern Europe. Fitter/Blamey. Harper Collins
Orchids of Britain and Europe. Buttler. Crowood

Animals
Mammals of Britain and Europe. Macdonald/Barrett. Harper Collins
Reptiles and Amphibians of Britain and Europe. Arnold/Burton. Collins

Insects
Butterflies. Whalley. Mitchell Beazley.
Butterflies and Day-flying Moths New Generation Guide. Chinery. Collins

Bibliography
Atlas dels Amfibis I Reftils de Catalunya i Andorra. Llorente et al. El Brau.
Els Grans Mamifers de Catalunya i Andorra. Ruiz-Olmo/Aguilar. Lynx.
Els Ocells del Delta del Llobregat. Guitierrez et al. Lynx.
Els Ocells del P.N. dels Aiguamolls de l'Empordà. Sargatal/Hoyo. Lynx.
La Grande Flore illustrée des Pyrénées. Saule. Red. Milan.
Grands Rapaces et Corvids dels Montagnes d'Europe. Dendaletche Ed. Acta Biologica Montana.
Oiseaux des Pyrénées 2. Dendaletche. ABM.
Col-loqui d'Ornitologia Pirinenca 1995. AND.

Birds

The following check list follows the sequence and nomenclature of the recently published *List of Birds of the Western Palearctic* (British Birds Ltd 1997), which follows those adopted for the new Concise Edition of *Birds of the Western Palearctic*. Extreme rarities and very occasional visitors have not been included.

Key to Symbols:

RB = Resident Breeder   MB = Migrant Breeder   OB = Occasional Breeder

PM = Passage Migrant   WV = Winter Visitor   AV = Accidental Visitor

English Name	Scientific Name	Status
Red-throated Diver	*Gavia stellata*	WV
Black-throated Diver	*Gavia arctaica*	WV
Great Northern Diver	*Gavia immer*	WV
Little Grebe	*Tachybapus ruficollis*	RB
Great Crested Grebe	*Podiceps cristatus*	RB
Black-necked Grebe	*Podiceps nigricollis*	RB
Cory's Shearwater	*Calonectris diomedea*	AV, WV
Balearic Shearwater	*Puffinus mauretanicus*	WV
European Storm-petrel	*Hydrobates pelagicus*	AV
Northern Gannet	*Morus bassana*	WV
Great Cormorant	*Phalacrocorax carbo*	WV
Shag	*Phalacrocorax aristotelis*	RB
Great Bittern	*Botaurus stellaris*	RB
Little Bittern	*Ixobrychus minutus*	MB
Night Heron	*Nycticorax nycticorax*	MB
Squacco Heron	*Ardeola ralloides*	OB, PM
Cattle Egret	*Bubulcus ibis*	RB
Little Egret	*Egretta garzetta*	RB
Grey Heron	*Ardea cinerea*	RB, WV
Purple Heron	*Ardea purpurea*	MB
Black Stork	*Ciconia nigra*	PM
White Stork	*Ciconia ciconia*	RB, PM
Glossy Ibis	*Plegadis falcinellus*	AV
Eurasian Spoonbill	*Platalea leucorodia*	AV
Greater Flamingo	*Phoenicopterus ruber*	AV
Mute Swan	*Cygnus olor*	RB
Greylag Goose	*Anser anser*	AV
Common Shelduck	*Tadorna tadorna*	RB
Eurasian Wigeon	*Anas penelope*	WV
Gadwall	*Anas strepera*	RB
Common Teal	*Anas crecca*	RB
Mallard	*Anas platyrhynchos*	RB
Pintail	*Anas acuta*	WV
Gargany (few breed in Emporda)	*Anas quequedula*	PM, MB
Northern Shoveler	*Anas clypeata*	WV
Red-crested Pochard	*Netta rufina*	RB, WV
Common Pochard	*Netta ferina*	WV
Ferruginous Duck	*Aythya nyroca*	AV
Tufted Duck	*Aythya fuligula*	WV
Greater Scaup	*Aythya marila*	AV, WV
Common Eider	*Somateria mollissima*	AV, WV
Common Scoter	*Melanitta nigra*	AV, WV
Velvet Scoter	*Melanitta fusca*	AV, WV
European Honey-buzzard	*Pernis apivorus*	PM, MB
Black-shouldered Kite	*Elanus caeruleus*	AV
Black Kite	*Milvus migrans*	PM, MB
Red Kite	*Milvus milvus*	PM, MB, WV
Lammergeier	*Gypaetus barbatus*	RB
Egyptian Vulture	*Neophran percnopterus*	MB
Griffon Vulture	*Gyps fulvus*	RB
Short-toed Eagle	*Circaetus gallicus*	MB, PM
Marsh Harrier	*Circus aeruginosus*	RB, WV, PM

English Name	Scientific Name	Status
Hen Harrier	*Circus cyaneus*	WV, RB, PM
Montagu's Harrier	*Circus pyrargus*	PM, MB
Northern Goshawk	*Accipiter gentilis*	RB
Eurasian Sparrowhawk	*Accipiter nisus*	RB
Common Buzzard	*Buteo buteo*	RB, PM
Golden Eagle	*Aguila chrysaetos*	RB
Booted Eagle	*Hieraaetus pennatus*	MB, PM
Bonelli's Eagle	*Hieraaetus fasciatus*	RB
Osprey	*Pandion haliaetus*	PM
Lesser Kestrel	*Falco naumanni*	MB (few)
Common Kestrel	*Falco tinnunculus*	RB
Red-footed Falcon	*Falco vespertinus*	AV, PM
Merlin	*Falco columbarius*	WV
Hobby	*Falco subbuteo*	MB, PM
Eleanora's Falcon	*Falco eleonorae*	AV
Peregrine Falcon	*Falco peregrinus*	RB
Ptarmigan	*Lagopus mutus*	RB
Capercaillie	*Tetrao urogallus*	RB
Red-legged Partridge	*Alectoris rufa*	RB
Grey Partridge	*Perdix perdix*	RB
Common Quail	*Cortunix cortunix*	MB
Water Rail	*Rallus aquaticus*	RB
Spotted Crake	*Porzana porzana*	PM, WV
Little Crake	*Porzana parva*	AV
Baillon's Crake	*Porzana pusilla*	AV
Corn Crake	*Crex crex*	PM, MB (few)
Moorhen	*Gallinula chloropus*	RB
Purple Swamp-hen (Gallinule)	*Porphyrio porphyrio*	RB
Common Coot	*Fulica atra*	RB
Common Crane	*Grus grus*	PM
Little Bustard	*Tetrax tetrax*	RB
Great Bustard	*Otis tarda*	RB
Oystercatcher	*Haematopus ostralegus*	RB
Black-winged Stilt	*Himantopus himantopus*	MB
Avocet	*Recurvirostra avosetta*	PM
Stone-curlew	*Burhinus oedicnemus*	RB
Collared Pratincole	*Glareola pratincola*	PM
Little Ringed Plover	*Charadrius dubius*	RB
Great Ringed Plover	*Charadrius hiaticula*	PM, WV
Kentish Plover	*Charadrius alexandrinus*	RB
Dotterel	*Charadrius morinellus*	MB,(few) PM
European Golden Plover	*Pluvialis apricaria*	WV
Grey Plover	*Pluvialis squatarola*	WV
Northern Lapwing	*Vanellus vanellus*	WV
Red Knot	*Calidris canutus*	PM
Sanderling	*Calidris alba*	PM
Little Stint	*Calidris minuta*	WV
Temminck's Stint	*Calidris temminckii*	AV
Pectoral Sandpiper	*Calidris melanotos*	AV
Curlew Sandpiper	*Calidris ferruginea*	PM
Dunlin	*Calidris alpina*	WV
Ruff	*Philomachus pugnax*	PM

English Name	Scientific Name	Status
Jack Snipe	*Lymnocryptes minimus*	AV
Common Snipe	*Gallinago gallinago*	WV
Woodcock	*Scolopax rusticola*	RB
Black-tailed Godwit	*Limosa limosa*	WV, PM
Bar-tailed Godwit	*Limosa lapponica*	PM
Whimbrel	*Numenius phaeopus*	PM
Eurasian Curlew	*Numenius arquata*	WV
Spotted Redshank	*Tringa erythropus*	PM
Common Redshank	*Tringa totanus*	RB
Marsh Sandpiper	*Tringa stagnatilis*	AV
Greenshank	*Tringa nebularia*	PM
Green Sandpiper	*Tringa ochropus*	PM
Wood Sandpiper	*Tringa glareola*	PM
Common Sandpiper	*Actitis hypoleucos*	RB
Turnstone	*Arenaria interpres*	AV
Great Skua	*Stercorarius skua*	AV
Mediterranean Gull	*Larus melanocephalus*	WV
Little Gull	*Larus minutus*	WV
Black-headed Gull	*Larus ridibundus*	RB
Slender-billed Gull	*Larus genei*	AV
Audouin's Gull	*Larus audouinii*	AV, PM
Common Gull	*Larus canus*	WV
Lesser Black-backed Gull	*Larus fuscus*	WV
Yellow-legged Gull	*Larus cachinnans*	RB
Great Black-backed Gull	*Larus marinus*	WV
Kittiwake	*Rissa tridactyla*	WV
Gull-billed Tern	*Sterna nilotica*	AV
Sandwich Tern	*Sterna sandvicensis*	RB
Common Tern	*Sterna hirundo*	PM
Little Tern	*Sterna albifrons*	MB
Whiskered Tern	*Chlidonias hybridus*	PM
Black Tern	*Chlidonias niger*	PM
White-winged Black Tern	*Chlidonias leucopterus*	AV
Razorbill	*Alca torda*	WV
Black-bellied Sandgrouse	*Pterocles orientalis*	RB
Pin-tailed Sandgrouse	*Pterocles alchata*	RB
Stock Dove	*Columba oenas*	RB
Wood Pigeon	*Columba palumbus*	RB
Collared Dove	*Streptopelia decaoto*	RB
Turtle Dove	*Streptopelia turtur*	PM, MB
Great Spotted Cuckoo	*Clamator glandarius*	MB
Common Cuckoo	*Cuculus canoris*	MB
Barn Owl	*Tyto alba*	RB
Eurasian Scops Owl	*Otus scops*	MB
Eagle Owl	*Bubo bubo*	RB
Little Owl	*Athene noctua*	RB
Tawny Owl	*Strix aluco*	RB
Long-eared Owl	*Asio otus*	RB
Short-eared Owl	*Asio flamius*	WV
Tengmalm's Owl	*Aegolius funereus*	RB
European Nightjar	*Caprimulgus europaeus*	MB
Red-necked Nightjar	*Caprimulgus ruficollis*	MB

English Name	Scientific Name	Status
Alpine Swift	*Tachymarptis melba*	MB
Common Swift	*Apus apus*	MB
Pallid Swift	*Apus pallidus*	MB
Common Kingfisher	*Alcedo atthis*	RB
European Bee-eater	*Merops apiaster*	MB
European Roller	*Coracias garrulus*	MB
Hoopoe (a few winter)	*Upupa epops*	MB
Green Woodpecker	*Picus viridis*	RB
Black Woodpecker	*Dryocopus martius*	RB
Great Spotted Woodpecker	*Dendrocopos major*	RB
Middle Spotted Woodpecker	*Dendrocopus medius*	RB (very few Fr.)
White-backed Woodpecker	*Dendrocopus leucotos*	RB (very local)
Lesser Spotted Woodpecker	*Dendrocopus minor*	RB (very local)
Dupont's Lark	*Chersophilus duponti*	RB
Calandra Lark	*Melanocorypha calandra*	RB
Short-toed Lark	*Calandrella brachydactyla*	MB
Lesser Short-toed Lark	*Calandrella rufescens*	RB
Crested Lark	*Galerida cristata*	RB
Thekla Lark	*Galerida theklae*	RB
Wood Lark	*Lullula arborea*	RB
Sky Lark	*Alauda arvensis*	RB
Sand Martin	*Riparia riparia*	MB
Crag Martin	*Ptyonoprogne rupestris*	RB
Barn Swallow	*Hirundo rustica*	MB
Red-rumped Swallow	*Hirundo daurica*	AV, OB
House Martin	*Delichon urbica*	MB
Tawny Pipit	*Anthus campestris*	MB
Tree Pipit	*Anthus trivialis*	MB
Meadow Pipit	*Anthus pratensis*	WV
Water Pipit	*Anthus spinoletta*	MB
Rock Pipit	*Anthus petrosus*	PM
Yellow Wagtail	*Motacilla flava*	PM, MB
Pied (White) Wagtail	*Motacilla alba*	RB
Grey Wagtail	*Motacilla cinerea*	RB
Dipper	*Cinclus cinclus*	RB
Wren	*Troglodytes troglodytes*	RB
Hedge Accentor (Dunnock)	*Prunella modularis*	RB
Alpine Accentor	*Prunella collaris*	RB
Rufous-tailed Scrub-robin	*Cercotrichas galactotes*	PM
Robin	*Erithacus rubecula*	RB
Rufous Nightingale	*Luscinia megarhynchos*	MB
Bluethroat	*Luscinia svecica*	PM, WV
Black Redstart	*Phoenicurus ochruros*	RB
Common Redstart	*Phoenicurus phoenicurus*	MB (local)
Common Stonechat	*Saxicola torquata*	RB
Whinchat	*Saxicola rubetra*	MB
Northern Wheatear	*Oenanthe oenanthe*	MB
Black-eared Wheatear	*Oenanthe hispanica*	MB
Black Wheatear	*Oenanthe leucura*	RB
Rock Thrush	*Monticola saxatilis*	MB
Blue Rock Thrush	*Monticola solitarius*	RB
Ring Ouzel	*Turdus torquatus*	MB

English Name	Scientific Name	Status
Blackbird	*Turdus merula*	RB
Fieldfare	*Turdus pilaris*	PM, WV
Song Thrush	*Turdus philomelos*	RB
Redwing	*Turdus iliacus*	PM, WV
Mistle Thrush	*Turdus viscivoris*	RB
Cetti's Warbler	*Cettia cetti*	RB
Zitting Cisticola (Fan-tailed Warbler)	*Cisticola juncidis*	RB
Moustached Warbler	*Acrocephalus melanopogon*	RB
Reed Warbler	*Acrocephalus scirpaceus*	MB
Great Reed Warbler	*Acrocephalus arundinaceus*	MB
Melodious Warbler	*Hippolais polyglotta*	MB
Dartford Warbler	*Sylvia undata*	RB
Spectacled Warbler	*Sylvia conspicillata*	MB
Subalpine Warbler	*Sylvia cantilans*	MB
Sardinian Warbler	*Sylvia melanocephala*	RB
Orphean Warbler	*Sylvia hortensis*	MB
Common Whitethroat	*Sylvia communis*	MB
Garden Warbler	*Sylvia borin*	MB
Blackcap	*Sylvia atricapilla*	MB, RB
Western Bonelli's Warbler	*Phylloscopus bonellii*	MB
Wood Warbler	*Phylloscopus sibilatrix*	PM
Common Chiffchaff	*Phylloscopus collybita*	MB, RB
Willow Warbler	*Phylloscopus trochilus*	PM
Goldcrest	*Regulus regulus*	RB
Firecrest	*Regulus ignicapillus*	RB
Spotted Flycatcher	*Muscicapa striata*	MB
Pied Flycatcher	*Ficedula hypoleuca*	MB (local, rare)
Bearded Tit	*Panurus biarmicus*	RB
Long-tailed Tit	*Aegithalos caudatus*	RB
Marsh Tit	*Parus palustris*	RB (local)
Crested Tit	*Parus cristatus*	RB
Coal Tit	*Parus ater*	RB
Blue Tit	*Parus caeruleus*	RB
Great Tit	*Parus major*	RB
European Nuthatch	*Sitta europaea*	RB
Wallcreeper	*Tichodroma muraria*	RB
Short-toed Treecreeper	*Certhia brachydactyla*	RB
Eurasian Treecreeper	*Certhia familiaris*	RB
Penduline Tit	*Remiz pendulinus*	RB
Golden Oriole	*Oriolus oriolus*	MB
Red-backed Shrike	*Lanius collurio*	MB
Lesser Grey Shrike	*Lanius minor*	MB (local)
Great Grey Shrike	*Lanius excubitor*	RB, WV
Woodchat Shrike	*Lanius senator*	MB
Eurasian Jay	*Garrulus glandarius*	RB
Magpie	*Pica pica*	RB
Red-billed Chough	*Pyrrhocorax pyrrhocorax*	RB
Yellow-billed Chough	*Pyrrhocorax graculus*	RB
Eurasian Jackdaw	*Corvus monedula*	RB
Carrion Crow	*Corvus corone corone*	RB
Common Raven	*Corvus corax*	RB
Spotless Starling	*Sturnus unicolor*	RB

English Name	Scientific Name	Status
Common Starling	*Sturnus vulgaris*	RB, WV
House Sparrow	*Passer domesticus*	RB
Tree Sparrow	*Passer montanus*	RB
Rock Sparrow	*Petronia petronia*	RB
Snowfinch	*Montifringilla nivalis*	RB
Common Chaffinch	*Fringilla coelebs*	RB
Brambling	*Fringilla montifringilla*	WV
European Serin	*Serinus serinus*	RB
Citril Finch	*Serinus citrinella*	RB
Greenfinch	*Carduelis chloris*	RB
Goldfinch	*Carduelis carduelis*	RB
Siskin	*Carduelis spinus*	WV, RB (local)
Linnet	*Acanthis cannaina*	RB
Common Crossbill	*Loxia curvirostra*	RB
Common Bullfinch	*Pyrrhula pyrrhula*	RB
Hawfinch	*Coccothraustes coccothraustes*	RB(local), WV
Yellowhammer	*Emberiza citrinella*	RB
Cirl Bunting	*Emberiza cirlus*	RB
Rock Bunting	*Emberiza cia*	RB
Ortolan Bunting	*Emberiza hortulana*	MB
Reed Bunting	*Emberiza schoeniclus*	RB
Corn Bunting	*Miliaria calandra*	RB

Mammals

English Name	Scientific Name
Western Hedgehog	*Erinaceus europaeus*
Pyrenean Desman	*Galemys pyrenaicus*
Northern Mole	*Talpa europaea*
Pygmy Shrew	*Sorex minutus*
Millet's Shrew	*S. coronatus*
Water Shrew	*Neomys fodiens*
Miller's Water Shrew	*N. anomalus*
Lesser White-toothed Shrew	*Crocidura suaveolens*
Greater White-toothed Shrew	*C. russula*
Pygmy White-toothed Shrew	*Suncus etruscus*
Lesser Horseshoe Bat	*Rhinolopus hipposideros*
Mediterranean Horseshoe Bat	*R. euryale*
Greater Horseshoe Bat	*R. ferrumequinum*
Daubenton's Bat	*Myotis daubentonii*
Long-fingered Bat	*M. capaccinii*
Natterer's Bat	*M. nattereri*
Geoffroy's Bat	*M. emarginatus*
Bechstein's Bat	*M. bechsteinii*
Greater Mouse-eared Bat	*M. myotis*
Lesser Mouse-eared Bat	*M. blythi*
Common Pipistrelle	*Pipistrellus pipistrellus*
Nathusius's Pipistrelle.	*P. nathusii*
Kuhl's Pipistrelle	*P. kuhlii*
Savi's Pipistrelle	*P. savii*
Leisler's Bat	*Nyctalus leisleri*
Noctule	*N. noctula*

				English Name	Scientific Name
				Serotine	*Eptesicus serotinus*
				Barbastelle	*Barbastella barbastellus*
				Grey Long-eared Bat	*Plecotus austriacus*
				Brown Long-eared Bat	*P. auritus*
				Schreiber's Bat	*Miniopterus schreibersi*
				Free-tailed Bat	*Tadarida teniotis*
				Brown Hare	*Lepus europaeus*
				Rabbit	*Oryctolagus cuniculus*
				Red Squirrel	*Sciurus vulgaris*
				Alpine Marmot	*Marmota marmota*
				Bank Vole	*Clethrionomys glareolus*
				Southern Water Vole	*Arvicola sapidus*
				Northern Water Vole	*A. terrestris*
				Field Vole	*Microtus agrestis*
				Common Vole	*M. arvalis*
				Pyrenean Pine Vole	*Microtus pyrenaicus*
				Snow Vole	*M. nivalis*
				Garden Dormouse	*Eliomys quercinus*
				Fat Dormouse	*Glis glis*
				Wood Mouse	*Apodemus sylvaticus*
				Yellow-necked Mouse	*A. flavicollis*
				Harvest Mouse	*Micromys minutus*
				Brown Rat	*Rattus norvegicus*
				Black Rat	*R. rattus*
				House Mouse	*Mus domesticus*
				Wild Boar	*Sus scrofa*
				Izard (Chamois)	*Rupicapra pyrenaica*
				Spanish Ibex	*Capra pyrenaica*
				Mouflon	*Ovis musimon*
				Red Deer	*Cervus elaphus*
				Fallow Deer	*Dama dama*
				Roe Deer	*Capreolus capreolus*
				Red Fox	*Vulpes vulpes*
				Brown Bear	*Ursus arctos*
				Weasel	*Mustela nivalis*
				Stoat	*M. erminea*
				Western Polecat	*Mustela putorius*
				Pine Marten	*Martes martes*
				Beech Marten	*M. foina*
				Badger	*Meles meles*
				Otter	*Lutra lutra*
				Genet	*Genetta genetta*
				Wild Cat	*Felis silvestris*
				Lynx	*Lynx lynx (possibly L. pardellus) (Extinct?)*

Amphibians and Reptiles

				English Name	Scientific Name
				Hermann's Tortoise	*Testudo hermanni*
				Stripe-necked Terrapin	*Mauremys leprosa*
				European Pond Terrapin	*Emys orbicularis*
				Moorish Gecko	*Tarentola mauritanica*

				English Name	Scientific Name
				Large Psammodromus	*Psammadromus algirus*
				Spanish Psammodromus	*P. hispanicus*
				Oscellated Lizard	*Lacerta lepida*
				Green Lizard	*L. viridis*
				Sand Lizard	*L. agilis*
				Viviparous Lizard	*L. vivipara*
				Iberian Rock Lizard	*L. monticola*
				Pyrenean Lizard	*L. bonnali (L. aurelioi)*
				Common Wall Lizard	*Podarcis muralis*
				Iberian Wall Lizard	*P. hispanica*
				Slow Worm	*Anguis fragilis*
				Three-toed Skink	*Chalcides chalcides (C. striatus)*
				Monpellier Snake	*Malpolon monspessulanus*
				Western Whip Snake	*Coluber viridiflavus*
				Aesculapian Snake	*Elaphe longissima*
				Ladder Snake	*E. scalris*
				Grass Snake	*Natrix natrix*
				Viperine Snake	*N. maura*
				Smooth Snake	*Coronella austriaca*
				Southern Smooth Snake	*C. girondica*
				Asp Viper	*Vipera aspis*
				Seoanei's Viper	*V. seoanei*
				Fire Salamander	*Salamandra salamandra*
				Pyrenean Brook Salamander	*Euproctus asper*
				Marbled Newt	*Triturus marmoratus*
				Palmate Newt	*Triturus helveticus*
				Yellow-bellied Toad	*Bombina variegata*
				Painted Frog	*Discoglossus pictus*
				Midwife Toad	*Alytes obstretaicans*
				Western Spadefoot	*Pelobates cultripes*
				Parsley Frog	*Pelodytes punctatus*
				Common Toad	*Bufo bufo*
				Natterjack	*B. calamita*
				Common Tree Frog	*Hyla arborea*
				Stripeless Tree Frog	*H. meridionalis*
				Grass Frog	*Rana temporaria*
				Marsh Frog	*R. perezi*

Butterflies

				English Name	Scientific Name
				PAPILLIONIDAE	
				Swallowtail	*Papilio machaon*
				Scarce Swallowtail	*Iphiclides podalirius*
				Spanish Festoon	*Zerynthia rumina*
				Apollo	*Parnassius apollo*
				Clouded Apollo	*Parnassius mnemosyne*
				PIERIDAE	
				Black-veined White	*Aporia crataegi*
				Large White	*Pieris brassicae*
				Small White	*Artogeia rapae*
				Southern Small White	*A. manii*

				English Name	Scientific Name
				Mountain Small White	*A. ergane*
				Green-veined White	*A. napi*
				Black-veined White	*Aporia crataegi*
				Bath White	*Pontia daplidice*
				Peak White	*P. callidice*
				Freyer's Dappled White	*Euchloe simplonia*
				Mountain Dappled White	*E. ausonia*
				Orange Tip	*Anthocharis cardamines*
				Moroccan Orange Tip	*A. belia*
				Mountain Clouded Yellow	*Colias phicomone*
				Clouded Yellow	*C. crocea*
				Pale Clouded Yellow	*C. hyale*
				Berger's Clouded Yellow	*C. australis*
				Brimstone	*Gonepteryx rhamni*
				Cleopatra	*G. cleapatra*
				Wood White	*Leptides sinapis*
				LIBYTHEIDAE	
				Nettle-tree Butterfly	*Libythea celtus*
				NYMPHALIDAE	
				Two-tailed Pasha	*Charaxes jasius*
				Purple Emperor	*Apatura iris*
				Lesser Purple Emperor	*A. ilia*
				White Admiral	*Lagoda camilla*
				Southern White Admiral	*Limenitis reducta*
				Camberwell Beauty	*Nyphalis antiopa*
				Large Tortoiseshell	*N. polychloros*
				Small Tortoishell	*Aglais urticae*
				Comma	*Polygonia c-album*
				Map Butterfly	*Araschnia levana*
				Painted Lady	*Cynthia cardui*
				American Painted Lady	*C. virginiensis*
				Red Admiral	*Vanessa atalanta*
				Indian Red Admiral	*V. indica vulcania*
				Peacock Butterfly	*Inachis io*
				Cardinal	*Pandoriana pandora*
				Silver-washed Fritillary	*Argynnis paphia*
				Dark Green Fritillary	*Mesoacidalia aglaja*
				High Brown Fritillary	*Fabriciana adippe*
				Niobe Fritillary	*F. niobe*
				Queen of Spain Fritillary	*Issoria lathonia*
				Twin-spot Fritillary	*Brenthis hecate*
				Marbled Fritillary	*B. daphne*
				Lesser Marbled Fritillary	*B. ino*
				Shepherd's Fritillary	*Boloria pales*
				Bog Fritillary	*Proclossiana eunomia*
				Pearl-bordered Fritillary	*Clossiana euphrosyne*
				Small Pearl-bordered Fritillary	*C. selene*
				Weaver's Fritillary	*C. dia*
				Glanville Fritillary	*Melitaea cinxia*
				Knapweed Fritillary	*M. phoebe*
				Spotted Fritillary	*M. didyma*
				Lesser Spotted Fritillary	*M. trivia*

English Name	Scientific Name
False Heath Fritillary	*M. diamina*
Heath Fritillary	*Mellicta aathalia*
Provencal Fritillary	*M. deione*
Meadow Fritillary	*M. parthenoides*
Marsh Fritillary	*Eurodryas aurinia*
Spanish Fritillary	*E. desfontainii*
SATYRIDAE	
Marbled White	*Menanargia galathea lachesis*
Esper's Marbled White	*M. russiae*
Western Marbled White	*M. occitanica*
Woodland Grayling	*Hipparchia fagi*
Rock Grayling	*H. alcyone*
Grayling	*H. semele cadmus*
Southern Grayling	*H. aristaeus*
Tree Grayling	*Neohipparchia statillinus*
Striped Grayling	*Pseudotergumia fidia*
The Hermit	*Chazara briseis*
Black Satyr	*Satyrus actaea*
Great Sooty Satry	*S. ferula*
Great Banded Grayling	*Brintesia circe*
False Grayling	*Arethusana arethusa*
Large Ringlet	*Erebia euryale*
Mountain Ringlet	*E. epiphron*
De Prunner's Ringlet	*E. triaria*
Silky Ringlet	*E. gorge*
Gavarnie Ringlet	*E. gorgone*
Spring Ringlet	*E. epistygne*
Common Brassy Ringlet	*E. cassioides*
Spanish Brassy Ringlet	*E. hispanica rondoui*
Water Ringlet	*E. pronoe*
Lefèbvre's Ringlet	*E. lefebvrei*
Autumn Ringlet	*E. neoridas*
Bright-eyed Ringlet	*E. oeme*
Piedmont Ringlet	*E. meolans*
Dewy Ringlet	*E. pandrose*
False Dewy ringlet	*E. sthennyo*
Arran Brown	*E. ligea*
Meadow Brown	*Maniola jurtina*
Dusky Meadow Brown	*Hyponephele lycaon*
Gatekeeper	*Pyronia tithonus*
Southern Gatekeeper	*P. cecilia*
Spanish Gatekeeper	*P. bathseba*
Ringlet	*Aphantopus hyperantus*
Small Heath	*Coenonympha pamphilus*
Dusky Heath	*C. dorus*
Pearly Heath	*C. arcania*
Chestnut Heath	*C. glycerion*
Spanish Heath	*C. iphioides*
Speckled Wood	*Pararge aegeria*
Wall Brown	*Lasiommata megera*
Large Wall Brown	*L. maera*
Northern Wall Brown	*L. petropolitana*

English Name	Scientific Name
RIODINIDAE	
Duke of Burgundy Fritillary	*Hameoris lucina*
LYCAENIDAE	
Brown Hairstreak	*Thecla betulae*
Purple Hairstreak	*Quercusia quercus*
Spanish Purple Hairstreak	*Laeosopis roboris*
Sloe Hairstreak	*Nordmannia acaciae*
Liex Hairstreak	*N. ilicis*
False Ilex Hairstreak	*N. esculi*
Blue-spot Hairstreak	*Strymonidia spini*
Black Hairstreak	*S. pruni*
White-letter Hairstreak	*S. w-album*
Green Hairstreak	*Callophrys rubi*
Small Copper	*Lycaena phlaeas*
Scarce Copper	*Heodes virgaureae*
Sooty Copper	*H. tityrus*
Purple-shot Copper	*H. alciphron*
Purple-edged Copper	*Palaeochrysophanus hippothoe*
Long-tailed Blue	*Lampides boeticus*
Lang's Short-tailed Blue	*Syntarucus pirithous*
Short-tailed Blue	*Everes argiades*
Provencal Short-tailed Blue	*E. alcetas*
Little Blue	*Cupido minimus*
Osiris Blue	*C. asiris (or sebrus)*
Holly Blue	*Celastrina argiolus*
Green-underside Blue	*Glaucopsyche alexis*
Black-eyed Blue	*G. melanops*
Alcon Blue	*Maculinea alcon*
Large Blue	*M. arion*
Iolas Blue	*Iolana iolas*
Baton Blue	*Pseudophilotes baton*
Panoptes Blue	*P. panoptes*
Chequered Blue	*Scolitantides orion*
Silver-studded Blue	*Plebejus argus*
Idas Blue	*Lycaeides idas*
Geranium Argus	*Eumedonia eumedon*
Brown Argus	*Aricia agestis*
Southern Brown Argus	*A. cramera*
Silvery Argus	*Pseudaricia nicias*
Glandon Blue	*Agriades glandon*
Gavarnie Blue	*A. pyrenaicus*
Mazarine Blue	*Cyaniris semiargus*
Furry Blue	*Agrodiaetus dolus*
Forster's Furry Blue	*A. ainsae*
Damon Blue	*A. damon*
Escher's Blue	*A. escheri*
Amanda's Blue	*A. amanda*
Chapman's Blue	*A. thersites*
Oberthur's Anomalous blue	*A. fabressei*
Ripart's Anomalous Blue	*A. ripartii*
Turquoise Blue	*Plebicula dorylas*
Mother-of-Pearl Blue	*P. nivescens*

English Name	Scientific Name
Chalk-hill Blue	*Lysandra corydon*
Provence Chalk-hill Blue	*L. hispana*
Spanish Chalk-hill Blue	*L. albicans*
Adonis Blue	*L. bellargus*
Common Blue	*Polyommatus icarus*
Eros Blue	*P. eros*
HESPERIIDAE	
Grizzled Skipper	*Pyrgus malvae*
Large Grizzled Skipper	*P. alveus*
Oberthur's Grizzled skipper	*P. armoricanus*
Foulquier's Grizzled Skipper	*P. foulquieri*
Olive Skipper	*P. serratulae*
Carline Skipper	*P. carlinae*
Cinquefoil Skipper	*P. cirsii*
Rosy Grizzled Skipper	*P. onopordi*
Safflower Skipper	*P. carthami*
Alpine Grizzled Skipper	*P. andromedae*
Dusky Grizzled Skipper	*P. cacaliae*
Red Underwing Skipper	*Spialia sertorius*
Sage Skipper	*Syrichtus proto*
Mallow Skipper	*Carcharodus alceae*
Marbled Skipper	*C. lavatherae*
Southern Marbled Skipper	*C. boeticus*
Tufted Marbled Skipper	*C. flocciferis*
Dingy Skipper	*Erynnis tages*
Large Chequered Skipper	*Heteropterus morpheus*
Chequered Skipper	*Carterocephalus palaemon*
Lulworth Skipper	*Thymelicus acteon*
Essex Skipper	*T. lineola*
Small Skipper	*T. flavus*
Silver-spotted Skipper	*Hesperia comma*
Large Skipper	*Ochlodes venatus*
Mediterranean Skipper	*Gegenes nostrodamus*

NOTES

NOTES